The Plays of Girish Karnad

De-Colonisation of Language and Techniques

The Plays of Girish Karnad

De-Colonisation of Language and Techniques

Krishna Singh

AUTHORSPRESS

Worldwide Circulation through Authorspress Global Network
First Published 2013
by
Authorspress

Editorial
Q-2A Hauz Khas Enclave
New Delhi-110 016

Marketing
E-35/103, Jawahar Park
Laxmi Nagar, Delhi-110 092

e-mails: authorspress@rediffmail.com; authorspress@hotmail.com
Website: www.authorspressbooks.com

The Plays of Girish Karnad:
De-Colonisation of Language and Techniques
ISBN 978-81-7273-694-1

Printed in India at: Sri Krishna Offset Press, D

Preface

The present book is a modified version of my UGC Research Project sponsored by UGC Regional Office, Bhopal. The project endeavours to explore Karnad's contribution to de-colonize Indian English drama and revitalize it. His strong advocacy to purposeful return to rich indigenous tradition and culture of dramas brought revolution in play texts and their performing techniques. Girish Karnad, a versatile genius, acclaimed as a noted actor, producer, director, TV artist and cultural administrator, occupies prominent place in Indian English Drama. His plays are the testimony of it. Karnad is appreciated as a playwright of myths and legends, history, subalternity, castesim, rituals, feminism, cultural issues and humanism. Despite these cultural roles Karnad definitely brought revolution in Indian English drama—discarding Eurocentric models and techniques altogether; boldly advocated and used Indian myths, legends, folk tales, history, socio-political and contemporary issues with Indianized English and folk theatre conventions with the motif to de-colonize Indian English drama, he gave it a new shape—Postcolonial Indian English Drama. All his plays from *Yayati* to *Wedding Album* illustrate this hypothesis. His views expressed in prefaces, introduction to his plays and interviews also endorse the argument.

While the project is focused on Karnad's cultural and literary contribution to advance postcolonial discourse, obviously it will help to understand his genius as a playwright, purpose of writing plays, his subjects, art of characterization, language, theatre techniques etc. and establish their academic validity. Analysis of experiments by Karnad, i.e., plot, character, thought, diction and theatre techniques will help to enlarge the scope of Indian English drama and their acknowledgement. Researchers and scholars of Indian English literature will find the study highly informative and useful. It will also work as a reference work on Karnad while he has been prescribed in most of the Indian universities. The project aims to highlight the potentiality of Karnad's plays, consequently, it will dwindle the 'sick man' image of Indian English drama.

The project has an interdisciplinary relevance while it aims to analyse socio-cultural and literary achievements of Karnad, it will be highly relevant to present day problems Indian society is facing largely: (i) Analysis of Karnad as a postcolonial writer of Indian English drama will facilitate to see, observe and understand the glory of India's past and its continuity in the present. (ii) It will also give impetus to overcome "colonial neurosis" and recognize indigenous culture, history and literature. (iii) Thematic concerns in Karnad's plays, which the project analyses will display their urgency in the present context in our country. (iv) The project also aims to explain the archetypal patterns embedded in Karnad's plays—obviously it will be an opportunity to understand Indian myths, legends, folktales, history and culture, narrative design and character-types and feel proud of them. The proposed research project will cater to the socio-political, cultural and literary needs of the society. Issues and problems discussed and analyzed will enlighten the society and help to meditate on those problems. Exposition of theatre techniques in Karnad will facilitate to enjoy and assess their validity in the modern context.

The proposed research project is focused on *Primary Research*—to define, to classify, to investigate and to analyse the concept, illustrating through the plays of Karnad; personal interviews, letters, prefaces and introductions to plays as well as *Secondary Research*—examination of erstwhile studies, books, articles, reviews, historical documents, electronic documents etc. for identifying, locating, assessing, analyzing, understanding and interpreting the primary sources. It is exploratory, analytical, explicative and comparative in nature—biographical, historical, socio-linguistic, archetypal, text-based criticism, psychoanalytical methods with postcolonial approach focusing on postcolonial dialectics, subalternization and nativitism have been applied to investigate and verify the project statement. Documentation conforms to *MLA Handbook for the Writers of Research Papers* (Seventh Edition). Academic library, library research source, reference works, online catalogue of library holdings, full-text databases, other library resources, and services, internet services etc. have been frequently used while conducting research.

The book has been developed into seven chapters: Chapter (1) Introduction: Life and Works deals with the life of Karnad, education and process of evolution of his dramatic generous; Chapter (2) De-Colonization of Indian English Drama has two sections—the first section briefly analyses the meaning, scope and ideologies of postcolonialism; and the second section exclusively analyses the plays of Karnad to verify postcoloniality which is inherent in his plays; Chapter (3) Themes / Subjects has five sub-chapters: (A) Genesis of Titles and Evolution of Themes in the Plays of Girish Karnad (B) Indian Myths, Legends, History, Culture and Polity in the Plays of Girish Karnad (C) Existentialist Dilemma in the Plays of Girish Karnad (D) Subaltern Issue in the Plays of Karnad and (E) Feminism and the Quest for Women's Emancipation in the Plays of Girish Karnad. These sub-chapters discuss the rich thematic contents in the plays of Karnad rooted in ancient culture of India but they have modern validity. Chapter (4) Characterization discusses Karnad's art of characterization; Chapter (5) Technique closely scrutinizes the theatre conventions and Karnad's handling of folk, classical and modern theatre conventions with emphasis on the theatre of roots; Chapter (6) Language highlights the Indianization of English thwarting King's English; Chapter (7) Conclusion sums up the entire discussion, followed by an updated Select Bibliography. Certain lines, expressions, quotations and remarks are repeated in more than one chapter because of their validity and high relevance under those heads.

Krishna Singh

Acknowledgement

I acknowledge my sincerest thanks to U.G.C. Central Regional Office, Bhopal for the financial support in initiating the research project. Books, journals, travel, field work, use of web material, contingency and special needs were amply fulfilled with the grant. I also thank Delhi University Library, J.N.U. Library, Lucknow University Library, Kanpur University Library, A.P.S. University, Rewa Library, Pt. S.N.S. Govt. P.G. College, Shahdol Library and Paradise Cyber Café for extending cooperation to procure study material in hard and soft copies. Dr. M.S. Kushwaha, former Professor and Head, Department of English and European Language, Lucknow University, Lucknow, Dr. B.K. Das, Professor of English, Burdhwan University, Burdhwan, Dr. G.K. Das, Professor of English, Delhi University, Delhi helped to mould the project report in the present form. The moral support of Dr. S.K. Saxena, Principal, Pt. S.N.S. Govt. P.G. College, Shahdol, M.P. deserve special mention; Prof. (Dr.) Vinay Kumar Singh, U.G.C. Academic Controller, Pt. S.N.S. Govt. P.G. College, Shahdol, M.P. proved catalytic to carry out the research project and the adulation of Dr. Karunesh Jha, Prof. and Head, Department of English, Pt. S.N.S. Govt. P.G. College, Shahdol, M.P. enthused me to accomplish my work. I express my grateful thanks to both of them for generosity they have displayed during my project work. Mr. K.S. Baghel, L.D.C., Mr. R.S. Gupta, Account, Pt. S.N.S. Govt. P.G. College, Shahdol, M.P, and Marina Typing Institute also deserve commendation for their cooperation.

My family members are entitled for special word of thanks, especially my parents and in-laws whose all time support and blessings motivated me to continue my academic pursuits. My wife, Chetana Singh, Assistant Professor of Political Science, Pt. S.N.S. Govt. P.G. College, Shahdol, M.P, who, despite her official duties and academic engagements, spared certain hours to my research project and went through proof-reading. My son Tejus, 10, maintained silence during my work. It would be unwise to eschew them from heart-felt thanks.

Lastly, it's my humble duty to display my indebtedness to the following esteemed journals for publishing research papers based on the present research project:

(i) "Myth and Modernity in the Plays of Girish Karnad", *Contemporary Vibes.* Volume No.:5, Issue No.: 20, July-September 2010.

(ii) "Existential Dilemma in the Plays of Girish Karnad", *Vishwabharati.* Vol 1, Issue 4, 2010 & *Literati.* Volume: IX Winter 2010 & Summer 2011.

(iii) "Postcolonial Subalternization in the Plays of Girish Karnad", *The Criterion.* Vol. II. Issue I April 2011 *<http: / /www.the-criterion.com>*

(iv) "Theatre Techniques in the Plays of Girish Karnad", *The Atlantic Literary Review.* January-March 2011, Volume 12 Number 1.

(v) "The Plays of Girish Karnad: De-Colonization of Indian English Drama", *The Atlantic Critical Review.* April-June 2011, Volume 10 Number 2.

(vi) "Karnad: A Man and Artist—Evolution of His Dramatic Genius", *The Criterion.* Vol. II, Issue III September 2011 *<http: / /www.the-criterion.com>*.

(vii) "Genesis of Titles and Evolution of Themes in the Plays of Girish Karnad", *Contemporary Vibes.* Volume No:7, Issue No. 25. October-December, 2011.

(viii) "The Plays of Girish Karnad: A Feminist Study", *Labyrinth.* Vol.2 / No 4-October 2011 & *The Atlantic Literary Review.* July-September 2011, Volume 12 Number 3.

(ix) "The Plays of Girish Karnad: Art of Characterization", *Thematics Journal of Indian Literature*. Vol. 1, Issue 3, Sep 2011.

(x) "The Plays Girish Karnad: A Socio-Linguistic Study", *Illuminati*. Dec 2011.

Authorspress, New Delhi deserves deserves special thanks to bring out the typescript in the present form in a very short span of time. I also thank those who were kind enough and convivial to me, but due to the paucity of space their names cannot be mentioned here.

Krishna Singh

Contents

1

Introduction: Life and Works

Girish Raghunath Karnad is a playwright, poet, actor, director, critic, translator and cultural administrator, all rolled into one. He has been rightly called the "renaissance man" (Kalidas & Merchant,"Renaissance Man") whose celebrity is based on decades of prolific and consistent output on native soil. He belongs to a generation that has produced Dharamveer Bharati, Mohan Rakesh and Vijay Tendulker who have created a national theatre for modern India which is the legacy of his generation.

Karnad is the most famous as a playwright. His plays written in Kannada have been widely translated into English and all major Indian languages. Karnad's plays are written neither in English, except few, in which he dreamed of earning international literary fame, nor in his mother tongue Konkani. Instead they are composed in his adopted language Kannada, thereafter translated by himself into English—a language of adulthood.

When Karnad started writing plays, Kannada literature was highly influenced by the renaissance in Western literature. Writers would choose a subject which looked entirely alien to manifestation of native soil. Conflicting ideologies, political freedom of India, modernity versus indigenous traditions supplied the specific backdrop to write plays.

During his formative years, Karnad went through diverse influences that went long way into shaping his dramatic taste and genius. The earliest influence was that of the Natak Company that was in vogue in Sirsi. The Yakshagana plays which he used to see with the servants also appealed to him by their buffoonery and horseplay. But the greater influence came from the naturalistic drama of Henrik Ibsen and through him of G.B. Shaw.

Karnad was also influenced by Shakespeare considerably. But the influence of Kannada drama was quite profound and deep on him.

Karnad represents the best traditions of the Kannada drama which was quite rich with romantic plays, tragedies, comedies, poetic and blank verse plays. He took keen interest in all these kinds of Kannada plays. He was exposed to a literary scene where there was a direct clash between Western and native tradition. It was the India of the fifties and sixties that surfaced two streams of thought in all walks of life—adoption of new modernistic techniques, a legacy of the colonial rule and adherence to the rich cultural past of the country. Karnad has acknowledged this fact:

> My generation was the first to come of age after India became independent of British rule. It therefore had to face a situation in which tensions implicit until then had come out in the open and demanded to be resolved without apologia or self-justification: tensions between the cultural past of the country and its colonial past, between the attractions of Western modes of thought and our own traditions, and finally between the various visions of the future that opened up once the common cause of political freedom was achieved. This is the historical context that gave rise to my plays and those of my contemporaries.
>
> ("Author's Introduction" *Three Plays.* 1)

Under such context, Karnad found, "a new approach like drawing historical and mythylogical sources to tackle contemporary themes" (Wikipedia "Girish Karnad"). R.K. Dhawan examines the impact of contemporary socio-cultural and literaray milieu: "Karnad was fascinated by the traditional plays; nonetheless the Western playwrights that he read during his college days opened up for him a new world of magical possibilities" (14). M.K. Nayak observes, "the most significant plays of the last two decades have come from two playwrights, who interestingly enough, represent a generation each: Girish

Karnad and Mahesh Dattani" (*Littcrit.* 43). Karnad's plays had effectively demonstrated how Indian English drama could revitalize itself by employing indigenous subjects, characters, language and folk and Natak Company conventions and de-colonize Indian English drama. M.K. Naik has justly commented that Karnad knew well that:

> If Indian English drama wishes to go ahead, it must go back first, that is, only a purposeful return to its own roots in the rich tradition of ancient Indian drama, both in Sanskrit and folk drama in Prakrits, can help it shed its lean and pale look, and increase its artistic haemoglobin count, and make it cease to be the 'sick man' of Indian English Literature.
>
> ("Author's Introduction", *Three plays* 43-44)

Karnad has emerged as a living legend in the contemporary Indian English drama. His output which ranges from *Yayati* to *Wedding Album* marks the evolution of Indian theatre since four decades. "He represents", Saryug Yadav considers, a "synthesis of cultures and his formal experiments have certainly been far more successful than those of some of his contemporaries" (9). His technical experiments with an indigenous dramatic form "opened up fresh lines of fruitful exploration for the Indian English playwright" (Naik. *A History of Indian English Literature* 263). P. Hari Padma Rani also gives credit to Karnad to Indianize the form of drama in English: " Girish Karnad has attempted to Indianize the form by using some of the conventions of Indian Classical drama and some of those of the folk theatre and by blending them in a singular style of his own" (15).

Karnad was born on 19 May 1938 in Matheran, a town near Mumbai. He hails from a Saraswat Konkani family of Manglore. His childhood was spent growing up in a small village, Sirsi, in Karnataka where he had first-hand experience of the indigenous folk theatre. The influence of the theatre was immense on the making of Karnad as a playwright. He happened to see with his father the performances of the touring Natak Companies. These Natak Companies were the offshoots of the Parsi theatre. Karnad wrote:

> In my childhood, in a small town in Karnataka, I was exposed to two theatre forms that seemed to represent irreconcilably different worlds. Father took the entire family to see plays staged by troupes of professional actors called *natal companies* which toured the countryside throughout the year. The plays were staged in semipermanent structures on proscenium stages, with wings and drop curtains, and illuminated by petromax lamps.
>
> Once the harvest was over, I went with the servants to sit up nights watching the more traditional *Yakshagana* performances. The stage, a platform with a black curtain, was erected in the open air and lit by torches.
>
> By the time I was in my early teens, the *natak companies* had cesed to function and *Yakshagana* had begun to seem quaint, even silly, to me. Soon we moved to a big city. This city had a college and electricity, but no professional theatre.
>
> ("Author's Introduction" *Three Plays.* 1)

As a young man studying at Karnataka University, Dharwar, where he earned a Bachelor of Arts Degree in Mathematics and Statistics in 1958, Karnad dreamed of earning international literary fame, but he thought that he would do so by writing in English. Upon graduation, he went to England and studied at Oxford where he earned a Rhodes scholarship and went on to receive a Master of Arts Degree in Philosophy, Politics and Economics.

During his stay at Magdalen College, Oxford, Karnad felt immensely interested in art and culture. On his return to India in 1963, he joined Oxford University Press, Madras. This offered him an opportunity to get exposed to various kinds of writings in India and elsewhere. Such influences made an indelible mark on the creative genius of Karnad. In 1974, he received an important assignment and was appointed Director of the Film and Television Institute of India, Pune. In 1987, he went to the U.S.A. as Fulbright Scholar-in-Residence at the Department of South Asian Languages and Civilizations, University of Chicago.

From 1988 to 1993, he worked as Chairman of the Sangeet Natak Akademi (National Akademy for Performing Arts), New

Delhi. In 1994, he was awarded Doctor of Letters degree by the Karnataka Uiversity, Dharwad. The awards conferred on Karnad testify to his recognisation as a contributor to art, literature and cinema. Karnad's awards include the Mysore State Award for *Yayati* (1962), the Government of Mysore Rajyotsava Award (1970), Presidents Gold Medal for the Best Indian film for *Samskara* (1970), the Homi Bhabha Fellowship for creative work in folk theatre (1970-72), the Sangeet Natak Academy (National Academy of the Performing Arts) Award for playwriting (1972), the Kamaladevi Award of the Bharatiya Natya Sangh for the Best Indian Play of the Year for *Hayavadana* (1972), the National Award for Excellence in Direction for *Vamsha Vriksha* (shared with B.V. Karanth-1972), the Mysore State Award for the Best Kannada film and the Best Direction for *Vamsha Vriksha* (1972), the Presidents Silver Medal for the Second Best Indian film for *Kaadu* (1974), the Padma Shri Award (1974), the National Award for the Best Kannada film for *Ondanondu Kaaladalli* (1978), the National Award for the Best Script for *Bhumika* (shared with Shyam Benegal and Satyadev Dubey-1978), the Film Fare Award for the Best Script for *Godhuli* (shared with B.V. Karanth-1978), the Best Bengal Film Journalists Association Award for the Best Actor in *Swami* (1978), the Karnataka Nataka Academy Award (1984), the Nandikar, Calcutta, Award for Playwriting (1989), the Golden Lotus for the Best Non-Feature Film for *Kanaka Purandara* (1989), the National Award for the Best Non-Feature Film on Social Issues for *The Lamp in the Niche* (1990), "Writer of the Year" Award from Granthaloka Journal of the Book Trade for *Taledanda* (1990), Karnataka State Award for the Best Supporting Actor in *Santa Shishunala Shareef* (1991), the Karnataka Sahitya Academy Award for the Most Creative Work for *Nagamandala* (1992), the B.H. Sridhar Award for *Tale-Danda* (1992), the Padma Bhushan Award (1992), the Karnataka Sahitya Academy Award for Best Play for *Tale-Danda* (1992), the Booksellers and Publishers Association of South India Award (1992), the National Award for the Best Film on Environmental Conservation for *Cheluvi* (1993), a Special Honour Award from the Karnataka Sahitya Academy (1994), the Sahitya Academi Award for *Tale-Danda* (1994), and the Gubbi Veeranna Award (1996-97), and the Jnanpith Award (1999).

Kannad also served as Director of the Film and Television Institute of India (1974-75), President of the Karnataka Nataka Academy (1976-78), Indian Co-Chairman for the Joint Media Committee of the Indo-U.S. Sub-Commission on Education and Culture (1984-93). In recognition of his meritorious contribution to art, culture and theatre, the President of India awarded him Padma Shri in 1974 and Padma Bhushan in 1992. He won the prestigious Gnanpith Award in 1999. He is a gifted genius and a man of excellent intellectual abilities. He strikes a balance between intellect and emotion in his plays.

When Karnad was preparing to go to England, amidst the intense emotional turmoil, he found himself writing play. It was just a chance that he became a dramatist. He himself tells us: "I wanted to be a poet, the greatest ambition in my life. At the age of 22, I realized I would not be a poet, but be only a playwright" (27). He finds it difficult to describe the trauma created by decision to go abroad for further studies. He was surprised to see that instead of becoming a poet he had become a playwright. He himself recounts some reasons behind it:

> Going abroad was a much rare occurrence in those days; besides, I came from a large, close-knit family and was the first member of the family ever to go abroad. My parents were worried lest I decide to settle down outside India, and even for me, though there was no need for an immediate decision, the terrible choice was implicit in the very act of going away....While still preparing for the trip, amidst the intense emotional turmoil, I found myself writing a play. This took me by surprise, for I had fancied myself a poet, had written poetry through my teens, and had trained myself to write in English, in preparation for the conquest of the West. But here I was writing a play and in Kannad, too, the language spoken by a few million people in South India, the language of my childhood. A greter surprise was the theme of the play, for it was taken from ancient Indian mythology from which I had believed myself alienated.
>
> ("Author's Introduction" *Three Plays.*2-3)

Karnad's plays include *Yayati* (1961), *Tughlaq* (1964). *Hayavadana* (1971), *Anjumallige,* Kannada version published by

Manohara Grantha Mala, Dharwad, 1977; the English translation by the playwright as "Driven Snow" is as yet unpublished, *Hittina Hunja* (1980), published as *Bali: The Sacrifice* [along with *The Dreams of Tipu Sultan*] New Delhi: OUP, 2003. *Nagamandala: A Play with a Cobra* (1990), *Tale-Danda* (1993), *The Fire and the Rain* (1998), "The Dreams of Tipu Sultan," *Theatre India*. No.1 May 2000: 47-85. *The Dreams of Tipu Sultan* and *Bali: The Sacrifice*. New Delhi: OUP, 2004. *Two Monologues: Flowers* and *Broken Images*. OUP, 2005. *Wedding Album*. OUP, Nov, 2008.

Karnad's first play *Yayati* was the result of intense emotional crisis he felt while going to England for further studies. To escape from his stressful situation, he began writing a play based on the myth of Yayati from *Mahabharata*. The play that reflects his mental condition at that time is a self-conscious existentialist drama on the theme of responsibility. He combines native subject with existential philosophy, and juxtaposes the past and the present together. The play reveals the existentialist view that each man is what he chooses to be or makes himself. The play doesn't glorify a son's obedience to his father who exchanges his curse with his son Pooru that is contrary to the original myth.

Karnad raises a practical question: what would be the reaction of Pooru's wife? Chitralekha's protest attacks male-chauvinism and subverts patriarchy. Karnad being a problem playwright deals with soci-political and cultural concerns of the contemporary life. Yayati is an unheroic hero who stands for modern man inhabitated by worldly desires, sensual pleasure, irresponsible exercise of power and utter forgetfulness of the imperishable values of life. In *Yayati* Karnad reinterprets an ancient myth from the Puranic past to make a statement in the form and structure he borrowed from the Western playwrights. The play was a great success on stage.

Karnad's second play *Tughlaq* is a historical play on the life of fourtheenth century Sultan of India, Muhammad-bin-Tughlaq. Karnad has always found it difficult to find a suitable subject for writing plays. He read the history of Kannada literature by Kirtinath Kurtkoti and learnt from him that Indian history has not been handled by any Indian writer the way it has been done by Shakespeare or Brecht. He was very much impressed by this statement; he went through a book of Indian history. And when he came to Tughlaq, he exclaimed, "Oh! Marvellous. That is what I wanted." That was a subject in tune with the times. In those days, existentialism was quite in vogue. Everything about Tughlaq seemed to fit into what Karnad had surmised from Kurtkoti. He felt that in Tughlaq he had hit upon a fantastic character. He realized that he had absorbed this character and it was growing in front of him:

> certainly the most brilliant individual ever to ascend the throne of Delhi and also one of the biggest failures. After a reign distinghuished for policies that today seem far-sighted to the point of genius, but which in their day earned him the title 'Muhammad the Mad,' the sultan ended his career in bloodshed and political chaos. In a sense, the play reflected the slow disillusionment my generation felt with the new politics of independent India: the gradual erosion of the ethical norms that had guided the movement for independence and the coming to terms with cynicism and realpolitik. ("Author's Introduction", *Three Plays.* 7)

R.K. Dhawan explores several resemblances between Karnad's *Tughlaq* and Shakespeare's *Richard II*:

> Like King Richard, Muhammad-bin-Tughlaq is temperamental and whimsical. Events in both the plays centre around the eccentricities of their protagonists. Again like Shakespeare, Karnad presents the historical events and complexities of the time with perfect objectivity of a true historian, throwing upon them the beautiful colouring of art. He exhibits without concealement the weakness of the king's character but spares no pain to evoke our whole-hearted pity for him in his fall. (16)

The political chaos which Karnad depicts in *Tughlaq* reminded many readers of the Nehru era in Indian history. Karnad finds this similiarity accidental. U.R. AnathaMurthy considers the play.

> more than a political allegory.it has an irreducible, puzzling quality which comes from the ambiguities of

> Tughlaq's character...all other characters are dramatized aspects of his complex personality....But it would be unjust to say that the play is about an 'interesting' character, for the play relates the character of Tughlaq to philosophical questions on the nature of man and the destiny of a whole kingdom which a dreamer like him controls.
>
> ("Introduction," *Tughlaq* viii-ix)

Tughlaq had a tremendous success wih the reading public and it achieved greater popularity on the stage as actors have liked to do the role of the emperor. As opposed to the first play, Karnad wrote this one in the convention of the Natak Company. For the form of the play, Karnad was no more interested in John Anouilh. He divided the play into scenes in the indigenous fashions of the natakas—*shallow* and *deep scenes.* The shallow scenes were played in the foreground of the stage with a painted curtain—normally depicting a street—as a backdrop. These scenes were reserved for 'lower class' characters with prominence given to comedy. They served as link scenes in the development of the plot, but the main purpose was to keep the audience engaged while the deep scenes, which showed interiors of palaces, royal parks, and other such visually opulent sets, being changed or decorated. The important characters rarely appeared in the street scenes, and in the deep scenes the lower classes strictly kept their place.

Hayavadana (1970) is the third and the most representative of his plays. It deals with archetypal theme, underlying mythical patterns, identifiable character, types, folk theatre conventions, i.e., use of mask, curtains, dolls, story within story, use of images of Kali, Ganesh, Rudra etc. Allegorical significance of the play is the characteristic feature of the play. It was originally written in Kannada and Karnad was persuaded by Rajinder Paul to translate the play into English and first published this translation in his journal *Enact*. It was Mrs. Laxmi Krishnamurthy and Mrs. Yamuna Prabhu who jointly produced it for the Madras Players at the Museum Theatre, Madras on 7 December 1972.

The plot of *Hayavadana* is derived from Somdeva's *Brihadkatha Saritasagar*, an ancient collection of stories in

Sanskrit. The central episode in the play—the story of Devadatta and Kapila—is based on a tale from *Vetala Panchavimshika,* but Karnad has borrowed it through Thomas Mann's novel *Transposed Heads,* a mock-heroic transcription of the original Sanskrit tales, whereas the sub-plot—horse-man's search for completeness, is Karnad's original invention. *Hayavadana* is a play on the "mad dance of incompleteness" (57) and search of identity in a world of tangled relationships. Devadatta, the intellectual, and Kapila, the man of body, are intimate friends who represent two extreme opposites—one Appolonian; another Dionysian tendency. Devadatta marries Padmini. Padmini and Kapila fall in love with each other. The two friends kill themselves. In a highly comic scene which is of great dramatic significance Padmini transposes their heads, giving Devadatta Kapila's body and viceversa. It results in a confusion of identities which reveals the ambiguous nature of human personality. The situation gets complicated. They fight a duel and kill themselves again. Padmini performs *sati.* Karnad delves deep into the traditional myths to spell out modern man's anguish and dilemmas that are created in his mind. S.Ramaswami has rightly commented:

> Karnad transmutes and transforms his source material to such an extent, being an actor and theatre man himself, that the modern, contemporary, individual talent incorporates the tradition into a transcreation that is rich and strange. The Rhodes scholar and practical man of theatre and cinema blend into a recreation of the myth and legend of India with a novel blend of traditional material and contemporary narrative technique which is quite challenging in bringing folk and elite theatres together. (21-22)

Karnad's play in a characteristic way begins where the 'Vetal' story ends. How would the woman take it if it really happened and would it ultimately solve the problem for her? These are the fascinating questions the artist in him faces. Karnad isn't satisfied with Pooru's acceptance of his father's old-age and uses this only as a starting point. If young Pooru had a wife how would she feel about Pooru's extraordinary decision? This becomes the nucleus of his exploration of the problem raised by the mythical story.

In *Hayavadana* what Karnad wants to suggest is that for us King Vikram's solution does not solve the problem. In fact, the real problem begins when it appears to be solved. That could be the reason why he dropped the version of *Vetala Panchavimshika* which had the "incest" theme at its core. He also makes significant departures from Mann's story. Shubhangi S. Raykar analyses thus: "In all his plays Karnad takes this kind of leap from the original story and develops it further. This further development is the play of artist's imagination and it challenges the glib solution offered in the original stories" (48).

Naga-Mandala: Play with a Cobra (1990) is a play based on two oral tales of Karnataka narrated by older women of the family while feeding their children in the kitchen or putting them to bed. The other adults present on these occasions are also women. Therefore these tales, though directed at the children, often serve as a parallel system of communication among the women in the family. These tales Karnad heard from Professor A.K. Ramanujan. Thereafter he transmuted them into a dramatic form. First is the traditional tale of a cobra turning into man at night and visiting a married woman; and the second is based on the popular belief that a night-long vigil in a temple can ward off death. Karnad himself commented on the role and significance of these tales:

> They also express a distinctly woman's understanding of the reality around her, a lived counterpart to the patriarchal structures of the classical texts and institutions. The position of Rani in the story of *Naga-Mandala*, for instance, can be seen as a metaphor for the situation of a young girl in the bosom of a joint family where she sees her husband only in two unconnected roles—as a stranger during the day and as a lover at night. Inevitably, the pattern of relationships she is forced to weave from these disjointed encounters must be something of a fiction. The empty house Rani is locked in could be the family she is married into. ("Author's Introduction" 17)

The play presents a tale of male chauvinism to give the message that it debilitates and degrades both sexes. In modern ambience, men and women have to work in tandem to maintain this pace of progress. Women have shown that they have drive and enterprise as much as men have. Though to our misfortune we find that there are innumerable cases of exploitation of women, yet it is more than clear that Rani cannot be incarcerated anymore. We shall be "worse than blind Kurudavva if we fail to give women their due place in the society and worse than Cobra if we fail to appreciate their potential. Rani's and Naga's ultimate act of reconciling with the situation is edifying. It is no wisdom to remain stuck to the past, when future beckons us" (Prem Sagar "Preface").

The play deals with gender-bias and the subjection of woman in patriarchal Indian orthodox society. The female protagonist, Rani, and Kurudavva, another female character, are generic creations who stand for Indian women. Though the play is a richly textured dramatic transmutation of two folk tales of Karnataka, Karnad delves deep to explore contemporary socio-cultural and philosophical concerns giving them modern validity. Rani is placed in a world where orthodox social conventions, cultural taboos and coercive forces work; patriarchy is established which proves the greatest blow to the existence of Rani. Apart from overt patriarchy, she is socialized to internalize the male superiority—an invisible conspiracy to derogate and marginalize her position in the society. She adopts new ways to transcend age-old subjection of women. Rani is surrounded by evil social forces where she finds herself helpless; tortured by alienation and despair but she never surrenders but continues her struggle for identity –as a woman, as a wife and as a mother. Karnad's solution appears, at the first observation odd, unconvincing and unconventional violating traditional mode of treatment. The message is clear: despite alienation, despair and antithetical conditions a woman must continue her struggle for her existence and transcend "nothingness" in life and manipulate co-existence as a means for self-existence. Patriarchy, socio-cultural practices, parents of Rani, Appanna, Village Elders, Naga, Dog, Mongoose etc. are the tools to perpetuate exploitation of Rani. M.K. Naik has explored the symbolism embedded in the play:

> The two folk-tales are deftly blended in presenting the two allied themes of the nature of art and the relationship between art and imagianation on the one hand and mundane reality on the other. The tale of the failed playwright seems to suggest that art demands everthything from the artist and that he will die if he cannot fulfil his mission. The Rani-Appanna-Cobra tale is evidently an allegory of the nexus between the world of art and the world of reality. Rani, who whiles away her time making up fairy tales, is the artist, and the Cobra, the power of imagination, while Appanna represents the work-a-day world. The fact that the Cobra assumes the form of Appanna suggests that Art is, and also is not, the same as reality. That the Cobra finally finds permanent refuge in the hair of Rani is perhaps indicative of the permanent alliance between Art and Imagination. (46)

Tale- Danda (1993) derives its story from the life of a Kannada saint, Basavanna, who resisted ideologically against the prevailing evils of caste hierarchy. Like *Tughlaq* and *The Dreams of Tipu Sultan,* it is a historical play. History and its urgent relevance to the present continuous have always fascinated Karnad, and *Tale-Danda* illustrates this fact. Explosive situations after the official endorsement of Mandal Commission Report and Mandir issue in 1989 motivated Karnad to work on the subaltern issue and highlight "how relevant the questions posed by these thinkers were for our age. The horror of subsequent events and the religious fanaticism that has griped our national life today have only proved how dangerous it is to ignore the solutions they offered" (Karnad "Preface"). And the historical context, deeply implanted in his mind, proved catalytic to his plays. Drawing our attention to the genesis of the present, the play illuminates the endemic affliction of the caste and class politics infecting our body politic in the medieval period of history. It was the strong sense of history which has nurtured in Karnad a dominant will for social justice, a sincere compassion for the socially oppressed and subaltern. Karnad doesn't offer any solution to the problem; but he raised the subaltern issue for discussion and common consensus. Basavanna, a social reformer of the twelfth century, assembled a congregation of poets, who mystics and social revolutionaries and philosophers, formed the *Lingayat* faith, giving impetus to courageous questioning and social commitment. The abolition of caste, equality of sexes, rejection of idol worship, repudiation of Brahminism, and of Sanskrit in favour of the mother tongues, i.e., Kannada were the main tenets of subaltern revolution. The resentment reaches its climax when Madhuvarsa, a brahmin, gives his daughter Kalavati in marriage to an untouchable—Sheelvanta. This last act opposing caste hierarchy, not just in theory but in practice also, brought upon him the wrath of the orthodox; the movement ended in terror and bloodshed. The playwright wants to suggest whenever such important issues are not considered seriously and solutions offered by these thinkers go unheeded, disastrous results would follow again. Rupalee Burke finds Karnad a playwright with a difference whose motive behind playwriting is to catch the:

> pulse of the socio-cultural-historical-political facets of India and Indian life...his pltays have always aimed at providing message in the contemporary context....In *Tughlaq* and *Tale-Danda* Karnad employs history to comment on the pathetic and corroded state of Indian modern day politics, and through which he engages in an intellectual debate of our time. (105-107)

Basvanna's vision of egalitarian society and spiritualized politics was the vision of Karnad himself. He raises many questions and provided few oblique suggestions but more are left to the audience to think and get them resolved.

The Fire and the Rain is a far more successful play based on the myth of Yavakri (or Yavakrita) which occurs in Chapters 135-138 of the Vana Parva (Forest Canto) of the *Mahabharata*. It is an English translation of a play in Kannada, *Agni Mattu, Male,* by the playwright himself. It took 37 years to live with a myth and develop into the present form for a workshop with professional actors at the Guthrie Theatre in Minneapolis. Years spent in the company of South Asian scholars at the University of Chicago stimulated his interest in orthodox Hinduism and the complex organization of the Hindu society. The most spectular and successful production of the play was by Arjun Sajnani in English (Bangalore, 1999), subsequently,

Sajnani reworked the play as a commercial Hindi film titled *Agnivarsha* (casting Amitabh Bachchan as Indra).

Aparna Bhargava Dharwadker has examined the genesis and evolution of the play: "Karnad reimagines the world of Hindu antiquity and constructs a story of passion, loss, and sacrifice in the contexts of Vedic ritual, spiritual discipline (*tapasya*), social and ethical differences between human agents, and interrelated forms of performance still close to their moments of origin" ("Introduction", Vol. Two xvii). The 'fire' in the title of the play is the fire of lust, anger, vengeance, envy, treachery, violence and death. The 'rain' symbolizes self-sacrifice, compassion, Divine Grace, forgiveness, revival and life. It is narrated by the ascetic Lomsha to the Pandavas during their exile. But Karnad gives a contemporary meaning to an old legend, which stresses the dangers of knowledge without wisdom and power without integrity. The myth cautions about the misappropiation of power that human beings receive from the gods after great penance.

Yavakri, the son of sage Bhardwaj, acquires knowledge of the *Vedas* directly from Indra after 10 years, rigorous penance. Though his father warns him regarding acquisition of divine power, Yavakri uses it to molest the daughter-in-law of Sage Raibhya, whom he resents. Raibhya in retaliation creates a demon (*Brahma Rakshasa*) and a spirit in the form of his daughter-in-law, Vishakha, both of whom pursue Yavakri and kill him. Bharadwaj curses Raibhya—that he will die at the hands of his own son—and then kills himself in remorse. Sometime later Paravasu indeed mistakes the deerskin his father Raibhya is wearing for a wild animal, and accidentally kills him. Involved with his younger brother Aravasu in a fire sacrifice, Paravasu initiates another cycle of evil when he falsely accuses the latter of patricide (hence of brahiminicide). Aravasu then begins his own penance to the Sun God, and when granted a boon, asks for Yavakri, Bharadwaj, and Raibhya to be restored to life. Lives that were destroyed due to human lapses are restored through divine intervention.

Karnad has forged closer connections between the principal characters and created them into rounded personalities.

Yavakri and Vishakha are not strangers but lovers whose relationship both precedes and follows Vishakha's marriage to Paravasu, making her more than merely a passive object of Yavakri's lust. Her marriage itself appears to be an arid contract: after a frenzy of sensual gratification Paravasu has left Vishakha to Raibhya's care, and the relationships between the three are startling in their lovelessness and malevolence. Similarly, Paravasu kills his father out of hatred rather than ignorance. Karnad has also invented a love episode between Aravasu and a tribal girl Nittilai, and develops a contrast between the life of discipline and sacrifice, and the life of instinct and emotion—opposition between brahmin and shudra, with Aravasu working as a connective link between the two appositive worlds. Karnad's note on "Drama and *Purushartha*" in *The Fire and the Rain* endorses his unequivocal interest in the doctrines of *Purushartha* towards which a work of art should draw mankind. Karnad himself has pointed out the structure of the play resembles that of Aeschyles's *Oresteia* triology, the chief motifs in which are the protagonist's homecoming after a prolonged absence; human fraility and temptation and crime; the operation of the supernatural in human life; and Divine Grace. With its solid thematic richness *the Fire and Rain* is "perhaps the finest of Karnad's plays so far" (Naik 48).

The Dreams of Tipu Sultan (1997) draws its plot from the history of Tipu Sultan. It follows the model of the history play established in *Tughlaq* and *Tale-Danda*. It was first written as a radio play for BBC to celebrate the fiftieth anniversary of India's independence in 1996. The plot obviously deals with some aspect of Indo-British relation. It primarily explores the secret inner world of a man whose public life was a continual war against British colonialism. It was late A.K. Ramanujan who drew his attention to the record of his dreams maintained by Tipu Sultan himself. Karnad, like many other playwrights, was fascinated by the valour of Tipu Sultan who continued to inspire folk ballads in Karnataka. Tipu Sultan is viewed as one of the most brave warriors, political visionary and dreamer; one of the most politically perceptive and tragic figures in modern Indian history.

The radio play was broadcast by the BBC on 15 August 1997 and was directed by Jatinder Verma of Tara Arts with Saeed Jaffrey playing the role of Tipu Sultan. Karnataka Nataka Rangayana staged the Kannad version in the periphery of Daria Daulat, Tipu's summer palace in Srirangapatna, to commemorate his 200th death anniversary in May 1999. Later it was entirely re-written for the stage.

The play blends historical sources to portrait major characters and develops an imaginative plot and resonant dialogue to reflect their experience. Tipu stands for a force fighting against British Colonialism. The image in the play of polity in crisis, both because of internal dissensions and the presence of a powerful alien adversary, "carries the same potential for application to contemporary problems that had made the history of *Tughlaq* and *Tale-Danda* politically relevant in present day India" (Dharwadker, Vol. Two xxiii). The characters, major as well as minor, are put together, language and dialogue are apt to create the air of the Sultanate period of India. The characters are Tipu, Haider Ali, Nana Phadnavis, Lord Cornwallis, Arthur and Richard Wellesley against a less prominent historical figures, i.e., Kirmani, Tipu's queen and sons, courtiers, ordinary citizens and soldiers. Karnad avoids any partisan parade of heroes and villains, rather creates a black sheep in both the camps. Aparna Bhargava Dharwadker rightly comments: "Karnad interlineates 'textualized' history with legend, lore, and memory because all these modes of transmission are germane to the story of Tipu" (Ibid. xxiv).

Karnad has also projected Tipu in multiple and contradictory roles—as a beloved ruler, legendry warrior, loving father, and visionary dreamer, but also a Machiavellian schemer who plots with the French against the British, the defeated soldier who enters into humiliating treaties with the enemy, and the gullible commander who is eventually betrayed by his own side. Tipu's decline destroyed a visionary who had progressive ideas to modernize his empire on the European line.

Bali: The Sacrifice discusses conflicting mindsets with religious beliefs, simultaneously exposes the hollowness and futility of age-old rituals. The plot of the play has drawn upon the thirteenth century Kannada epic *Yashodhara Charite* by Janna, which in turn refers back through an eleventh century Sanskrit epic by Vadiraja to the ninth-century Sanskrit epic *Yashastilaka*, by Somdeva Suri. The play is "a tribute to astuteness and sensitivity of Mahatama Gandhi that he saw so clearly the insistence of non-violence to the cultural and political survival of India" (Karnad. *Two Plays* 69). Anshuman Khanna observes that the play "Offers a fresh perspective of approach vis-à-vis man's psychological struggle and manoeuvres. It presents the cultural, moral and religious dialogic in the context of the warfare between the losing grounds of reality and conscious right to social survival—a conflict between the effete essentialist position and the conceptualized work of living" (106).

It explores the existential dilemma of passion and violence posed by an ancient Jain myth. The myth is less concerned with actual violence than with the morality of substitution, which permits violence, a wider and subtler play by masking its true nature. Violence has been the one of the crucial subjects of debate in the history of Indian civilization. Vedic sacrifices, conducted by brahmin priests, involved the slaughter of animals as offerings to the gods, which the Jains found repugnant. To the Jain, indulging in any kind of violence, however minor or accidental, meant forfeiting one's moral status as a human being. Later Buddhists too advocated non-violence. The issue found some resolution when the brahmins renounced blood sacrifice. Miniature figurines, made of dough, were substituted for live animals, a practice that continues to this day. Despite this change, Jains objected to this process of substitution that carries the original violent impulse within them which was no less dehumanizing.

Karnad came across the myth of the Cock of Dough when he was in his teens and the mÿth littered with discarded drafts of dramatized versions of it. The myth revealed unexpected meanings with long ponderings over it, and *Bali: The Sacrifice* is the result of over two decades evolution. Karnad transforms the story of the dough figurine that comes alive at the moment of sacrifice into a mature philosophical exploration of love, jealously, desire, betrayal and violence between men and women who are bound by the ties of blood and marriage, or encounter each other in the perfect freedom of anonymity.

The novelty of the play lies in the unconventionality of its major characters, and the seriousness with which it yokes intimate personal acts to structures of religious belief and practice. Subaltern issue and the feminist study also make the play more valid in the present context. The Mahout represents subalternity, and his anger, frustration and disgust are very much generic; whereas old Queen (King's mother) and Queen Amritawati underline two sets of women—one traditional, blind adherent to age-old rituals indulging in sacrificial acts for material gains; the other a woman of practical vision thwarting any form of violence. She even ridicules the morality of substitution. All the four characters are sets of opposites—old Queen and Queen; King and Mahout. Vinod Mishra finds in the play, "a voice of reason against a saga of myths" (104). Subha Mishra has seen Foucault's Panopticism in *Bali: The Sacrifice* which implies deconstructing the established beliefs.

The two short monologues in English—*Broken Images* (2004) and *Flowers* (2004)—mark a significant change in subjects and forms. *Broken Images* takes up a debate on the politics of language in Indian literary culture, particularly in relation to the respective claims of the modern Indian languages and English which must also be recognized now as an Indian, though not an indigenous language. Manjula Nayak, the play's only character, is a writer of short and long fiction in Kannada and a teacher of English in a Banglore college. She succumbs to the temptation of larger audience and money making. She involves in plagiarism and is exposed thereafter. She herself confesses while talking to her own television image that she is an imposter who has passed off her dead sister Malini's novel as her own. She has tried to cash in on a dead sibling's talent. This Anglophilic attitude, comments Dharwadker, "can only lead the Indian language author to prostitute herself" ("Introduction" Vol. Two xxvii). It deals with problems of authenticity and bad faith created by globalization, through a confrontation between a writer and her electronic image.

When Karnad takes on literary politics in the play he immediately relates language to genre. The central issue in the play doesn't involve drama at all but the radically unequal status of fiction written in two contemporary languages, Kannada and English. Manjula Nayak is an epitome of an Indian woman emerging in a changed world order. How can modern women lag behind their male counterparts even in literary writing or plagiarism? Both Majula and Malini are contrasted—one is an invalid and the other ready to exploit whatever is commercially significant.

Flowers (2004), in contrast, returns to the world of folk-tale, and is the first work in this genre to focus on male rather than female desire, thus registering a small but important shift in Karnad's dramaturgy. The legend of Veeranna on which the play is based belongs to the Chitradurg region. It became widely known when a Kannada writer T.R. Subbanna included it in his novel *Hamsageete* (1952). The married priest has been passionately in love with a mistress to whom he takes the offerings from the temple after every prayer. One day the *palegar* (chieftain) discovers a hair in the *prasada* and demands an explanation from Veeranna, who claims that the hair belongs to God. Challenged by the chieftain to prove the truth of his claim the priest in turn challenges God to display hair or accept his head in punishment, and enters a meditative trance to the accompaniment of Venkatashubhayya's song. When the chieftain arrives the next day to expose Veeranna's lie, the *shivalinga* has indeed sprouted long silken hair, and when (urged by the singer) he pulls out a tuft to test its authenticity, blood begins to ooze from the crown of the *lingam*. Overwhelmed by a sense of sin at having injured his deity, Veeranna beheads himself in the sanctum. The conflict between religious devotion and erotic love, the mingling of spiritual and carnal, is central. The miracle of the *shivalinga* confirms the power of the priest's worship and marks him as one of the chosen, but it also ends his life. Sudhir K. Arora has pertly commented:

> Thematically, both the monologues are sound and once again, Karnad has introduced his well-known confrontation—between love and duty in *Flowers* and anthenticity and duplicity in *Broken Images*. Hence, *Folwers* spiritualises the aesthetics of floweres while

> *Broken Images* breaks the ethics of pseudo-images regarding the questions related to languages and the originality in literary world. (233)

Both the monologues were originally written in English and later translated into Kannada which reversed the common feature of Karnad's writing. *Flowers* is a narrative and *Broken Images* is dramatic in technique. Both are the result of complex structural design and thematic innovation which mark a turning point in the long dramatic career of Karnad.

Wedding Album (2008) is the latest play of Karnad directed by Lillette Dubey and performed in Bangalore July 10-11, 2008 thereafter in Delhi, Chandigarh and Ludhiana with grand success. It's a contemporary play with "humourous insight into the country's traditions and culture...explores the traditional Indian wedding in a globalised and technologically advanced India" ("Express News service"). It's a delightfully poignant tale of love and longing in a shining India. According to Karnad:

> This play has been, in a sense, 30 to 40 years in the making. When his sister got married, he watched the members of his family gathering together, and observed the resultant interpersonal dynamics and tensions...he found it a combination of "celebration and anxiety", and tucked it away in his mind, to emerge much later. He didn't want to write it as a "story" play, though, and the form that it has taken now is satisfying to him.
>
> (citizenmatters.in)

Wedding Album deals with an urban middle-class Saraswat brahmin family of Nadkarni: a daughter who lives in Australia (Hema) with her professional husband, a son (Rohit) who is a software designer, a younger daughter (Vidula) willing to marry a suitable boy from America she has never met, a doting mother (Mother) and a cook (Radhabai). The family is educated, liberal and modern. Each snapshot shows its members "frozen in an attitude of respectability, yet each figure has a double image with a penumbra of a hidden life... It's a wonderful comic drama that is deeply revelatory about the India that we live in today" (Deopti "Wedding Album"). According to Lillette Dubey, director of the play, "*Wedding Album* is full of sharp, pithy, and observant comments. Just because the play is not heavy, it doesn't mean it doesn't have muscle and content" (Qtd. in Deepa Mohan). *Wedding Album* which is structured into nine scenes deals primarily with women and their two different worlds, i.e., traditional and modern cyber world. But both of them merge into each other. Even the traditional older women are fused with energy, hope and modern sensibility. The younger sorts enjoy liberty in education, love, courtship via 'distance' technology; and marriage. The play marks the highest evolution of feminine psyche. Amrit Srinivasan has observed:

> the consetellation of sexual, conjugal, caste, class, and age-related behaviours and attitudes of selfishness and sacrifice, chastity and commerce, obedience and authority, all integral to modern Hindu marriage, forms *Wedding Album*'s central narrative thread...works as modern myth, whose condensed logic straddles both the real and the tech-simulated world of today, to help us confront our own mixed-up, amoral, craven, unhappy selves...*Wedding Album* encourages us to examine the growing fundamentalism of the Hindu *middle class* family, which is largely 'missing' from social science scholarship on India today.
>
> ("Foreword" ix).

Karnad is an innovative, multifaceted and problem playwright who imbibes several personalities in one. He has contributed a lot to enrich Indian English drama through playtext, performance, acting, and direction. Moreover, like his contemporary playwrights Vijay Tendulker, Badal Sircar and Mahesh Dattani he has reshaped Indian English drama. But unlike his contemporaries, he adapts mythical and historicl material with a view to giving it a psychological interpretation. As a modern playwright, Karnad is always engaged in the act of "deconstructing myths. He takes up mythical and legendary tales from his own culture and unfolds them in the light of modern sensibility. This deconstructing myth becomes an act of self-searching for the playwright...he combines the past and the present into a unity that bespeaks of tradition and modernity in his art of playwriting" (Gill 8).

Karnad upholds the rich cultural heritage of India and endeavours to fight against the legacy of colonialism by advocating Indian values and cultural ethos of India. Subjects from the native soil, characters deeply rooted in indigenous culture, English very much Indianised to suit the context and create feel of Indianness, and folk and classical theatre traditions endorse his well- thought design to set free Indian English drama from the colonial yoke. Indian imagination and sensibility can be easily seen throughout his plays.

Works Cited

Arora, Sudhir K. "Spiritualising the Aesthetics (of Flowers) versus Breaking the Ethics (of Image): A Critical Study of Karnad's Two Monologues *Flowers* and *Broken Images*", *Thunder on Stage: A Study of Girish Karnad's Plays* (Eds.) Khatri, C.L. & Arora, Sudhir K.Jaipur: Book Enclave, 2008.

Burke, Rupalee. "India Then and Now: The Contemporary Relevance of Girish Karnad's *Tale-Danda", Studies in Indian Drama in English* (Eds.) Prasad, Amar Nath and Yadav, Saryug. Bareilly: Prakash Book Depot, 2003.

Deopti "Wedding Album" <banglore.metblogs.com> 18.01.2011.

Dhawan, R.K. "Girish Karnad: The Man and the Writer", *The Plays of Girish* (Ed.) Dodiya, J. Prestige: New Delhi, 2009.

Dharwadker, Aparna Bhargava. "Introduction", *Collected Plays.* Volume Two (Ed.) New Delhi: Oxford University Press, 2005.

"Express News Service" *<www.Indianewsexpress.com>* 18.01.2011.

Gill, L.S. *Girish Karnad's Hayavadana: A Critical Study.* New Delhi: Asia Book Club, 2005.

Kalida & Rahmat "Renaissance Man" <India-today.com/itoday/.../arts.html> 20.10.2010.

Karnad, Girish. "Author's Introduction", *Three Plays: Naga-Mandala, Hayavadana, Tughlaq.* (Eighth impression) New Delhi: Oxford University Press, 2002.

__________. "Preface", *Tale-Danda.* Delhi: Ravi Dayal, 1993.

Khanna, Anshuman. "Dialogic Ramifications in Karnad's Bali: The Sacrifice", Thunder on Stage: A Study of Girish Karnad's Plays. (Eds.) op.cit.

Mishra, Vinod. "Girish Karnad's *Bali: The Sacrifice*: A Voice of Reason against a Saga of Myth", *Thunder on Stage: A Study of Girish Karnad's Plays.* op.cit.

Mohan, Deepa "Wedding Album at Chowdiah" <banglore.citizenmatters.in> 17.01.2011.

Murthy, U.R. Anantha. "Introduction" to *Tughlaq*. Chennai: Oxford University Press, 1998.

Naik, M.K. "Cinderella Still: Recent Indian English Drama". *Littcrit*. Volume 27, Number 1&2, June-Dec. 2001.

__________. *A History of Indian English Literature*. New Delhi: Sahitya Akademi, 1995.

Padma Rani, P. Hari. "The Form of Indian drama in English: A Few Problems", *Indian English Drama: Critical Perspectives* (Eds.) Dodiya, K. Jaydipsingh and Surendran, K.V. New Delhi: Sarup and Sons, 2002.

Ramaswami, S. "The New and the Old: Indian Writing at the Turn of the Century", *Indian Writing in the New Millennium*. (Ed.) Dhawan, R.K. New Delhi: Indian Association for English Studies, 2000.

Raykar, S Shubhangi. "The Development of Girish Karnad as a Dramatist", *Contemporary Indian Drama*. (Ed.) Pandey, Sudhaker and Taraporewala, Freya. New Delhi: Prestige, 1990.

Sagar, Prem. (Ed.) *Girish Karnad: Naga-Mandala*. Agra: Lakshmi Narain Agarwal, n.d.

Srinivasan, Amrit. "Foreword", *Wedding Album*. New Delhi: Oxford University Press, 2009.

Wikipedia "Girish Karnad"<en.wikipedia.org/wiki/Girish_Karnad> 21.08.2010.

Yadav, Saryug. "Indian English Drama: Tradition and Achievement" *Indian English Drama: Critical Perspectives*.op.cit.

2

De-Colonization of Indian English Drama

I

De-colonization is a process that is paralled with postcolonialism; it is more a cultural and psychological than historical and political phenomenon. De-colonization begins with the strong notion to thwart the colonial dominance and possess an independent status. Though political independence was a landmark in the history of a country once dominated by the Eurocetric force (s) and provided an opportunity to express and establish the native culture, history, polity and literature, intellectual thought process is the real marker of de-colonization. Postcolonial, writes Dennis Walder:

> Has come to be thought appropriate, because of the implication that the colonial experience persists despite the withdrawal of political control, as a result of the continuing strategic and economic power of the former colonizers. The new global dispositions which keep groups of poorer states in thrall...the impact of empire upon a particular people in the long perspective, it has always left its imprint. (3)

B.K. Das explores postcolonialism as a "historical marker of the period following decolonization and second, as an embodiment of intellectual approaches" (131). The process of de-colonization dates earlier to postcolonialism; even during the colonial period there were attempts in the form of ideological as well as physical resistance to dethrown the colonialism which operated in various forms—polity, history writing of the native people, interpretations of native literatures, introduction of English language etc. as part of colonial discourse. Postcolonial phase in the history of a country definitely accelerated the growth and process of de-colonization. De-colonization and postcolonialism are closely and reciprocally linked and gave impetus to each other. Leela Gandhi has closely analysed the relationship between postcoloniality and postcolonialism in terms of the decolonizing process:

> The emergence of anti-colonial and 'independent' nation-States after colonialism is frequently accompanied by a desire to forget the colonial past. This 'will-to-forget' takes a number of historical forms, and is impelled by a variety of cultural and political motivations. Principally, postcolonial amnesia is symptomatic of the urge for historical self-invention or the need to make a new start—to erase painful memories of colonial subordination. As it happens, histories, much as families, cannot be freely chosen by a simple act of will, and newly emergent postcolonial nation-States are often deluded and unsuccessful in their attempts to disown the burdens of their colonial inheritance. The mere repression of colonial memories is never, in itself, tantamount to a surpassing of or emancipation from the uncomfortable realities of the colonial encounter. In response, postcolonialism can be seen as a theoretical resistance to the mystifying amnesia of the colonial aftermath. It is a disciplinary project devoted to the academic task of revisiting, remembering and, crucially, integorrating the colonial past. The process of returning to the colonial scene discloses a relationship of reciprocal antagonism and desire between colonizer and colonized....The colonial aftermath is marked by the range of ambivalent cultural moods and formations which accompany periods of transition and translation. It is, in the first place, a celebrated moment of arrival—charged with the rhetoric of independence and the creative euphoria of self-invention. (4-5)

Postcolonialism bears the seeds of de-colonization, hece it's urgently needed to explore its mechanism. 'Postcolonialism' is a theory and the condition it addresses is best conveyed through the notion of 'postcoloniality'. Postcolonialism explores strategies of resistance and independence or a counterdiscourse in native texts against colonialism; it looks at colonialism's modes of representation of the native; the epistemological underpinnings of colonial projects; the writing of colonial histories; the feminization, marginalization and dehumanization of the native; the rise of nationalist and/or nativist discourse; the psychological effects of colonialism on both the colonizer and the colonized; the role of apparatuses like education, English studies, historiography, art and architecture in the execution of the colonial project.

Postcolonialism or sometimes hyphenated form 'post-' colonialism, indicates a temporal marker of the decolonizing process, the age or period after colonization, especially decolonized state. It therefore functions as a historical category that suggests a chronology—from the colonized to the decolonized or postcolonial. Others fiercely query the implied chronological separation between colonialism and its aftermath—on the grounds that the postcolonial condition is inaugurated with the onset rather than the end of colonial occupation.

Postcolonialism also refers to an oppositional analytic procedure in which colonial texts were re-read for colonial ideologies imbedded in them. Postcolonialism after Edward Said analyses the European "construction" of the East/Orient is a discursive field called "Orientalism". The European colonial power "creates" the Orient as an epistemological category before dominationg it militarily, politically and economically. That is, Europe first produces a category designated as the Other or the Orient through certain specific practices of knowledge and formation which rely upon a series of binary oppositions, all of which treat the native as the negative/dark opposite of Europe: civilized/barbaric, white/black, mature/immature, strong/weak, masculine/effeminate, rational/emotional, and progressive/primitive. The first term signifies to the European, and the second to the native.

Adapting ideas from poststructuralism, postcolonial studies focuses on the discursive and linguistic construction of reality. This meant that representation of the native in Europe was hardly "innocent" or "true", but essentially an exercise that preceded more concrete alterations in the material reality of the native: the discourse that representated the native also ruled the native. Said makes a pert comment: "The nexus of knowledge creating "the Orient" and in a sense obliterating him as a human being is therefore not for me an exclusively academic matter. Yet it is an intellectual matter of some very pbvious importance" (27). This link between representation, epistemology and political practices becomes the subject of analysis in postcolonial studies.

Ashcroft and others characterize writing emerging from the once-colonised nations as postcolonial. They cover "all the culture affected by the imperial process from the moment of colonization to the present day" (*The Empire Writes Back* 2) and still find the colonial operation to in a new world order:

> All post-colonial societies are still subject in one way or another to overt or subtle forms of neo-colonial domination, and independence has not solved this problem. The development of new elites within independent societies, often buttressed by neo-colonial institutions; the development of internal divisions based on racial, linguistic or religious discriminations; the continuing unequal treatment of indigenous peoples in settler/invader societies—all these testify to the fact that post-colonialism is a continuing process of resistance and reconstruction.
>
> (*The Post-Colonial Studies Reader* 1-2)

They identify three major characteristics of postcolonial writing:

(a) The silencing and marginalization of the postcolonial voice by the imperial centre.

(b) The abrogation of the imperial centre within the text and;

(c) The active appropriation of the language and culture of that centre.

Postcolonial studies especially in the 1980s and 1990s questioned the nationalist protest to colonialism and argued that cultural independence also relied on categories that were themselves European, i.e., the idea of modernization, development and nation-state. Later developments added issues of ethnicity, displacement, gender, and race as categories for analysis. Thus the study was focused on, comments Pramod K Nayar:

> How the nationalist project in colonial times and decolonized nation-state replicated/extended certain fundamental oppressive structures in class, gender and (in India) caste. The decolonized nation, argue the postcolonials, under the guise of homogenizing, national stability, federalism, elide differences and perpetuate oppression of the marganalised—the women, the lower classes/castes. This, they argue, is essentially the same technique as that of colonialism. Under the rubric of postcolonial studies, we thus have an ongoing attempt to retrieve histories that have silenced/erased by both colonial and nationalist powers. This is the subaltern studies project in India, which seeks to write the history of the subaltern as against/alternative (to) the history of the upper classes/castes, a "history from below". (167)

Postcolonial studies analyse representations and identity formations of the colonizer and the colonized in literary and cultural texts. Further, the adoption of postcolonial studies as a discipline in Western academies, the dangers of neocolonialism and cultural imperialism in the age of global capital and information networks, the role of the nation-state in such a globalizing context, the issues of multiculturalism are also addressed. Avadhesh K. Singh considers postcolonialism "unattended by intellectual independence does not mean much...postcolonial state is a mirage, postcolonialism is ever always present. Only its colour, external appearance or demeaner changes. Its nature remains the same. Colonialism yields place to neo, new or newer colonialism", he further cautions us:

> What is needed is to understand it and its condition (s), its strategies, receive and respond to it. Our literature and criticism can play their own roles in bearing its ugly hidden face by penetrating under the skein of its connivance and thereby resisting whatever is inimical to our national and social interest with our counter-strategies...accept pragmatically whatever is of use to us in it; and we can think of alternatives to it, and redefine it or reconstruct our theory or model from our texts.
>
> (Presidential Address)

The consciousness of binary oppositional structures retained by colonial forces is, according to Avadesh K. Singh, "the first and an indispensable stage of decolonization. This is the stage of reaction....This is to be followed by the stage of consruction of the ideal... [i.e.] being healthy and being located in our self, i.e. traditions and roots" (*Interventions* 36-37). Prof. S.Z.H. Abidi has evolved a formula to explain the psychology and operative mechanism of postcolonialism:

> T3+PS+SE+CB>CC+A3 which is elaborated as:
>
> Trade, Thief, Translator+Prospero Syndrome+Surrogate English+ Cultural Bards> Caliban Complex+Adopt, Adapt, Adept.
>
> (Plenary Lecture)

Resistance to colonialism and its discourse can be defined in part as the rejection of foreign cultures and the celebration of the indigenous tradition. Helen Tiffin has argued that the focus of postcolonial writing is to "establish or rehabilitate self against either European appropriation or rejection" (169). It can be realized through a number of strategies, which comes from a writer's conscious awareness of the use and abuse of history and tradition which was moulded by the colonial powers to justify their superiority. Hence postcolonial intellectuals challenge their "master narrative" by fracturing them into two distinct different ways, depending on the nature of cultural system to which they belong. The first way goes to the countries like Africa, Australia, and India, which have well developed metaphysical systems. Here the writers use their indigenous resources to challenge European perspectives, as it constantly reflects in their conscious use of myth, history, and folktales. The second way goes to those countries, which do not have such systems. Here the challenge operates through the counter culture of the imagination, in which the writers resort to the dismantling of the narrative through interrogation of history and textuality, polyphony and by proposing varieties of re-readings. In colonial and postcolonial societies, comment Mallikarjuna Rao et al: "the nationalist aspiration of liberation and active resistance to colonialism is closely linked, in one way or another, to the socio-political movement of decolonization" (v).

Indian literary encounters of the last 50 years show that there have been a series of efforts to grapple with the postcolonial situation. K.Satchidanandan has briefly and coherently epitomized this process:

> Paradigms are tried and given up; communities are imagined and dissolved; traditions are consctructed and deconstructed; the principles of unity and of difference are alternately tried out; the West's presence is acknowledged and negated; radical European concepts and models are alternated with return to the indigeneous roots; the classical and folk elements of the heritage, the written and the oral/performed are explored one after the other. Our creativity has thus been dialogic, and our literary discoures marked by the negotiation of a necessary heterogeneity, by a conception of identity that lives through difference and hybridity. It has been a continuous process of mediation between "the self" and "the other" using, what Foucault terms, 'the technologies of the self'. (25)

After India's political Independence, Indian cultural nationalists' arguments about drama, theatre, and performance approach the issue of modernity and Western influences on the basis of the perceived relation of the colonial to pre-colonial. Cultural nationalists argue that modern Westernized culture of realistic, secular, urban and commercial performances disrupted and dislocated the indegenous theatrical traditions that had developed continuously from two millennia. This new:

> Western theatrical form forced the indigeneous theatrical forms like classical, devotional, ritual, and folk performance to accommodate realism and urban proscenium stage. The Westernised mode of production and representation led to a rejection of popular folk forms like jatra, bhavai, tamasha, yakshagana, nautanki, manch, and ramlila as "debased" and "corrupted".
>
> (Saurabh K. Singh 49)

The colonial discourse which created polarity of theatre as low (Indian) and high (European) was also condemned. The impulse to return to roots has motivated many writers to confront the issues of race, class, nationhood—*svadeshvada*. Dr. Suresh Awasthi, the spirit behind the 'theatre of roots' movement in India, has commented:

> As part of the great cultural renaissance of the post independence period, there has been a most meaningful encounter with tradition in various fields of creative activity. The return to and discovery of tradition is inspired by a search for roots and a quest for identity. This is part of whole process of decolonization of life style, social institutions, creative forms, and cultural modes. (48)

The end of colonialism provided an opportunity to classical or folk traditions to resume their due place in national culture and drama. The great cultural upsurge of the post-Independence period has resulted in cultural decolonization, and traditional art has asserted their vitality and relevance. Criticism of realism in Western theatre, and the emergence of various theatre forms, such as expressionism, theatre of absurd, and Brecht's epic theatre reflect the superiority of anti-realist, anti-Aristotlean aesthetic of Indian theatre over Western theatre. On the other hand, the modern and postmodern theatres and their techniques have been outmoded and there is stress on the traditonal theatrical forms which possess revitalizing energy and high aesthetic quality. Theatre personalities like Eugenio Barba, Jerzy Grotowsky, Richard Schechner and Peter Brooke, and their emphasis on traditional theatre forms alarms Indian playwrights to continue their new enterprise. Suresh Awasthi observes: "Theatre of roots has finally made its preence felt. It has compelling power, it thrills audience, and it is receiving institutional recognition. It is deeply rooted in regional theatre culture, but cuts across linguistic barriers, and has an all-India character in design" (48). Cultural renaissance after Independence led Girish Karnad, Badal Sircar, Vijay Tendulker, Habib Tanvir and Mudrarakshasa, and directors like B.V. Karanth, Ratan Thiyam, and K.N. Panikkar to reject Western influences, and to create the space for indigenous culture and traditions of performing art.

II

In Karnad's plays, the choice of indigeneous subjects, myths, legends, history and folklore; characters rooted in Indian cultural soil, yakshagana and Natak Company conventions fused with Indian classical theatre techniques, Indianised English to suit the context and milieu definitely proved detrimental to colonial stereotyped models, theories of drama and cultural hegemony. He not only reacted against colonialism but also constructed an ideal for writing; it is a brilliant instance to further the cause of intellectual and cultural independence and accomplish the process of "decanonization and decolonization" (Avadhesh K. Singh. *Interventions.* 13).

Karnad sets out to write plays with a definite purpose—to revitalize Indian history and culture and free them from Eurocentric domination and de-colonize Indian English drama. Postcolonial dialectics, subalternization of Indian English drama and nativism are the most important characteristics of his plays. Selecting native subjects for dramatic art is not a new thing; his predecessors have also experimented with it. But his superiority rests in his use of Indian myths, legends and history developing contemporaneity; correlating past with the present, subjects of the past and medieval transcend time and age, enjoy validity not only in the past but also in the present continuous.

Karnad finds a voice and a distinct identity for Indian English drama by reclaiming the past of the country. His plays are the lens through which he tries to view the emerging cultural consciousness and germination of indigenous sensibility; condemns Western literary imagination politically motivated then part of the relationship between culture and empire. Karnad diffused the "cultural bomb"—the biggest weapon of the West targeted to annihilate the people's beliefs in their indigenous names, unity, capacities and heritage; it makes native people see their past as a waste land of non-achievement. More importantly, it makes them want to identify themselves with other peoples' language and culture.

Karnad also resisted the colonizer's strategy for mental enslavement by (a) Destruction or undervaluing of a people's culture, art etc. (b) The conscious elevation of the language of the colonizer. Together these two resulted in the dissociation of the sensibility of the native from his natural and social environment—"colonial alienation" (the term is used by Ngugi wa Thiong'o). Karnad used English as a means to express his anguish, resistance and protest as Caliban did. "Centrality" of Europe in literature, history, geography, culture, polity all were challenged by Karnad who projects Indian history, myths, legends and culture all at the forefront to defy this centrality and give response to "discourse of Orientalism" (Edward Said). He proved it successfully and showed, if handled artistically, "local" (native) subjects also can entertain the majority. Like Frantz Fanon, he agrees that a "national literature", perhaps a *negritude*, would enable the development of a national consciousness and overcome "dreadful secondariness" (Edward Said). He adopts ideological resistance to save or restore the sense and the fact of community against colonial system. His quest for cultural independence, de-construction of the European "construction" of the East/Orient as the Dark Other is well illustrated in his plays.

Karnad has great insight into human nature which made him a great actor and playwright. He is well aware of the paradoxes in human nature and has thorough understanding of life's little ironies. He originally belongs to the Kannada theatre. He represents the best traditions of Kannada drama which found its finest expression in the plays of T.P. Kailasam, Huyilgal, Samsa and Adya. Various dramatic genres grew and developed in Kannada literature. Karnad was highly influenced by these trends and he took myth, legend and history for his plays. *Yayati* (1961), his first play, reinterprets an ancient myth from Adiparva of *Mahabharata* in modern context. It is self-consciously existentialist drama on the theme of responsibility and human relationship. Yayati, unheroic hero stands for modern man inhabitated by worldly desires, sensual pleasure, and irresponsible exercise of power and utter forgetfulness of the imperishable values of life. It provides "fleeting glimpses of the fears and desires sleepless within us" ("Prologue" 6).

Tughlaq (1972) deals with life and turbulent reign of Mohammad-bin-Tughlaq who ruled over India for about 26 years; but for the sake of dramatic precision and brevity, Karnad spans only five years from 1327 to 1332. The action begins in Delhi in 1327, then on the road from Delhi to Daultabad, and lastly in and around the fort of Daultabad. *Caligula* legend supplied the substance for the play, and the readings of Camu and Sartre accounted for the existentialist character of his plays.

History plays written earlier were costume plays in which no attempt was made to relate a historical episode to modern sensibility. Tughlaq, both in history and in the play, is a great scholar, idealist and visionary. He stands for administrative reforms, for implementing the policy of Hindu-Muslim amity, recognition of merit, reorganization of administrative machinery, taxation structure, etc. *Tughlaq* develops as a tragedy of the limits of human power in a predominantly psychological context. Karnad was fascinated by the history of Tughlaq's reign which reflected the "political mood of disillusionment which followed the Nehru era of idealism in the country" (Murthy viii). The treatment of history and its reinterpretation in the light of current political situation distinguishes Karnad from the rest. The play was performed in Natak Company conventions.

Hayavadana (1975) is based on Thomas Mann's *The Transposed Heads*, adapted on a tale from Somdeva's *Brihadkatha Saritasagar*, an ancient collection of stories in Sanskrit. The central episode in the play—the story of Devdatta and Kapil—is based on a tale from *Vetalapan Chavimshika*, but Karnad has borrowed it from Thomas Mann's mock-heroic transcription of the original Sanskrit tales—*The Transposed Heads*, whereas the sub-plot—the horseman's search for completeness, is Karnad's original invention. *Hayavadana* is essentially a play on "the search of identity in a world of tangled relationships" (Kurtkoti vi). P. Dhanavel finds that "*Hayavadana* gives expression to the Indian imagination in its richest colours and profound meanings" ("Preface"). The play was presented in Yakshagana conventions. Saurabh Kumar Singh cites *Hayavadana* as frontrunners in the theatre of roots movement:

> The play *Hayavadana* is rich in its theatrical language; complex in its multidimensional thematic aspects of

> identity; search for ideal and the question of completeness. Girish Karnad's consistent loyalty to indigenous theatrical performance, folklores, and myths has placed him among the front-runners in the 'return to roots' movement of contemporary Indian theatre practioners. (53)

Naga-mandala (1990) is a socio-psychological study of Indian woman; richly textured dramatic transmutation of two-folk tales of Karnataka. It deals with gender-bias and the subjection of woman in patriarchal Indian orthodox society. The female protagonist—Rani and Kurudavva, other female characters, are generic creations stand for Indian woman. Use of folk-tale to discuss such important issue and suggesting a lot shows Karnad's involvement in the social problems of the society. The woman's understanding of the reality around her, a lived counterpoint to the "patriarchal structures of classical texts and institutions" ("Author's Introduction" 17) have been obliquely suggested.

Tale-Danda (1993) draws its story from the life of a Kannada saint Basavanna who resisted ideologically against the prevailing evils of caste hierarchy. Explosive situations after the official endorsement of Mandal Commission Report and Mandir issue in 1989 motivated Karnad to concentrate on subaltern issue and expose "the horror of subsequent events and the religious fanaticism that has gripped our national life today have only proved how dangerous it is to ignore the solution they offered" ("Preface"). And the historical context, deeply implanted in his mind, proved catalytic to his plays. Drawing our attention to the genesis of the present, the play illuminates the endemic affliction of the caste and class politics infecting our body politic in the medieval period of history. Karnad doesn't offer any solution to the problem; but raised the subaltern issue for discussion and common consensus.

In *Fire and the Rain* (1998), which is a far more successful play, Karnad draws upon a story from the *Mahabharata*. But in the best traditions of moderinism, he gives a contemporary meaning to an old legend which stresses on the dangers of knowledge without wisdom and power without integrity. The 'fire' in the title of the play is the fire of lust, anger, vengeance, envy, treachery, violence and death. The 'rain' symbolizes self-sacrifice, compassion, Divine Grace, forgiveness, revival and life. The myth of Yavakri has been dramatized with new dimensions, and the presentation is amply successful to create ancient atmosphere and link past with present. Dharwadker writes:

> Karnad reimagines the world of Hindu antiquity and constructs a story of passion, love, and sacrifice in the contexts of Vedic ritual, spiritual discipline *(tapasya),* social and ethical differences between human agents, and interrelated forms of performance still close to their moments of origin.
>
> (Vol. Two. xvi-xvii).

The Dreams of Tipu Sultan (1997) was first written as a radio play for BBC to celebrate the fiftieth anniversary of India's independence in 1996. Later it was entirely re-written for the stage. The plot obviously deals with some aspect of Indo-British relation. It primarily explores the secret inner world of a man whose public life was a continual war against British colonialism. It follows the model of the history play established in *Tughlaq* and *Tale-danda*. Tipu Sultan is viewed as one of the most brave warriors, political visionary and dreamer; "one of the most politically perceptive and tragic figures in modern Indian history" ("Preface"). It was first presented by the Madras Players at the YMCA Ampitheatre Chennai, on 17 February 2000.

Bali:The Sacrifice has drawn upon the thirteenth century Kannada epic *Yashodhara Charite* by Janna, which in turn refers back through an eleventh century Sanskrit epic by Vadiraja to the ninth-century Sanskrit epic *Yashastilaka*, by Somdeva Suri. The play is "a tribute to astuteness and sensitivity of Mahatama Gandhi that he saw so clearly the insistance of non-violence to the cultural and political survival of India" (Preface). It explores the existential dilemma of passion and violence posed by an ancient Jain myth. The myth is less concerned with actual violence than with the morality of substitution, which permits violence a wider and more subtle play by masking its true nature. It was first presented at the Haymarket Theatre, Liecester, on 31 May, 2002. The two short monologues in English—*Broken Images* (2004) and *Flowers* (2004) form a radical coda to Karnad's 40-year career as a playwright because they initiate new subjects and forms.

Broken Images takes up a debate that has grown edgier since independence—the politics of language in Indian literary culture. Specifically in relation to the respective claims of the modern Indian languages and English, which must also be recognized now as an Indian though not an indigenous language. Manjula Nayak, the only character of the play, is a successful author of short and long fiction in Kannada and teacher of English in a Bangalore college succumbs to the temptation of larger audience and money making; involves in playgiarism and exposed later. It deals with problems of authenticity and bad faith created by globalization, through a confrontation between a writer and her electronic image. When Karnad takes on literary politics in the play he immediately relates language to genre. The central issue in the play doesn't involve drama at all but the radically unequal status of fiction written in two contemporary languages, Kannada and English.

Flowers (2004) in contrast, returns to the world of folktale, and is the first work in this genre to focus on male rather than female desire, thus registering a small but important shift in Karnad's dramaturgy. The legend of Veeranna on which the play is based belongs to the Chitradurg region, and became widely known when a Kannada writer, T.R. Subbanna included it in his novel *Hamsageete* (1952). The married priest has been passionately in love with a mistress to whom he takes the offerings from the temple after the every prayer. One day the *palegar* (chieftain) discovers a hair in the *prasada* and demands an explanation from Veeranna, who claims that the hair belongs to God. Challenged by the chieftain to prove the truth of his claim, the priest in turn challenges God to display hair or accept his head in punishment, and enters a meditative trance to the accompaniment of Venkatashubhayya's song. When the chieftain arrives the next day to expose Veeranna's lie, the *shivalinga* has indeed sprouted long silken hair, and when (urged by the singer) he pulls out a tuft to test its authenticity, blood begins to ooze from the crown of the *lingam*. Overwhelmed by a sense of sin at having injured his deity, Veeranna beheads himself in the sanctum. The conflict between religious devotion and erotic love, mingling of spiritual and carnal, is central. The miracle of the *shivalinga* confirms the power of the priest's worship and marks him as one of the chosen, but it also ends his life.

Wedding Album (2008) is the latest play of Karnad. It's a delightfully poignant tale of love and longing in a shining India. It explores the traditional Indian wedding in a globalized, technologically advanced India. It took more than 30 years to transform the memory of Karnad's sister's marriage which was marked by celebration and anxiety into a full-length play. The marriage of Vidula Nadkarni belonging to an urban middle class Saraswat family of Dharwad represents the indigenous socio-cultural practices, though she belongs to a different world—cyber world of modern youth to whom "marriage is a gamble" (89). Subha Mishra's comment on Karnad's plays is worthquoting:

> His plays are innovative and use folk techniques and folk philosophy to speak to a contemporary audience. He focuses on selected moments of cultural and historical crisis, which individuals have to confront as the 'burden of culture'. His creativity lies in exploring new aspects of life and philosophy, while his plays constantly depict social drama of the world and the aesthetic drama in the character's conscience. The concepts of time and space, traditional style of performance, the ability to transform space into many places are some qualities of Karnad's plays. (128)

Myths, legends, history and character-types have been portrayed using folk theatre conventions—*Yakshagana*; occasionally Natak Company conventions blending folk, classical and modern theatre devices have been employed to suit the context. Indianized English with (a) Vocabulary: Sanskrit, Kannada, Arabic, Persian, Hindi, dialectic words (b) Idioms and phrases (c) Structure of sentences (d) Imagery (e) Metaphors (f) Symbols etc. create a congenial atmosphere to transport the audience in that dramatic realm. Savita Goel has rightly judged the contribution of Karnad to drama:

> Girish Karnad is among those Indian playwrights who have rejected the imitative pursuit of the West and have ventured into indigenous territory for their themes and techniques. Karnad has sought for an appropriate approach, style and form of the theatre which is closer to the consciousness of people, consistent with our cultural traditions, entertaining and yet aesthetically satisfying. He thought over the fact as to how the paraphernalia of folk theatre can become meaningful outside its context and become relevant in the modern context. (204).

The potent underlying features, techniques, character delineation and choice of language directly targeted against colonial neurosis and centrality of the West, definitely pave the way for literary and cultural independence. The observation of P. Obula Reddy is highly significant in this regard:

> The Indian dramatiss like Karnad, Tanvir, Panikkar, and Karanth in their works return to the tradition....It is something to be lived and grappled with, adapted and even transformed, in order to create new forms of drama which relate to Indian people...their return to the past is an immediate response to to the immediate historical reality of 'Westernization' in India. There is also an attempt to 'decolonize the mind' in the sense that Ngugi wa Thiong'o might advocate; by decolonizing definitions of culture, aesthetics and representational forms and techniques; by combing rather than separating the various languages, idioms, forms and techniques, narratives and histories that make up popular and regional cultures of India. This process of decolonization involves the practice of interculturalism at the most essential level....They produce plays in the spirit of decolonization. They draw from the *Ramayana* and *Mahabharata* and from the dramas of Kalidas and Bhasa. But they do not uphold the Hindu hegemony by this. (34-35)

The stature and role of Karnad as a de-colonizer of Indian English drama must be acknowledged and appreciated without any altercation. Karnad freely develops his plots, characters, themes, choses a performing technique specific to the play; even he adopts modern theare technique of the West to make the performance effective rather than make a blind imitation of the

West, and fuses indigenous cultural sensibility. For instance, *Broken Images* and *Wedding Album* require modern theatre conventions to perform them well. He unhesitatingly, goes for modern theatre equipped with high technology, revolving theatre and high acoustic quality. But it is a medium only that he picks up for specific purposes, never forgets what he has to do. He has brought cultural facets of Indian society to the theatre and filled them with new energy and vitality. Vanashree Tripathi has discovered the growth of creativity of Karnad in postcolonial milieu:

> In Girish Karnad, we discover the creative urgencies of a highly complex postcolonial intellectual temper endeavouring to come to terms with its cultural legacy, muddled up in several versions and misinterpretations. Karnad's formidable erudition dedicated to the construction of an Indian theatre in the contemporary times springs from a desire to reflect the collective aspirations of innumerable generations, and give our relationship to art and culture an overall orientation. (7-8)

Karnad's major accomplishment lies in his "artistic revival of the ceremonial content of drama as ritual; he gives theatrical performance the dignity of a religious rite to counter its reputation as mere mimetic entertainment" (Tripathi 14). His narrative matrix seemingly takes to Brecht's epic realism to project the conflicting cultural mores, yet excercises rigid economy of form and content recalling elegance of classical theatre. Most importantly, Karnad's imagination is "thoroughly and originally Indian in every one of its blood cells" (Dhanavel 96), for he has declared courageously: "my three years in England had convinced me Western theatre had nothing to offer us" (Qtd. in Dhanavel 96). Rupalee Burke comments on the motive of Karnad's playwrighting: "Karnad's motive behind his playwrighting is to catch the pulse of the socio-cultural-historical-political facets of India and Indian life....Karnad has, from the beginning, been pre-occupied with history and myth, albeit with a purpose" (106-107). K. Chandrashekhar has rightly observed: "The likes of Girish Karnad enable us to pretend that there is such a thing as a truly 'Indian' theatre which can be true to its traditions and at the same time responsive to contemporary concerns" (xv).

Works Cited

Abidi, S.Z.H. Plenary Lecture in International Conference on "Postcolonial Literatures and Transnational" at C.C.S. University, Meerut, April 9-10, 2010.

Ashcroft, Bill, Griffiths & Tiffin, Helen. *The Empire Writes Back: Theory and Practice in Post-colonial Literatures.* (2nd edition) London/New York: Routledge, 2010.

________. *The Post-colonial Studies Reader.* (2nd edition) London/New York: Routledge, 2006.

Awasthi, Suresh. "Theatre of Roots", Encounter with Tradition, *TDR* (1988), Vol. 33, No. 4 (Winter, 1989).

Burke, Rupalee. "India Then and Now: The Contemporary Relevance of Girish Karnad's *Tale-Danda*" *Studies in Indian Drama in English.* (Eds) Prasad, Amar Nath & Yadav, Saryug. Bareilly: Prakash Book Depot, 2003.

Chandrashekhar, K. "Before the Curtain Call", *The Hindu.* New Delhi, March 21, 1999.

Dhanavel, P. "Preface", *The Indian Imagination of Girish Karnad.* New Delhi: Prestige, 2000.

Das, B.K. *Twentieth Century Literary Criticism.* (Fifth revised and enlarged edition), New Delhi: Atlantic Publishers and Distributors, 2005.

Dharwadker, Aparna Bhargava. (Ed.) With an Introduction *Collected Plays.* Volume One: *Tughlaq, Hayavadana, Bali: The Sacrifice, Naga-Mandala.* New Delhi: O.U.P., Fourth Impression, 2008.

________. (Ed.) With an Introduction Collected Plays. Volume Two: *Tale-Danda, The Fire and the Rain, The Dreams of Tipu Sultan, Two Monologues, Flowers, Broken Images.* New Delhi: O.U.P., 2005.

Gandhi, Leela. (Sixth Impression) *Postcolonial Theory: A Critical Introduction.* New Delhi: Oxford University Press, 2005.

Goel, Savita. "Folk Theatre Strategies in *Hayavadana*", *The Plays of Girish Karnad: Critical Perspectives.* (Ed) Dodiya, Jaydipsinh. New Delhi: Prestige, 2009.

Karnad, Girish. *Yayati.* New Delhi: Oxford University Press, 2008.

________. *Tughlaq.* Chennai: Oxford University Press, 1998.

________. *Hayavadana.* (Fourteenth Impression), Chennai: Oxford University Press, 1998.

________."Inroduction" to *Three Plays: Naga-Mandala, Hayavadana, Tughlaq.* New Delhi: O.U.P., 2002. *Naga-Mandala* has been extensively used and referred from this edition.

________. "Preface", *Dream of Tipu Sultan in Two Plays: Dream of Tipu Sultan, Bali: The Sacrifice*. New Delhi: O.U.P., Fourth Impression, 2005.

________. "Preface", Tale-Danada. Delhi: Ravi Dayal, 1993. This edition has *been extensively used* and referred in.

________. *Wedding Album*. New Delhi: Oxford University Press, 2009.

Kurtkoti, Kirtinath. "Introduction" *Hayavadana* (Fourteenth Impression), Chennai: Oxford University Press, 1998.

Mishra, Shubha. "Reading and (Mis) reading Girish Karnad'a *Bali: The Sacrifice* in the Light of Foucault's Panopticism", *Thunder on Stage: A Study of Girish Karnad's Plays*. (Eds) Khatri, C.L. & Arora, Sudhir K. Jaipur: Book Enclave, 2008.

Murthy, U.R. Anantha. "Introduction", *Tughlaq*. Chennai: Oxford University Press, 1998.

Nayar, Pramod K. *Literary Theory Today*. New Delhi: Asia Book Club, 2002.

Rao, Mallikarjuna, Mittapalli, R., Rao, Damodar K. (Eds) *Postcolonial Theory and Literature*. New Delhi: Atlantic Publishers and Distributors, 2003.

Reddy, Obula P. "Cultural Heterogeneity in Indian Drama", *Flowering of Indian Drama: Growth and Development*. (Eds) Reddy, Venkata K. & Dhawan, R.K., New Delhi: Prestige, 2004.

Said, Edward W. *Orientalism: Western Conceptions of the Orient*. New Delhi: Penguin, 2001.

Satchidanandan, K. *Indian Literature: Positions and Propositions*. Delhi: Pencraft International, 1999.

Singh, Avadhesh K. *Interventions: Literary and Critical Discourses*. New Delhi: Creative Books, 2007.

________. Presidential Address: "Writing Postmodernism and Postcolonialism in India" in National Seminar (February 6-7, 2009) at Nabira Mahavidyayalaya Katol, Nagpur.

Singh, Saurabh K. "Theatre of Roots: A Resistance to Colonial Discourse", *The Atlantic Critical Review*. Volume 8 Number 1, January-March 2009.

Tiffin, Helen. "Post-colonialism, Post-Modernism—Rehabilitation of Post Colonial History" *Journal of Commonwealth Literature*. 23.1, 1988.

Tripathi, Vanashree. *Three Plays of Girish Karnad: Hayavadana, Tale-Danda, The Fire and the Rain*. New Delhi: Prestige, 2004.

Walder, Dennis. *Post-colonial Literatures in English: History, Language, Theory*. (Second Indian Reprint) Delhi: Atlantic Publishers and Distributors, 2005.

3

Genesis of Titles and Evolution of Themes

Girish Karnad, a versatile genius acclaimed as a noted actor, producer, director, TV artist and cultural administrator, occupies a prominent place in Indian English drama. His plays are the medium where through he discusses socio-political and cultural problems of India conforming to the tradition of Henrik Ibsen, John Galsworthy and G.B. Shaw. He is appreciated as a playwright of myths and legends, history, subalternity, castesim, rituals, feminism, cultural issues and humanism. Despite these cultural roles he definitely brought revolution in Indian English drama—discarding Eurocentric models and techniques altogether; boldly advocated and used Indian myths, legends, folk tales, history, socio-political and contemporary issues with Indianized English and folk theatre conventions with the motif to de-colonize Indian English drama, he gave it a new shape—postcolonial Indian English drama in the real sense. All his plays from *Yayati* to *Wedding Album* illustrate this hypothesis. His views expressed in Prefaces, Introduction to his plays and Interviews also endorse the argument. Hence his role as a de-colonizer of Indian English drama is to be explored in the present chapter.

Even the titles of Karnad's plays are pregnant with the body of thought which can be expanded into several volumes. The titles are apt and very suggestive, they epitomize the Indian subjects and sensibility, and rooted in the cultural past of the country go beyond the limits of time and space. They connect one world, i.e., of myth, legend, history or folklore to another world, i.e., modern with its own characteristics and problems. They are wellchosen to correlate past with the present continuous. Titles are named after a mythical legendry historical or folklore character or a socio-political issue of the contemporary India. They instantly connote the proposition of the play, though the treatment often reverses the traditional message, yet elaboration, exemplification and conclusion (without offering any clear cut solution) make his plays more suggestive and thought-provoking which leads to public discourse regarding problems raised through his plays. His plays are real problem plays in which contemporary socio-cultural and political problems are dealt with dramatic action, and the final solution is left to the audience.

Yayati (1961), the first play of Karnad, gets its title from the myth of Yayati which figures in Adiparva of *Mahabharata*. Karnad has reinterpreted the myth of Yayati to give it modern meaning and significance. It is self-consciously existentialist drama on the theme of responsibility and human relationship. Yayati, unheroic hero the stands for modern man inhabited by worldly desires, sensual pleasures, and irresponsible exercise of power and utter forgetfulness of the imperishable values of life. The play also deals with the question of women's struggle for emancipation and identity in an orthodox Indian society. Karnad himself has commented on the genesis of the plot of *Yayati:*

> The story of King Yayati that I used occurs in Mahabharata. The King, for a moral transgression he has committed, is cursed to old age in the prime of life. Distraught at losing his youth, he approaches his son, pleading with to lend him his youth in exchange for old age. The son accepts the exchange and the curse, and thus becomes old, older than his father. But the old age brings no knowledge, no self-realization, only the senselessness of a punishment meted out for an act in which he had not even participated. The father is left to face the consequences of shirking responsibility for his own actions.
>
> ("Afterword" to *Yayati*, 73).

The play reflects the stressful situation while he was writing the play. The play enabled him to develop a set of values rationally. He was not satisfied with the traditional glorification of son's obedience. Contrary to it he connects the story with real life situations. He deviates from the original story—in *Mahabharata* King Yayati has five sons; after the older four refuse their father, the youngest Pooru yields to his entreaties. Karnad has restructured the story as an ironic drama of discontent, futility and death.

Yayati is a self-centred epicurean who invites the curse because he fails to overcome his lust for Sharmishtha (the Asura Princess who is a rival and slave of his wife, Sage Shukracharya's daughter Devayani), although Devayani has warned him about the dire consequences of his transgression. Pooru is a philosopher who feels unsettled by the questionable legitimacy of his birth, and oppressed by the weight of dynastic tradition. He accepts the curse of his father and ends the play on a note of stark bewilderment, unable to peruse the point of what he has endured.

Karnad's version of the myth makes itself an original due to his rejection of traditional glorification of son's 'self-sacrifice' and, against the backdrop of lust, jealously, and racial tensions, the tragic choices with which the young Prince and his bride Chitralekha are closely confronted. Devayani, the brahmin Queen, Sharmishtha, the slave Princess, Chitralekha, Pooru's new bride succeed in subverting the male world through an assertion of their rights and privileges. Chitralekha emerges as a New Woman who defies all sorts of traditional taboos and subjugation, and overtly fights against them to secure a "room" for her. She condemns Pooru's decision and Yayati's false rhetoric for the sake of dynastic glory. She is a woman who lives in the real world, confronted with practical problems vis-à-vis after Pooru's decision. But she never yields before them; rather she prefers to die. In the Prologue to *Yayati* Karnad has explained the choice of an ancient myth: "We turn to ancient lore not because it offers any blinding revelation or hope of consolation, but because it provides fleeting glimpses of the fears and desires sleepless within us. It is a good way to get introduced to ourselves" (6).

Tughlaq (1972) deals with the life and turbulent reign of Mohammad-bin-Tughlaq. The title of the play is named after him which is apt, and epitomizes the life and history of Tughlaq and suggests multiple connotations. *Tughlaq* is a historical play which confines, for the sake of dramatic precision, to five years reign of Tughlaq, from 1327 to 1332. The action begins in Delhi in 1327, then on the road from Delhi to Daultabad, and finally in and around the fort of Daultabad. *Caligula* legend supplied the substance for the play, and Camu and Sartre accounted for the existentialist character of Karnad's plays. History plays were also written before Karnad but there was no serious attempt to relate history to modern problems and sensibility. Karnad himself has commented on the genesis of the play and its multifold meanings:

> What struck me absolutely about Tughlaq's history was that it was contemporary. The fact that here was the most idealistic, the most intelligent king ever to come on the throne of Delhi...and one of the greatest failures also. And within a span of twenty years this tremendously capable man had gone to pieces. This seemed to be both due to his idealism as well as the shortcomings within him, such as his impatience, his cruelty, his feeling that he had the only correct answer. And I felt in the early sixties India had also come very far in the same direction—the twenty year period seemed to me very much a striking parallel.
>
> (Qtd. in Murthy, Viii).
>
> And when I came to Tughlaq I said Oh! Marvelous! That is what I wanted. In those days existentialism was very much in the air. To be considered mad was very much fashionable. Everything about Tughlaq seemed to fit into what I had read was the correct thing to do, which was to be mad and do impossible things and so on. So I started reading about Tughlaq. But as I started reading about Tughlaq, I suddenly realized what a fantastic character I had hit upon, I started with Ishwari Prasad and then went on to all the contemporary material and suddenly felt possessed. I felt this character was growing in front of me.
>
> (Qtd. in Tilak, 25)

The play has an interesting story, a complex plot and scope for spectacle and several dramatic conventions. Further, the play is of the sixties, and it reflects, observes U.R. Ananthamurthy:

"the political mood of disillusionment which followed the Nehru era of idealism in the country" (viii). Though Karnad denies having contemporaneity of the play in mind, it attracted the attention of the audience. As regards Tughlaq's idealism, scholarship, visionary temperament, zeal for innovation, religious tolerance and generosity, Karnad closely follows historical sources. A rationalist in politics and religion, Tughlaq was a victim of the wrath of orthodox Muslims, like Barani thought him to be a non-believer in Islam.

Karnad depends on ancient historical sources in delineating Tughlaq's character and ignores modern researches which help in presenting Tughlaq's character in an unbiased manner. According to both history and Karnad, Tughlaq is guilty of parricide and fratricide, a ruthless monarch who murders on suspicion and inflicts untold sufferings on his subjects by change of capital and introduction on token currency. His reign was full of rebellions.

In history as well as in Karnad, Tughlaq has been presented as a bundle of contradictions and paradoxes which are put to great artistic and dramatic use. For dramatic purposes, Karnad deviates from history. The episodes of Aziz and Aazam too have been included in view to creating humour, irony, paradoxes, parallels to highlight Karnad's account of Tughlaq's administration. But the play is, comments U.R. Ananthamurthy: "more than political allegory. It has an irreducible, puzzling quality which comes from the ambiguities of Tughlaq's character, the dominating character of the play" (viii). All the characters are dramatized aspects of his complex personality; they also exist in their own right. The character of Tughlaq has been projected in great psychological depth and signifying philosophical questions on the nature of man, and the destiny of a whole kingdom which a dreamer like him controls. The external action throughout enacts the inner drama of Tughlaq. Both Tughlaq and his rivals appear to be idealists; yet, in the pursuit of ideal, they perpetrate its opposite. The whole play is structured on these opposites: the ideal and real; the divine aspiration and the deft intrigue.

Hayavadana (1975) gets its title from the Sanskrit words, i.e., *Haya* (horse) and *Vadana* (head)—the story of a horse-headed man which constitutes the sub-plot of the play. The plot of *Hayavadana* is based on Thomas Mann's *The Transposed Heads*, adapted on a tale from Somdeva's *Brihadkatha Saritasagar*, an ancient collection of stories in Sanskrit. The Sanskrit tale, narrated by a ghost to an adventurous king, gains a further mock-heroic dimension in Mann's rendering. The original poses a moral problem whereas Mann uses it to ridicule the mechanical conception of life which distinguishes between body and soul. Mann laughs at the philosophy which holds the head superior to the body. He further maintains that the human body is fit instrument for the fulfilment of human destiny. Even the transposition of heads will not liberate the protagonists from the psychological limits imposed by nature. The central episode in the play—the story of Devadatta and Kapil—is based on a tale from *Vetalapan Chavimshika*, but Karnad has borrowed it from Thomas Mann's mock-heroic transcription of the original Sanskrit tales—*The Transposed Heads*—whereas the sub-plot, the horseman's search for completeness, is Karnad's original invention.

Hayavadana is essentially a play on the search of identity in a world of tangled relationships. Devadatta, the intellectual, and Kapil, the man of body, are very intimate friends. Devadatta marries Padmini. Kapil and Padmini fall in love with each other. The two friends kill themselves. In a highly comic scene which is of great significance Padmini transposes their heads, giving Devadatta Kapil's body and Kapil Devadatta's. It results in a confusion of identities, which reveals the ambiguous nature of human personality. The situation gets complicated. They fight a duel and kill themselves again. Padmini performs *sati*. Karnad delves deep into the traditional myths to spell out modern man's anguish and dilemmas that are created in his mind. In *Hayavadana* he is seized with the theme of incompleteness, "mad dance of incompleteness" (57) and depicts Devadatta, Kapil and Hayavadana (horse-man) yearning for completeness.

Karnad's play in a characteristic way begins where the 'Vetal' story ends. "How would the woman take it if it really happened and would it ultimately solve the problem for her?" are the fascinating questions the artist in him faces. Shubhangi

S. Raykar analyses thus: "In all his plays Karnad takes this kind of leap from the original story and develops it further... this further development is the play of the artist's imagination and it challenges the glib solutions offered in the original stories" (48). Kirtinath Kurtkoti rightly commented that the play is a "world of incomplete individuals, indifferent gods, dolls that speak and children who cannot, a world indifferent to the desires and frustrations, joys and sorrows of human beings" (vii). The use of folk-theatre conventions, i.e., use of masks, curtains, dolls, the story- within-a-story transport the audience into a bizarre world. The theme of extra-marital relationship is also treated which develops complication and entanglement in human relationship.

Naga-Mandala (1990) is a richly textured dramatic transmutation of two folk-tales of Karnataka. The title is apt and well-chosen to deal with the story of Naga with its symbolic connotations. It deals with gender-bias and the subjection of women in patriarchal Indian orthodox society. The female protagonist—Rani and Kurudavva, other female characters, are generic creations stand for Indian woman. Though the play is a dramatic transmutation of two folk-tales of Karnataka, Karnad delves deep to explore contemporary socio-cultural and philosophical concerns giving them modern validity. Rani is placed in a world where orthodox social conventions, cultural taboos and coercive forces work; patriarchy is established which proves greatest blow to the existence of Rani. Apart from overt patriarchy, she is socialized to internalize the male superiority—an invisible conspiracy to derogate and marginalize her position in the society. She adopts new ways to transcend age-old subjection of women. She is surrounded by evil social forces where she finds herself helpless; tortured by alienation and despair but she never surrenders and continues her struggle for identity –as a woman, as a wife and as a mother.

Karnad's solution appears, at the first observation odd, unconvincing and unconventional violating traditional mode of treatment. The message is clear: despite alienation, despair and antithetical conditions a woman must continue her struggle for her existence and transcend "nothingness" in life and manipulate co-existence as a means for self-existence. Patriarchy, socio-cultural practices, parents of Rani, Appanna, Village Elders, Naga, Dog, and Mongoose etc are the tools to perpetuate exploitation of Rani.

Like Kate Millet's *Sexual Politics* (1969), Karnad's *Naga-Mandala* exposes the mechanisms that express and enforce the relations of power in society, and further analyses the social arrangements and institutions as covert ways of manipulating power so as to establish and perpetuate the dominance of man and the subordination of woman.

The Prologue introduces Four Flames, which are animated, symbolic representations employed to report the sufferings of women. Man and Story are identical to Greek Chorus. Throughout the play they go on commenting and supplying important information and remain on the stage. Act I unfolds to show Rani, well known for her tresses; married to a man who was "rich and his parents were both dead" (27). Her parents are least concerned about the character and wrong doings of Appanna. They are equally responsible for her atrocities, and after marriage they never visit her. Neither welcome ceremony, nor bridal song is there. Rani is nonplussed to hear: "Well, then, I will be back tomorrow at noon. Keep my lunch ready. I shall eat and go" (27). Appanna pays no attention to her, goes out, shuts the door, and locks it from outside and goes away. She runs to the door, finds it locked. She doesn't know what is happening, stands perplexed. She can't even weep. She goes and sits in a corner of her room, talks to herself indistinctly; tired and exhausted goes into sleep; sees nightmares, cries for parents. Next morning when Appanna comes, Rani tries to explain the pains of loneliness, and tries to win his sympathy, but he very coldly rebukes her. He finishes his meal and goes out, locks her. Thus the days rolled by.

Rani, mechanically, goes into the kitchen, starts cooking and talks to herself. She becomes a caged bird whereas Appanna is a philanderer; regularly visiting his concubine. Kurudavva emerges as the rescuer and friend to Rani; sensing that Rani and her husband have no physical relation, she decides to help Rani.

Rani is treated in a slavish manner, imprisoned like a caged bird, neither is she allowed to talk to any outsider nor is any outsider allowed to do the same. Despite her chastity and fidelity, she is forced to face the Naga Ordeal.

In course of time, Rani becomes pregnant. It is news of joy for her as a fulfilment of a woman's dream. But her search for identity as a mother is not fulfilled; on the contrary, Appanna reacts violently knowing that she is pregnant for he has never made love to her. He is out of himself, calls her a strumpet, a whore, drags her out of the house, and threatens to give her extreme punishment for cuckolding him. Appanna publicly questions Rani's chastity and registers a case in the village court where the village elders sit to judge. Rani is forced to face an ordeal to prove her chastity. She finally accepts the Cobra who gave her love and motherhood: "You don't know how heavy you are. Let me get used to you.... This hair is the symbol of my wedded bliss. Live in there happily, for ever" (64). Rani's acceptance of Naga as her own is a curt reply to the question of extra-marital relation in which only males are allowed to go freely, even after getting married, to concubine (as Appanna does) whereas the yardstick of morality is imposed upon women.

J.D. Soni judiciously comments that Karnad in the play tries to "fuse artistically dialectical relationship between tradition and modernity" (76). A. Jagmohanchari has studied *Hayavadana* and *Naga-Mandala* as postcolonial dialectics. The postcolonial matrix "embedded in the play *Naga-Mandala* opens up yet another space for the working out of the theme of patriarchal oppression.... This (Appanna's) vulgar display of power instead of love and treating woman as a disposable object accrues to him owing to the post colonialist ethos and the mystique of tradition" (182). Krishnamayi attempts to redefine the insurgent female psyche in an androgenic milieu and concluded: "Gender equality still remains a myth...the discussion of the relationship between man and woman have been prescribed by man not by woman. Her limits have been imposed on her by man who is ruled by the mastery-motive. She accepts it because of biosocial reasons" (64-65), Karnad himself commented: "They (tales) also express a distinctly woman's understanding of the reality around her, a lived counterpart to the patriarchal structures of classical texts and institutions" ("Introduction" *Three Plays* 17). Prem Sagar observes, "*Naga-Mandala* presents a tale of male chauvinism to give the message that it debilitates and degrades both sexes" (Preface).

Tale-Danda literally means death by beheading. Offering one's head, either on completion of a vow or in penitence, was a common practice in medieval Karnataka. Basavanna often uses the word to express his outrage at a particularly unpleasant situation or accusation, to mean something like 'May my head roll' or 'I offer my head'. The play draws its title and story from the life of Kannada saint Basavanna who resisted ideologically against the prevailing evils of caste hierarchy. Explosive situations after the official endorsement of Mandal Commission Report and Mandir issue in 1989 motivated Karnad to concentrate on subaltern issue. And the historical context, deeply implanted in his mind, which proved the catalyst to the plays of Karnad was predominated with, Karnad himself explains: "...tensions between the cultural past of the country and its colonial past, between the attractions of Western modes of thought and our own traditions, and finally between the various visions of the future that opened up once the common cause of the political freedom was achieved" ("Introduction" *Three Plays* 1). Drawing our attention to the genesis of the present, the play illuminates the endemic affliction of the caste and class politics infecting our body politic in the medieval period of history. It was the strong sense of history, which has nurtured in Karnad a dominant will for social justice, a sincere compassion for the socially oppressed and subaltern. Karnad doesn't offer any solution to the problem; but raised the subaltern issue for discussion and common consensus. Under Basavanna, a social reformer of the twelfth century assembled a congregation of poets, mystics and social revolutionaries and philosophers formed the *Lingayat* faith, giving impetus to courageous questioning and social commitment. The abolition of caste, equality of sexes, rejection of idol worship, repudiation of brahminism, and of Sanskrit in favour of the mother tongues, i.e., Kannada, were the main tenets of subaltern revolution.

The resentment reaches its climax when Madhuvarsa, a brahmin, gives his daughter Kalavati in a marriage to an untouchable—Sheelvanta. This last act opposing caste hierarchy, not just in theory but in practice also, brought down upon the wrath of orthodox; the movement ended in terror and bloodshed. The playwright wants to suggest whenever such important issues are not considered seriously and solutions offered by these thinkers go unheeded, disastrous results would follow again.

The play reveals, in the name of Varnashrama Dharma, lower caste people are socialized to internalize the reigning superiority of upper caste. Though mallibomma adopts *Lingayat* faith, he can't think to enter Jagdeva's, a brahmin, house. King Bijjala tried to ascend to higher varna from barber to kshatriya but failed:

> For ten generations my forefathers ravaged the land as robber barrons. For another five they ruled as the trusted feudatories of the Emperor himself. They married into every royal family in sight. Bribed generations of Brahmins with millions of cows. All this so they could have the caste of Kshastriya branded on their foreheads. And yet you ask the most innocent child...what is Bijjala?...instant reply will be barber. One's caste is like the skin on one's body. You can peel it off top to toe, but when the new skin forms, there you are again; a barber –a shepherd. (14-15)

among subalterns tribals, shepherds, cowherds and low caste untouchables figure. Resistance has two forms: ideological and physical. It was *Lingayat* faith (Shaivistic) in sharp opposition to brahminical faith (better known as Sanatana Dharma) founded on humanitarian grounds, open to all groups, austerity in living, trying to crumble the wall of untouchability, exposing rigidity and discrimination in traditional faith. They rejected anything "static in favour of the principle of movement and progress in human enterprise" ("Preface" *Tale-Danda).* They tried to come out of caste venom and religious fanaticism. The devotee of the faith was called *Sharana*. Antagonistic forces were *vis-à-vis* to gain power – hence hegemonic war began. Physical resistance of *Sharanas* came to a dismal end. It was a conflict between deep-rooted orthodoxy and new and innovative ideas. The movement was not mature enough. Even Basavanna doubts the success of the marriage, i.e., hypergamous (*Pratilom*); it (movement) went into young hands of Jagadeva—a violent revolutionary who killed King Bijjala and finally commited suicide. *Sharanas* lost their drive, mutual differences and infights; prompt reaction from orthodox against *Sharanas* led by young Sovideva; Basavanna's resignation from the movement and power politics bring failure to the subalterns' resistance.

The violent reaction of brahmins suggests even now subalterns are no match to defy the exploitation and discriminating behaviour of the orthodox Hindu society. Basavanna obseves: "We have a long way to go" (39) and "we are not ready for the kind of revolution this wedding is. We haven't worked long enough or hard enough" (44). Damodara Bahatta, Queen's priest and Manchanna Karmita, a brahmin adviser to the King represent Hindu fanaticism and strongly plead for conformity with Vedic tradition—a measure to suppress subaltern revolution. Sovideva, the Prince, wins the game of power politics exploiting the Hindu brahminical sentiments; but subtly used to perpetuate Vedic traditions. With the coronation of Sovideva the triumph of the oppressor rings loud. Sanskrit chanting from ancient scriptures denotes the re-estabilization of caste order at least for the time being till another revolution. Pranav Joshipura has criticized the play: "...instead of deliberating on how to abolish the Varna system, Karnad presents it in a startling manner without any solution...to treat an age-old problem without suggesting any solution raises serious doubts about the capacity of a writer" (69). Karnad, who extends the tradition of Henrik Ibsen and G.B. Shaw, obviously leaves it to the audience to decide; yet he gives remedial suggestions through Basavanna's speeches. Basavanna's doubts, concerns and embarrassment regarding subaltern revolution clearly reflect platwright's concerns. Vanashree Tripathi judiciously comments: "*Tale-Danda* highlights the neglected portion of history that has immense bearing on the history and politics of contemporary times. Focusing on the class, caste, and gender configurations in AD1166, the play proves the subalterranean and insidious motivations driving the diverse caste groups in complex power equation" (28). Rupalee Burke finds Karnad a playwright with a difference whose motive behind playwriting is to catch the.

> Pulse of the socio-cultural-historical-political facets of India and Indian life...his plays have always aimed at providing message in the contemporary context....In *Tughlaq* and *Tale-Danda* Karnad employs history to comment on the pathetic and corroded state of Indian modern day politics, and through which he engages in an intellectual debate of our time. (105-107)

Basvanna's vision of egalitarian society and spiritualized politics was the vision of Karnad himself, expressed by Bijjala: "Basavanna wants to eradicate the caste structure. Annihilate the Varna system. What a vision! And what prodigious courage! And he has the ability.... All hard-working people from the common stock. They sit together, indifferent to caste, birth of station. (15). "*Tale-Danda*", Karnad acknowledged in an interview, "is not necessarily an attack on caste. It is a question of 'Why', why is it that some of our problems seem perennial" (Reddy and Dhawan 138). He raises many questions and few oblique suggestions provide but more are left to the audience to think and get them resolved.

The Fire and the Rain (1998) is a very apt and thought-provoking title which has deep, symbolic and allegorical meanings. The 'fire' in the title of the play is the fire of lust, anger, vengeance, envy, treachery, violence and death. The 'rain' symbolizes self-sacrifice, compassion, Divine Grace, forgiveness, revival and life. *Fire and the Rain* is a far more successful play; Karnad draws upon a story from Chapters 135-138 of the Vana Parva (Forest Canto) of the *Mahabharata*. It is narrated by the ascetic Lomsha to the Pandavas during their exile. But in the best traditions of modernism, Karnad gives a contemporary meaning to an old legend, which stresses the dangers of knowledge without wisdom and power without integrity. The myth cautions about the misapplication of power that human beings receive from the gods after great penance. Yavakri, the son of sage Bhardwaj, acquires knowledge of the Vedas directly from Indra after ten years rigorous penance.

Though his father regarding acquisition of divine power warns him, Yavakri uses it to molest the daughter-in-law of sage Raibhya, whom he resents. Raibhya in retaliation creates a demon (*Brahma Rakshasa*) and a spirit in the form of his daughter-in-law, Vishakha, both of whom pursue Yavakri and kill him. Bharadwaj curses Raibhya – that he will die at the hands of his own son—and then kills himself in remorse. Sometime later Paravasu indeed mistakes the deerskin his father Raibhya is wearing for a wild animal, and accidentally kills him. Involved with his younger brother Aravasu in a fire sacrifice, Paravasu initiates another cycle of evil when he falsely accuses the latter of patricide (hence of brahiminicide). Aravasu then begins his own penance to the Sun God, and when granted a boon, asks for Yavakri, Bhardwaj, and Raibhya to be restored to life. Lives that were destroyed due to human lapses are restored through divine intervention. Karnad has forged closer connections between the principal characters and created them into rounded personalities. Yavakri and Vishakha are not strangers but lovers whose relationship both precedes and follows. Vishakha's marriage to Paravasu, making her more than merely a passive object of Yavakri's lust. Her marriage itself appears to be an arid contract: after a frenzy of sensual gratification Paravasu has left Vishakha to Raibhya's care, and the relationships between the three are startling in their lovelessness and malevolence. Similarly, Paravasu kills his father out of hatred rather than ignorance. Karnad has also invented a love episode between Aravasu and a tribal girl Nittilai, and develops a contrast between the life of discipline and sacrifice with the life of instinct and emotion—opposition between brahmin and sudra, with Aravasu working as a connective link between the two appositive worlds. Karnad's note on "Drama and *Purushartha*" in *The Fire and the Rain* endorses his unequivocal interest in the doctrines of *Purushartha* towards which a work of art should draw mankind.

The Dreams of Tipu Sultan (1997) draws its title and story from the history of Tipu Sultan. It follows the model of the history play established in *Tughlaq* and *Tale-Danda*. It was first written as a radio play for BBC to celebrate the fiftieth anniversary of independence in 1996. Later it was entirely re-written for the stage. The plot obviously deals with some aspect of Indo-British relation. It primarily explores the secret inner world of a man whose public life was a continual war against British colonialism. Tipu Sultan is viewed as one of the most brave warriors, political visionary and dreamer; one of the most politically perceptive and tragic figures in modern Indian history.

Bali: The Sacrifice has drawn upon the thirteenth century Kannada epic *Yashodhara Charite* by Janna, which in turn refers back through an eleventh century Sanskrit epic by Vadiraja to the ninth-century Sanskrit epic *Yashastilaka*, by Somdeva Suri. The play is a tribute to astuteness and sensitivity of Mahatma Gandhi that he saw so clearly the insistence of non-violence to the "cultural and political survival of India" (Karnad. *Two Plays.* 69). It explores the existential dilemma of passion and violence posed by an ancient Jain myth. The myth is less concerned with actual violence than with the morality of substitution, which permits violence, a wider and subtler play by masking its true nature. Violence has been the one of the crucial subjects of debate in the history of Indian civilization. Vedic sacrifices, conducted by Brahmin priests, involved the slaughter of animals as offerings to the gods, which the Jains found repugnant. To the Jain, indulging in any kind of violence, however minor or accidental, meant forfeiting one's moral status as a human being. Later Buddhists too advocated non-violence. The issue found some resolution when the brahmins renounced blood sacrifice. Miniature figurines, made of dough, were substituted for live animals, a practice that continues to this day. Despite this change, Jains objected this process of substitution that carries the original violent impulse within them which was no less dehumanizing. Karnad came across the myth of the Cock of Dough when he was in his teens and the myth littered with discarded drafts of dramatized versions of it. The myth revealed unexpected meanings with long ponderings over it and *Bali: The Sacrifice* is the result of over two decades evolution. Karnad transforms the story of the dough figurine that comes alive at the moment of sacrifice into a mature philosophical exploration of love, jealously, desire, betrayal and violence between men and women who are bound by the ties of blood and marriage, or encounter each other in the perfect freedom of anonymity. Novelty of the play lies in the unconventionality of its major characters, and the seriousness with which it yokes intimate personal acts to structures of religious belief and practice.

The two short monologues in English—*Broken Images* (2004) and *Flowers* (2004) form a radical addendum to Karnad's forty -years career as a playwright because they initiate new subjects and forms. The title of *Broken Images* is derived from Karnad's study of spilt personality—disintegrated due to complex mind sets and takes up a debate that has grown edgier since independence—the politics of language in Indian literary culture. Manjula Nayak, the play's only character, is a successful author of short and long fiction in Kannada and teacher of English in a Banglore college, succumbs to the temptation of larger audience and money making; involves in plagiarism and exposed later. It deals with problems of authenticity and bad faith created by globalization, through a confrontation between a writer and her electronic image. When Karnad takes on literary politics in the play he immediately relates language to genre. The central issue in the play doesn't involve drama at all but the radically unequal status of fiction written in two contemporary languages, Kannad and English. *Flowers* (2004) in contrast, returns to the world of folktale, and is the first work in this genre to focus on male rather than female desire, thus registering a small but important shift in Karnad's dramaturgy. The tiltle is very apt and symbolic; it is offered for devotional purposes as well as for sensual desires. The legend of Veeranna on which the play is based belongs to the Chitradurg region, and became widely known when a Kannad writer T.R.Subbanna included it in his novel *Hamsageete* (1952). The married priest has been passionately in love with a mistress to whom he takes the offerings from the temple after the every prayer. One day the *palegar* (chieftain) discovers a hair in the *prasada* and demands an explanation from Veeranna, who claims that the hair belongs to God. Challenged by the chieftain to prove the truth of his claim the priest in turn challenges god to display hair or accept his head in punishment, and enters a meditative trance to the accompaniment of Venkatashubhayya's song. When the chieftain arrives the next day to expose Veeranna's lie, the *shivalinga* has indeed sprouted long silken hair, and when (urged by the singer) he pulls out a tuft to test its authenticity, blood begins to ooze from the crown of the *lingam*. Overwhelmed by a sense of sin at having injured his deity, Veeranna beheads himself in the sanctum. The conflict between religious devotion and erotic love—mingling of spiritual and carnal is central. The miracle of the *shivalinga* confirms the power of the priest's worship and marks him as one of the chosen, but it also ends his life.

Wedding Album (2008) is the latest play of Karnad. It's a delightfully poignant tale of love and longing in a shining India. It explores the traditional Indian wedding in a globalized, technologically advanced India. The *Wedding Album* which is structured into nine scenes deals primarily with women and their two different worlds i.e. traditional and modern cyber world. But both of them merge into each other. Even the traditional elder women are fused with energy, hope and modern sensibility. Younger sorts enjoy liberty in education, love, courtship via 'distance' technology; and marriage. The play marks the highest evolution of feminine psyche.

The backdrop of the play is unlike of *Yayati, Hayavadana, Naga-Mandala,* and *The Fire and the Rain* which also treat feminine issue. Wedding Album deals with middle class Saraswat Brahmin family—an epitome of multiculturalism and cosmopolitan ideology. The play also examines the fundamentalism of the Hindu middle class family weakening. The family comprises Father Nadkarni, a doctor, Mother, an intelligent housewife, progressive in her ideas who sacrificed her talent for the sake of the family, conscious of children's career. Hema, the eldest daughter married and lives in Australia; Vidula, younger daughter has done BA in Geography, Rohit, son who writes stories and script for teleplays, is seeking better future prospects, and Radhabai, a cook in Nadkarni's family is antitype of rest of the women.

Vidula Nadkarni is exposed to modern education, social culture and science and technology. She is twenty-two, and a half; has done BA in Geography and presently doing nothing. She is the product of modern cyber world. She regularly visits the Internet Café to find her life partner. Of the surprise of Pratibha Khan she, "agrees to consider marrying a man whom she has never met…in this day and age?" (8). Like Westernized Indian youths, she is facilitated by video tapes, SMSs, phone calls and webcam to decide her husband. Aswin Panje, a Sarswat brahmin, is her choice, finally their marriage is materialized. Unlike Vidula, Pratibah Khan is a modern self-made Oriya woman of forty who develops her own business in Bangalore and takes tough decision to marry a Khan. And for being successful producer of television serials, she understands the psychology and emotional appetite of the audience and rejects out rightly the story of Vidula as a possible theme for future episode: "PRATIBHA: Rohit, we have an audience which is predominantly young. College going. Or young professionals. Westernized. At least potentially" (8). She has a practical approach to life. She wonders over Vidula's decision to marry a man without meeting him. Pratibha is an important figure in modern corporate world symbolizing modern Indian woman's emerging role and image. Hema, though born in modern age, educated and married and lives in Australia, is rooted in conservative practices and customs of Sarswat Brahmin family. She disapproves Rohit's advances to Isabel, a Christian girl. She is satisfied as a housewife. As a fair sex, she has bitter experience of how, first, her father-in-law observes her body; secondly, Vivan, a young boy, younger to her son feels crazy about her: "VIVAN: The moment I saw you the other day, I fell desperately in love. I want to die kissing you. I want to die with my hand inside your blouse…" (45). She feels humiliated and slaps on his cheek. These two instances prove a woman is always a prey to male sexual desire irrespective of age or relation.

Mother is a fusion of tradition and modernity. She maintains age-old social conventions prevalent in Saraswat brahmins. The most remarkable feature of her character is that she understands the need of the time and proper human resource development. Despite limitations of middle class family, she has "skill at management" (91). She is talented who sacrificed it for the sake of the family. She has learnt a lot from life. Consequently, she insists on, especially to Vidula, to make sound career and become self-reliant: "MOTHER: ...so many opportunities in today's world. We couldn't even dream of such world...there are lots of openings in America....Don't throw away your talents in just bearing children" (90). Mother has developed a cosmopolitan vision which refutes any caste or religious distinction: "I don't see any difference between Christian girls and Hindu girls these days" (43).

Radhabai, Mira and Vatsala have been characterized to depict first set of woman in Indian society. Mira and Vatsala regiser their presence in Scene Three. They are generic and typed characters. Radhabai, a widow, is a cook in Nadkarni's family who takes personal care of the family and serves delicious dishes to children and is reminded of her own daughter Yamuna she has shamelessly left, naked and abused on the road. At the end of the Scene Nine she finds her daughter in the street below in a very pitiable condition: "RADHABAI: ...There she was— this mad woman—stark raving mad. Shouting foul abuses at the kids who were throwing stones at her....Yamuna! She was shouting and screaming: 'Where is Amma? Where is Amma's house," (92-93). Radhabai is paralyzed to see her and avoids from her eyes apprehending the loss of job; and engages in kitchen menials. The gloomy image of the widow and her mad daughter figure in the last page of the wedding album leaves us to think over their lot seriously.

Karnad is widely known as a playwright, but he is also a highly talented film-maker, a versatile actor, an able cultural administrator, a noted communicator and a person of wide accomplishments and interests. Based on his serious explorations of folklore, mythology and history, the subjects of his plays reflect the problems and challenges of the contemporary life, and endeavour to forge a link between the past and the present. The creative intellectual that Karnad is, he obviously, "views the subjects of his plays from his own perspective, develops them in the crucible of his own imagination and personal experiences, and employs them as a medium to communicate his own-independent and original feelings, thoughts and interpretations" ("Girish Karnad").

Works Cited

Burke, Rupalee. "India Then and Now: The Contemporary Relevance of Girish Karnad's *Tale-Danda" Studies in Indian Drama in English.*Eds. Prasad, Amar Nath and Saryug Yadav. Bareilly: Prakash Book Depot, 2003.

Dharwadker, Aparna Bhargava. Ed. With an Introduction *Collected Plays.*Vol. One: *Tughlaq, Hayavadana, Bali: The Sacrifice, Naga-Mandala.* New Delhi: O.U.P., Fourth Impression, 2008.

__________. Ed. With an Introduction Collected Plays. Vol. Two: *Tale-Danda, The Fire and the Rain, The Dreams of Tipu sultan, Two Monologues, Flowers, Broken Images.* New Delhi: O.U.P., 2005.

"Girish Karnad" <karnatakavision.com/girish-karnad.php> 20.10.2010.

Jagamonarchari, A. "Karnad's *Hayavadana* and *Naga-Mandala*: A Study in Post Colonial Dialectics" *New Directions in Indian Drama.* (Eds.) Pandey, Sudhaker & Barua, Freya. New Delhi: Prestige, 1994.

Joshipura, Pranav. "*Tale-Danda:* A Problem Play" *Indian English Drama: Critical Perspectives.* (Eds.) Dondiya & Sunderan. New Delhi: Sarup & Sons, 2000.

Karnad, Girish. *Yayati.* New Delhi: Oxford University Press, 2008.

__________. *Tughlaq.* Chennai: Oxford University Press, 1998.

__________. *Hayavadana.* Chennai: Oxford University Press, (Fourteenth Impression), 1998.

__________. "Inroduction" to *Three Plays: Naga-Mandala, Hayavadana, Tughlaq.* New Delhi: O.U.P., 2002. *Naga-Mandala* has been extensively used and referred from this edition.

__________. Two Plays: Dream of Tipu Sultan, Bali: The Sacrifice. New Delhi: O.U.P., Fourth Impression, 2005.

__________. *Tale-Danada.* Delhi: Ravi Dayal, 1993. This edition has been extensively used and referred in.

__________. *Two Monologues: Flowers, Broken Images.* Collected Plays. Vol. Two: *Tale-Danda, The Fire and the Rain, The Dreams of Tipu sultan, Two Monologues, Flowers, Broken Images.* (Ed.) With an Introduction by Dharwadker, Aparna Bharagava. New Delhi: O.U.P., 2005.

__________. *Wedding Album.* New Delhi: Oxford University Press, 2009.

Krishanamayi. "Redefinig the Insurgent Female Psyche in an Androcentric milieu" *The Indian Journal of English Studies.* Vol. XLI, 2003-04.

Kurtkoti, Kirtinath. "Introduction" to *Hayavadana.* Chennai: Oxford University Press, (Fourteenth Impression), 1998.

Murthy, U.R. Anantha. "Introduction" *Tughlaq.* Chennai: Oxford University Press, 1998.

Raykar, Shubhangi S. "The Development of Girish Karnad as a Dramatist: *Hayavadana*" *Contemporary Indian Drama.* (Eds.) Pandey, sudhaker & Taraporewala, Freya. New Delhi: Prestige, 1990.

Reddy, K Venkata & Dhawan, R.K. (Eds.) *Flowering of Indian English Drama: Growth and Development.* New Delhi: Prestige, 2004.

Sagar, Prem. (Ed.) *Naga- Mandala* (Narain's Series). Agra: Lakshmi Narain Agarwal, n.d.

Soni, J.D. "Girish Karnad's *Naga-Mandala*: An Experiment in Technique" *Indian Writing in the New Millenium.* Ed.Dhawan, R.K. New Delhi: Indian Association for English Studies, 2000.

Tilak, Raghukul. *Tughlaq: A Critical Study.* New Delhi: Rama Brothers, 1998.

Tripathi, Vanashree. *Three plays of Girish Karnad: A Study in Poetics and Culture: Hayavadana, Tale-Danda, The Fire and the Rain.* New Delhi: Prestige Books, 2004.

4

Indian Myths, Legends, Folklore, History, Culture and Polity

Girish Karnad is one of the most prominent Indian English playwrights who superbly blends Indian philosophy, myths, legends, history and dramatic transmutation with a definite purpose—to revitalize Indian history and culture and free them from Euro centric domination and de-colonizes Indian English Drama. His world of myth is varied and complex. It's not a mere primitive or archetypal belief or story but a correlative—a link connecting past with the present. It embodies a body of thoughts and ideas inviting dialogic discourse; a living reality manifestly concerned with contemporary socio-cultural and political problems. Plot, character types, narrative design or technique, though identifiable with texts already in existence, are fused with modern sensibility and ethos attempting to involve audience and seek remedial measures with common consensus. Aligned to myths, legends, folklore and history enrich his dramatic realm with similar objectives. *Yayati, Hayavadana, Naga-Mandala, Tale-Danda, Bali: The Sacrifice, The Fire and the Rain, Flowers* etc. amply illustrate the above proposition. Karnad finds a voice and a distinct identity for Indian English Drama by reclaiming the past of the country. Aparna Bhargava Dharwadker has explored the evolution of Karnad's dramatic genius:

> The dominant presence of the ancient and the medieval past in Karnad's drama is a result of both personal and cultural compulsions. He has argued from the beginning that the deep-rooted narratives of myth, oral history, and

> legend constitute a vital connection between an author and his or her audience, and theatre is a particularly powerful medium for the communication of such culturally resonant fictions. Karnad belongs perhaps to the last generation of *urban* Indian writers who encountered the 'great' and 'little' traditions of myth, poetry, history, legend, and folklore at first hand in their earliest childhood, and internalized them deeply enough to have their adult authorial selves shaped by them. Such a vibrant culture of orality is no longer available to the western playwright, and Karnad is fully aware that it is being rapidly eroded in India by the processes of urbanization, Westernized education, and economic development.
>
> ("Introduction" *Collected Plays.* Vol.One. x).

The plays of Karnad are the lens through which he tries to view the emerging cultural consciousness and germination of indigenous sensibility; condemns Western literary imagination politically motivated then part of the relationship between culture and empire. Karnad diffused the "cultural bomb"—the biggest weapon of the West targeted to annihilate the people's beliefs in their indigenous names, unity, capacities and heritage; it makes native people see their past as a wasteland of non-achievement. Myths, legends, history and character-types have been portrayed using folk theatre conventions—*Yakshagana*; occasionally *Natak Company* conventions blending folk, classical and modern theatre devices have been employed to suit the context. The present section aims at highlighting Karnad's handling of myths, history, folklore and polity—its objectives and techniques.

Karnad has great insight into human nature, which made him a great actor and playwright. He is well aware of the paradoxes in human nature and has thorough understanding of life's little ironies. Vanashree Tripathi pertly remarked:

> Karnad's plays testify to a larger cultural matrix of mythic modes, oral folk forms and narrative conventions than any other plays written and performed in the recent times. His re-writing of myths and folktales instills unique emotional and intellectual angle to the given prototypes and thus attains a larger frame of reference—psychologically

> complex. The stories of the past from X century B.C. to the present intersect and in displacement and reverberation we sense their presence in our personal and public life in the contemporary world. (19)

Yayati (1961), Karnad's first play, reinterprets an ancient myth from Adiparva of *Mahabharata* in modern context. It is self-consciously existentialist drama on the theme of responsibility and human relationship. Yayati, unheroic hero, stands for modern man inhabited by worldly desires, sensual pleasure, and irresponsible exercise of power and utter forgetfulness of the imperishable values of life. The story centres round the character of Yayati. "Karnad's interpretation of the familiar old myth on the exchange of ages between father and son", remarked U.R. Ananthmurthy, "baffled and angered many conventional critics but, for others, who were trying to root their contemporary concerns in old myths, Karnad's unheroic hero, Pooru, was a great experience" (vii). The interpretation of myth no doubt irritated the orthodox viewers but the more enlightened critics appreciated the new approach of the play. What impressed the modern spectators of the play was the reinterpretation of the ancient myth in the light of the contemporary context. Existential dilemma inherent in the play makes it a complex and didactic. Karnad himself commented on the theme of the play:

> The story of King Yayati that I used occurs in the *Mahabharata*. The king, for a moral transgression he has committed, is cursed to old age in the prime of life. Distraught at losing his youth, he approaches his son, pleading with him to lend him his youth in exchange for old age. The son accepts the exchange and the curse, and thus becomes old, older than his father. But the old age brings no knowledge, no self-realization, only the senselessness of a punishment meted out for an act in which he had not even participated. The father is left to face the consequences of shirking responsibility for his own actions.
>
> ("Afterword" 73)

It was written on the way to England and Karnad was only 23 years old. He was under stressful situation and engagement with the play escaped him from it. He noted: "the myth enabled me to articulate to myself a set of values that I had been unable to arrive at rationally" ("Author's Introduction" 3). Anouilh, Sartre, O'Neill and Greeks provided Karnad dramatic structure for *Yayati.* He couldn't find appropriate structure in our dramatic tradition to relate his anxieties. Aparna Bhargava Dharwadker observes: "The play itself resolved, as a literary work, the existential crisis that had generated and shaped it" ("Introduction" *Collected Plays.* Volume One. xv). Karnad restructures the story as an ironic drama of discontent, futility, and death. Yayati is a self-centred epicurean who invites the curse because he can't overcome his desire for Sharmishtha (the Asura Princess who is rival and slave of his wife, Sage Shukracharya's daughter Devayani) although Devayani has warned him about the destructive consequences of his choice. Pooru is a philosopher but self-hating 'outsider' who feels unsettled by the questionable legitimacy of his birth, and oppressed by the weight of dynastic tradition. He accepts the curse of his father. Puru ends the play on a note of stark bewilderment, unable to comprehend the point of what he has endured. Devayani the Brahman Queen, Sharmishtha the slave Princess, Chitrlekha, Pooru's new bride succeed in subverting the male world through an assertion of their rights and privileges. Seema Suneel has very judiciously commented: "Karnad takes refuge in the Indian myths and legends and makes them vehicle of a new vision, by using these myths; he tries to show the absurdity of life with all its elemental passions and conflicts, and man's eternal struggle to achieve perfection" (125). What makes his version of the tale so resonant, and startlingly original, is that he rejects the traditional glorification of the son's 'self-sacrifice' and, against a backdrop of lust, jealously, and racial tensions, foregrounds the tragic choices with which the young prince and his bride are confronted.

Tughlaq (1972) deals with life and turbulent reign of Mohammad-bin-Tughlaq who ruled over India for about twenty-six years; but for the sake of dramatic precision and brevity, Karnad spans only five years from 1327 to 1332. The action begins in Delhi in 1327, then on the road from Delhi to Daultabad and lastly in and around the fort of Daultabad.

Caligula legend supplied the substance for the play and the readings of Camu and Sartre accounted for the existentialist character of Karnad's plays. History plays written earlier were costume plays in which no attempt was made to relate a historical episode to modern sensibility. Karnad, in an interview to Tutun Mukherjee reacted: "the play certainly reflects the disillusionment that my generation felt with the new politics of independent India, the realpolitik, the cynicism, the gradual erosion of ethical norms" (36). Tughlaq, both in history and in the play is a great scholar, idealist and visionary. He stands for administrative reforms, for implementing the policy of Hindu-Muslim amity, recognition of merit, reorganization of administrative machinery and taxation structure etc. *Tughlaq* develops as a tragedy of the limits of human power in a predominantly psychological context. Karnad was fascinated by the history of Tughlaq's reign which reflected the political mood of disillusionment prevailing in the sixties in India. The treatment of history and its reinterpretation in the light of current political situation distinguishes Karnad from the rest.

Interesting story, a complex plot, scope for spectacle, reflection of the political mood of disillusionment which followed the Nehru era of idealism in the country attracted the applause of Indian audiences. *Tughlaq*'s "...elusive and haunting quality which it gets from the character of Tughlaq who has been realized in great philosophical depth...philosophical questions on the nature of man and the destiny of a whole kingdom which a dreamer like him controls" (Murthy viii-ix). Tughlaq has been portrayed with great psychological truth and depth. The dramatist deftly projects the paradoxes in the complex personality of Tughlaq who is at once a dreamer and a man of action, benevolent and cruel, devout and godless. He himself reveals his idealism, scholarship, and secularism in his various speeches. When his idealism and administrative reforms are frustrated a psychological change comes over him. In order to realize his plans and administrative reforms he resorts to murder and bloodshed; gets frustrated and disillusioned: "I am teetering on the brink of madness, Barani, but the madness of God still eludes me. (*Shouting)* And why should I deserve that madness? I have condemned my mother to death and I'm not even sure she was guilty of the crime..." (68). Barani, the scholarly historian, and Najib, the shrewd politician represent the two opposite selves of Sultan. Tughlaq's experiments and administrative reforms are just means to assert and prove his identity. The play has an irreducible, puzzling quality, which comes from the ambiguities of Tughlaq's character.

Hayavadana (1975) is based on Thomas Mann's *The Transposed Heads*, adapted on a tale from Somdeva's *Brihadkatha Saritasagar*, an ancient collection of stories in Sanskrit. The central episode in the play—the story of Devadatta and Kapil—is based on a tale from *Vetalapan Chavimshika*, but Karnad has borrowed it from Thomas Mann's mock-heroic transcription of the original Sanskrit tales—*The Transposed Heads* whereas the sub-plot –the horseman's search for completeness, is Karnad's original invention. The play has various archetypal patterns—plot, character-types, narrative design and identifiableness with connect erstwhile literatures to present text. *Hayavadana* is essentially a play on the search of identity in a world of tangled relationships. Devadatta, the intellectual, and Kapil, the man of body, are very intimate friends. Devadatta marries Padmini. Kapil and Padmini fall in love with each other. The two friends kill themselves. In a highly comic scene which is of great significance Padmini transposes their heads, giving Devadatta Kapil's body and Kapil Devadatta's. It results in a confusion of identities, which reveals the ambiguous nature of human personality. The situation gets complicated. They fight a duel and themselves again. Padmini performs *sati*. Karnad delves deep into the traditional myths to spell out modern man's anguish and dilemmas that are created in his mind. In *Hayavadana* he is seized with the theme of incompleteness and depicts Devadatta, Kapil and Hayavadana (horse-man) yearning for completeness. Theme of the *Vasavadatta*, the finest play of Sri Auribindo, depicting the development of love between Prince Udayana and Princess Vasavadatta has also been borrowed from Somedeva's *Brhadkatha Saritasagar* but his treatment of the original differs from Karnad's. S. Ramaswamy has pertly commented:

> Sri Aurobindo's wide ranging eclecticism is seen in one of his plays like *Perseus the Deliverer, Vasavadatta,* etc. his treatment of myth and legend in the genre of drama and theatre differs considerably the way Girish Karnad uses similar material in his English plays like *Hayavadana* and *Naga-Mandala*. Karnad transmutes and transforms his source material to such an extent, being an actor and theatre man himself, that the modern, contemporary, individual talent incorporates the tradition into a transcreation that is rich and strange...blend into a recreation of the myth and legend of India with a novel blend of traditional material and contemporary narrative technique which is quite challenging in bringing folk and elite theatres together. (21-22)

Karnad's play in a characteristic way begins where the 'Vetal' story ends. "How would the woman take it if it really happened and would it ultimately solve the problem for her?" are the fascinating questions the artist in him faces. Shubhangi S. Raykar analyses thus: "In all his plays Karnad takes this kind of leap from the original story and develops it further... this further development is the play of the artist's imagination and it challenges the glib solutions offered in the original stories" (48).

Naga-mandala (1990) is a richly textured dramatic transmutation of two folk-tales of Karnataka. It deals with gender-bias and the subjection of woman in patriarchal Indian orthodox society. Karnad delves deep to explore contemporary socio-cultural and philosophical concerns giving them modern validity. The female protagonist—Rani and Kurudavva, other female character, are generic creations stand for Indian woman. Rani is placed in a world where orthodox social conventions, cultural taboos and coercive forces work; patriarchy is established which proves greatest blow to the existence of Rani. Apart from overt patriarchy, she is socialized to internalize the male superiority—an invisible conspiracy to derogate and marginalize her position in the society. Unlike G.B.Shaw's Candida she adopts new ways to transcend age-old subjection of woman. She is surrounded by evil social forces where she finds herself helpless; tortured by alienation and despair but she never surrenders and continues her struggle for identity – as a woman, as a wife and as a mother. Karnad's solution appears, at the first instance odd, unconvincing and unconventional violating traditional mode of treatment. Patriarchy, socio-cultural practices, parents of Rani, Appanna, Village Elders, Naga, Dog, and Mongoose etc are the tools to perpetuate exploitation of Rani. Karnad's *Naga- Mandala* exposes the mechanisms that express and enforce the relations of power in society and further analyses the social arrangements and institutions as covert ways of manipulating power so as to establish and perpetuate the dominance of man and the subordination of woman.

Prologue introduces Four Flames, which are symbolic representations employed to report the sufferings of women; they also comment on their mental conflicts as Dolls do in *Hayavadana* . Man and Story are identical to Greek Chorus, throughout the play they go on commenting and supplying important information and remain on the stage. Act I unfolds Rani, well known for her tresses; married to a man who was "rich and his parents were both dead" (27); Rani's parents are least concerned about the character and wrong doings of Appanna, they are equally responsible for her atrocities, after marriage they never visit Rani. No welcome ceremony, nor bridal song is there. Rani is nonplussed to hear: "Well, then, I will be back tomorrow at noon. Keep my lunch ready. I shall eat and go" (27) He pays no attention to her, goes out, shuts the door, locks it from outside and goes away. She runs to the door, finds it locked. She doesn't know what are happening, stands perplexed. She can't even weep. She goes and sits in a corner of her room, talks to herself indistinctly; tired and exhausted goes into sleep; sees nightmares, cries for parents. Next morning when Appanna comes, Rani tries to explain the pains of loneliness, and tries to win the sympathy of Appanna, he very coldly rebukes: "What is there to be scared of .... Look, I don't like idle chatter. Do as you are told, you understand" (28). He finishes his meal and goes out, locks her. Thus the days rolled by. Rani, mechanically, goes into the kitchen, starts cooking and talks to herself. She becomes a caged bird whereas Appanna is a philanderer; regularly visits to his concubine.

When Kurudavva, a blind woman calls at her, and asks about Appanna's treatment to her:

> KURUDAVVA: Does he...talk to you?
>
> RANI: Oh that he does. But not a syllable more than required 'Do this', 'Do that', 'Serve the food'. Apart from him, you are the first person I have seen since coming here. I am bored to death. There is no one to talk to. (31)

Kurudavva emerges as the rescuer and friend to Rani; sensing between Rani and her husband has no relation, she decides to help Rani. Rani is treated in a slavish manner, imprisoned like a caged bird, neither is she did not allow talking to outsider nor outsider is allowed to do the same. Despite her chastity and fidelity, she is forced to face the Naga Ordeal. In course of time, Rani becomes pregnant. Appanna reacts violently knowing her pregnant that he has never made love with her. He is out of himself, publicly questions Rani's chastity and registers a case in the village court where Village Elders (all male) sit to judge. Rani is forced to face an Ordeal to prove her chastity. Rani finally accepts Cobra who gave her love and motherhood: "You don't know how heavy you are. Let me get used to you.... This hair is the symbol of my wedded bliss. Live in there happily, for ever" (64). Rani's acceptance of Naga as her own is a curt reply to the question of extra-marital relation in which only males are allowed to go freely, even after getting married, to concubine (as Appanna does) whereas the yardstick of morality is imposed upon women. J.D.Soni judiciously comments that Karnad in the play tries to "fuse artistically dialectical relationship between tradition and modernity" (76). A. Jagmohanchari has studied *Hayavadana* and *Naga- Mandala* as post colonial dialectics. The post colonial matrix "embedded in the play *Naga- Mandala* opens up yet another space for the working out of the theme of patriarchal oppression.... This (Appanna's) vulgar display of power instead of love and treating woman as a disposable object accrues to him owing to the post colonialist ethos and the mystique of tradition." (182). Krishnamayi attempted to redefine the insurgent female psyche in an androgenic milieu and concluded: "Gender equality still remains a myth...the discussion of the relationship between man and woman have been prescribed by man not by woman. Her limits have been imposed on her by man who is ruled by the mastery-motive. She accepts it because of biosocial reasons" (64-65). "The play", M.K. Naik has commented "moves at a brisk pace, and the dialogue, which is clear, simple everyday English without any conscious straining after Indian-ness; suits the rustic folk tale it presents as a surface structure, without causing harm to the deep structure of the symbolism beneath" (46). Karnad himself commented: "They (tales) also express a distinctly woman's understanding of the reality around her, a lived counterpart to the patriarchal structures of classical texts and institutions" ("Introduction" *Three Plays* 17).

Tale-Danda is a history play and it continues the tradition of history play that begins with *Tughlaq* and extends to *The Dreams of Tipu Sultan. Tale- Danda* draws its story from the life of Kannada saint Basavanna of the 12th century A.D. who resisted ideologically against the prevailing evils of caste hierarchy. Explosive situations after the official endorsement of Mandal Commission Report and Mandir issue in 1989 motivated Karnad to concentrate on subaltern issue. And the historical context, deeply implanted in his mind, which proved catalyst to the plays of Karnad was predominated with, Karnad himself explains: "...tensions between the cultural past of the country and its colonial past, between the attractions of Western modes of thought and our own traditions, and finally between the various visions of the future that opened up once the common cause of the political freedom was achieved" ("Introduction" *Three Plays* 1) It deals with caste and class politics infecting our body politic in the medieval period of history. It was the strong sense of history, which has nurtured in Karnad a dominant will for social justice, a sincere compassion for the socially oppressed and subaltern. Karnad's astute transformation of the metaphysical into the contemporary dimensions and history into trans-historical perspective is, not linked to the Western philosophical matrix, but, Vanashree Tripathi observes, "playwright's understanding of a long tradition of humanism in India...since the earliest periods" (25). Karnad doesn't offer any solution to the problem; but raised the subaltern issue for discussion and common consensus. Under Basavanna, a social reformer of the 12th century assembled a congregation of poets, mystics and social revolutionaries and philosophers formed the *Lingayat* faith, giving impetus to courageous questioning and social commitment. The abolition of caste, equality of sexes, rejection of idol worship, repudiation of Brahaminism, and of Sanskrit in favour of the mother tongue i.e. Kannad; were the main tenets of subaltern revolution. The resentment reaches its climax when Madhuvarsa, a Brahmin gives his daughter Kalavati in a marriage to an untouchable—Sheelvanta. This last act opposing caste hierarchy, not just in theory but in practice also, brought down upon the wrath of orthodox; the movement ended in terror and bloodshed. The playwright wants to suggest whenever such important issues are not considered seriously and solutions offered by these thinkers go unattended disastrous results would follow again.

The subaltern issue is strongly highlighted; they have been brought from margin to centre and put before higher section of the society. The subalterns are led by Basavanna. The caste distinction is so deep-rooted that even King Bijjala tried to ascend to higher Varna from barber to Kshatriya but failed:

> For ten generations my forefathers ravaged the land as robber Barrons. For another five they ruled as the trusted feudatories of the Emperor himself. They married into every royal family in sight. Bribed generations of Brahmins with millions of cows. All this so they could have the caste of Kshastriya branded on their foreheads. And yet you ask the most innocent child...what is Bijjala?...instant reply will be barber. One's caste is like the skin on one's body. You can peel it off top to toe, but when the new skin forms, there you are again; a barber –a shepherd. (14-15)

among subalterns tribals, shepherds, cowherds and low caste untouchables figure. Resistance has two forms: ideological and physical. It was *Lingayat* faith (Shaivistic) in sharp opposition to Brahminical faith; founded on humanitarian grounds, open to all groups, austerity in living, trying to crumble the wall of untouchability, exposing rigidity and discrimination in traditional faith. They rejected anything "static in favour of the principle of movement and progress in human enterprise" ("Preface" *Tale- Danda).* They tried to come out of caste venom and religious fanaticism. The devotee of the faith was called *Sharana*. Physical resistance of *Sharanas* comes to dismal end. It was a conflict between deep-rooted orthodoxy and new and innovative ideas. The movement was not matured enough. Even Basavanna doubts the success of the marriage—i.e. hypergamous (*Pratilom*); movement went into young hands of Jagadeva- a violent revolutionary who kills King Bijjala and finally commits suicide. *Sharanas* lost their drive, mutual differences and infighhts, prompt reaction from orthodox against *Sharanas* led by young Sovideva; Basavanna's resignation from the movement and power politics brings failure to the subalterns' resistance. The violent reaction of Brahmins suggests even now subalterns are no match to defy the exploitation and discriminating behaviour of the orthodox Hindu society. Basavanna also anticipates:

> Until now it was only a matter of theoretical speculation. But this—this is real. The orthodox will see this mingling of castes as a blow at the very roots of varnashrma dharma. Bigotry has not faced such a challenge into two thousand years. I need hardly describe what venom will gush out, what hatred will erupt once the news spreads. (38)

He adds further: "we have a long way to go" (39) "we are not ready for the kind of revolution this wedding is. We haven't worked long enough or hard enough" (44). Damodara Bahatta, Queen's priest and Manchanna Karmita, a brahmin adviser to the King impose Vedic tradition—a measure to suppress subaltern revolution:

> ...Civilization has been made possible because our Vedic tradition controls and directs that self-destructive energy. How large-hearted is our dharma! To each person it says you don't have to be anyone but yourself. One's caste is like one's home – meant for one's self and one's family. It is shaped to one's needs, one's comforts, and one's traditions. And that is why the Vedic tradition can absorb and accommodate all differences, from Kashmir to Kanya Kumari. And even those said to be its victims have embraced its logic of inequality. (56)

Sovideva, the Prince, wins the game of power politics exploiting the Hindu Braminical sentiments; but subtly used to perpetuate Vedic traditions. With the coronation of Sovideva the triumph of the oppressor rings loud. Sanskrit chanting from ancient scriptures denotes the re-estabilization of caste order at least for the time being till another revolution. M.K. Naik has criticised the play because, he considers, "It fails to offer solution to the problem" (45); Pranav Joshipura has also expressed the similar view: "...instead of deliberating on how to abolish the Varna system, Karnad presents it in a startling manner without any solution...to treat an age-old problem without suggesting any solution raises serious doubts about the capacity of a writer" (69). Karnad leaves the problem to the audience to decide; yet he gives remedial suggestions through Basavanna's speeches. Basavanna's doubts, concerns and embarrassment regarding subaltern revolution clearly reflect platwright's concerns. Vanashree Tripathi judiciously comments: "*Tale-Danda* highlights the neglected portion of history that has immense bearing on the history and politics of contemporary times. Focusing on the class, caste, and gender configurations in A.D.1166, the play proves the subalterranean and insidious motivations driving the diverse caste groups in complex power equation" (28). She further observes that *Tale-Danda* is:

> a thesis play that intends to revive upon the Indian stage the age old debate on the virtues and vices of casteism ...an endeavour to do justice to history—a stark reminder of our past, of the struggles and movements that bestowed upon us the freedom to think and question. The play is an invitation to look at ourselves—our empty present and our futurelessness. (91-92)

Sharanas lived a life of contradiction because of their mixed identity. They had taken on their new sharana identity without shedding off their old one completely, so that the ones from the upper castes still looked down upon those from the lower castes and those from the lower castes could not forget that they were untouchables and detestable. Rupalee Burke finds Karnad a playwright with a difference whose motive behind playwriting is to catch the

> pulse of the socio-cultural-historical-political facets of India and Indian life...his plays have always aimed at providing message in the contemporary context....In *Tughlaq* and *Tale-Danda* Karnad employs history to comment on the pathetic and corroded state of Indian modern day politics, and through which he engages in an intellectual debate of our time. (105-107)

Basvanna's vision of egalitarian society and spiritualized politics was the vision of Karnad himself, expressed by Bijjala:

> Basvanna wants to eradicate the caste structure. Annihilate the varna system.What a vision! And what prodigious courage! And he has the ability. Look at those he has gathered around him: poets, mystics, and visionaries. And nothing airy-fairy about them, mind you. All hard-working people from the common stock. They sit together, indifferent to caste, birth of station. (15)

Post-Independence Indian literature has had social, economic and political concerns and the plays of Karnad are also expressive of a variety of issues treated in such a way to enable the audience to understand them. "*Tale-Danda*", Karnad acknowledged in an interview, "is not necessarily an attack on caste. It is a question of 'Why', why is it that some of our problems seem perennial" (Reddy and Dhawan138). He raises many questions and few oblique suggestions provide but more are left to the audience to think and get them resolved. He is rightly called the 'cultural administrator'. Y. Somalata's observation of *Tale-Danda* is remarkable:

> In this play, Karnad discovers the vital relationship between contemporary society and literature...adept in choosing the dialectical opposites such as tradition and modernity; conservative and reformist; spiritual and physical; ideal and pragmatic; constancy and flux for unfolding a logical sequence in poetic terms...centrifugal and centripetal forces of change and resistance are directed against caste order in Hindu society.
>
> (*Ibid.* 137-138)

In *Fire and the Rain* (1998), which is a far more successful play, Karnad draws upon a story from Chapters 135-138 of the Vana

Parva (forest Canto) of the *Mahabharata.* The play uses the myth of Yavakri and Vritri (in Epilogue). The myth of Yavakri is narrated by the ascetic Lomsha to the Pandavas during their exile. But in the best traditions of modernism, Karnad gives a contemporary meaning to an old legend, which stresses the dangers of knowledge without wisdom and power without integrity. The 'fire' in the title of the play is the fire of lust, anger, vengeance, envy, treachery, violence and death. The 'rain' symbolizes self-sacrifice, compassion, Divine Grace, forgiveness, revival and life. The myth cautions about the misapplication of power that human beings receive from the gods after great penance. Yavakri, the son of sage Bhardwaj, acquires knowledge of the Vedas directly from Indra after ten years rigorous penance. Though his father regarding acquisition of divine power warns him, Yavakri uses it to molest the daughter-in-law of sage Raibhya, whom he resents. Raibhya in retaliation creates a demon (*Brahma Rakshasa*) and a spirit in the form of his daughter-in-law, Vishakha, both of whom pursue Yavakri and kill him. Bhardwaj curses Raibhya –that he will die at the hands of his own son—and then kills himself in remorse. Sometime later Paravasu indeed mistakes the deerskin his father Raibhya is wearing for a wild animal, and accidentally kills him. Involved with his younger brother Aravasu in a fire sacrifice, Paravasu initiates another cycle of evil when he falsely accuses the latter of patricide (hence of brahiminicide). Aravasu then begins his own penance to the Sun God, and when granted a boon, asks for Yavakri, Bhardwaj, and Raibhya to be restored to life. Lives that were destroyed due to human lapses are restored through divine intervention. Karnad has forged closer connections between the principal characters and created them into rounded personalities. Yavakri and Vishakha are not strangers but lovers whose relationship both precedes and follows Vishakha's marriage to Paravasu, making her more than merely a passive object of Yavakri's lust. Her marriage itself appears to be an arid contract: after a frenzy of sensual gratification Paravasu has left Vishakha to Raibhya's care, and the relationships between the three are startling in their lovelessnss and malevolence. Similarly, Paravasu kills his father out of hatred rather than ignorance. Karnad has also invented a love episode between Aravasu and a tribal girl Nittilai, and develops a contrast between the life of discipline and sacrifice with the life of instinct and emotion—opposition between Brahmin and sudra, with Aravasu working as a connective link between the two appositive worlds. Karnad's note on "Drama and *Purushartha*" in *The Fire and the Rain* endorses his unequivocal interest in the doctrines of *Purushartha* towards which a work of art should draw mankind. Myth of Vritri constitutes the substance of play-within-the –play which is performed in the Epilogue parallel to fire sacrifice to please Indra, God of Rain.

The Dreams of Tipu Sultan (1997) was first written as a radio play for BBC to celebrate the fiftieth anniversary of independence in 1996. Later it was entirely re-written for the stage. The plot obviously deals with some aspect of Indo-British relation. It primarily explores the secret inner world of a man whose public life was a continual war against British colonialism. It follows the model of the history play established in *Tughlaq* and *Tale- Danda*. Tipu Sultan is viewed as one of the most brave warriors, political visionary and dreamer; one of the most politically perceptive and tragic figures in modern Indian history. It was first presented by the Madras Players at the YMCA Ampitheatre Chennai, on 17 February 2000. The costant struggle of Tipu against Marathas, Nizam and English develops his personality and his vision for future India is appreciable. The history of Tipu Sultan is highly captivating force to all of us. The dreams that Tipu recorded in his diary reveal Tipu's far-sightedness and blueprint for political strategy.

Bali: The Sacrifice has drawn upon the thirteenth century Kannada epic *Yashodhara Charite* by Janna, which in turn refers back through an eleventh century Sanskrit epic by Vadiraja to the ninth-century Sanskrit epic *Yashastilaka*, by Somdeva Suri. It explores the existential dilemma of passion and violence posed by an ancient Jain myth. The play is a tribute to astuteness and sensitivity of Mahatma Gandhi that he saw so clearly the insistence of non-violence to the "cultural and political survival of India" (Karnad. *Two Plays.* 69). The myth is less concerned with actual violence than with the morality of substitution, which permits violence, a wider and subtler play by masking its true nature. It was first presented at the Haymarket Theatre, Leicester, on 31 May 2002. Violence has been the one of the crucial subjects of debate in the history of Indian civilization. Vedic sacrifices, conducted by Brahmin priests, involved the slaughter of animals as offerings to the gods, which the Jains found repugnant. To the Jain, indulging in any kind of violence, however minor or accidental, meant forfeiting one's moral status as a human being. Later Buddhists too advocated non-violence. The issue found some resolution when the Brahmins renounced blood sacrifice. Miniature figurines, made of dough, were substituted for live animals, a practice that continues to this day. Despite this change, Jains objected this process of substitution that carries the original violent impulse within them which was no less dehumanizing. Karnad came across the myth of the Cock of Dough when he was in his teens and the myth littered with discarded drafts of dramatized versions of it. The myth revealed unexpected meanings with long ponderings over it and *Bali: The Sacrifice* is the result of over two decades evolution. Karnad transforms the story of the dough figurine that comes alive at the moment of sacrifice into a mature philosophical exploration of love, jealously, desire, betrayal, and violence between men and women who are bound by the ties of blood and marriage, or encounter each other in the perfect freedom of anonymity. Novelty of the play lies in the unconventionality of its major characters, and the seriousness with which it yokes intimate personal acts to structures of religious belief and practice. Mother Queen and Queen are juxtaposed vis-à-vis who represent two opposite extremes—one indulges in animal sacrifice while the another condemns at any cost.

Flowers (2004) derives the plot from the legend of Veeranna of Chitradurg region, which was popularized by Kannad writer T.R.Subbanna who included it in his novel *Hamsageete* (1952). The married priest has been passionately in love with a mistress to whom he takes the offerings from the temple after the every prayer. One day the *palegar* (chieftain) discovers a hair in the *prasada* and demands an explanation from Veeranna, who claims that the hair belongs to God. Challenged by the chieftain to prove the truth of his claim the priest in turn challenges god to display hair or accept his head in punishment, and enters a meditative trance to the accompaniment of Venkatashubhayya's song. When the chieftain arrives the next day to expose Veeranna's lie, the *shivalinga* has indeed sprouted long silken hair, and when (urged by the singer) he pulls out a tuft to test its authenticity, blood begins to ooze from the crown of the *lingam*. Overwhelmed by a sense of sin at having injured his deity, Veeranna beheads himself in the sanctum. The conflict between religious devotion and erotic love—mingling of spiritual and carnal is central. The miracle of the *shivalinga* confirms the power of the priest's worship and marks him as one of the chosen, but it also ends his life.

Thematic concerns discussed through myths, legends, history and folklore in Karnad's plays display their urgency in the present context in our country. The archetypal patterns embedded in Karnad's plays—obviously it will be an opportunity to understand Indian myths, legends, folktales, history and culture, narrative design and character-types and feel proud of them. Veena Noble Das has rightly observed the significance of the use of myths, legends and folktales in the plays of Karnad:

> ...myth and folktale merge and come together and weave a rich tapestry of meaning that explores the modern predicament. Myth can never be dismissed as belonging to the past, because a great deal of its charm lies in its principal quality—that of repeating itself. Thus the age-old myth reappears in disguise form to confront us" (125-26).

The plays with rich mythical, legendry and historical stuff will cater the socio-political, cultural and literary needs of the society. Issues and problems discussed and analyzed will enlighten the society and help to meditate on those problems.

Works Cited

Burke, Rupalee. "India Then and Now: The Contemporary Relevance of Girish Karnad's *Tale-Danda" Studies in Indian Drama in English.* (Eds.) Prasad, Amar Nath and Yadav, Saryug. Bareilly: Prakash Book Depot, 2003.

Das, Veena Noble. "A Re-Reading of Girish Karnad's Plays with Reference to Myth and Folktale" *Flowering of Indian English Drama: Growth and Development*. (Eds.) Reddey, Venkata K & Dhawan, R.K. New Delhi: Prestige, 2004.

Dharwadker, Aparna Bhargava. (Ed.) With an Introduction *Collected Plays*.Vol. One: *Tughlaq, Hayavadana, Bali: The Sacrifice, Naga-Mandala*. New Delhi: O.U.P., Fourth Impression, 2008.

_______. (Ed.) With an Introduction Collected Plays. Vol. Two: *Tale-Danda, The Fire and the Rain, The Dreams of Tipu sultan, Two Monologues, Flowers, Broken Images*. New Delhi: O.U.P., 2005.

Jagamonarchari, A. "Karnad's *Hayavadana* and *Naga-Mandala*: A Study in Post Colonial Dialectics" *New Directions in Indian Drama*. Eds. Sudhaker Pandey & Freya Barua. New Delhi: Prestige, 1994.

Joshipura, Pranav. "*Tale-Danda:* A Problem Play" *Indian English Drama: Critical Perspectives*. (Eds.) Dondiya & Sunderan. New Delhi: Sarup & Sons, 2000.

Karnad, Girish. *Two Plays: Dream of Tipu Sultan, Bali: The Sacrifice*. New Delhi: O.U.P., Fourth Impression, 2005.

_______. "Inroduction" to *Three Plays: Naga-Mandala, Hayavadana, Tughlaq*. New Delhi: O.U.P., 2002. *Naga-Mandala* has been extensively used and referred from this edition.

_______. *Tale-Danada*. Delhi: Ravi Dayal, 1993. This edition has been extensively used and referred in.

_______. *Yayati*. New Delhi: O.U.P., 2008. This edition has been used and subsequent references are from this edition.

Krishanamayi. "Redefinig the Insurgent Female Psyche in an Andrcentric milieu" *The Indian Journal of English Studies*. Vol. XLI, 2003-04.

Mukherjee, Tutun. (Ed.) Girish Karnad's Plays: Performance and Critical Perspectives. Delhi: Pencraft International, 2006.

Murthy, U.R. Anantha. "Introduction" *Tughlaq*. Delhi: O.U.P., (Twenty Second Impression), 1998. This edition has been used and referred.

Naik, M. K . *Littcrit*. Vol 23, Number1&2 , June-Dec , 2001.

Ramaswamy, S. "The New and the Old: Indian Writing at the Turn of the Century" *Indian Writing in the New Millennium*. (Ed.) Dhawan, R.K. New Delhi: Indian Association for English Studies, 2000.

Raykar, Shubhangi S. "The Development of Girish Karnad as a Dramatist: *Hayavadana*" *Contemporary Indian Drama*. (Eds.) Pandey, sudhaker & Taraporewala, Freya. New Delhi: Prestige, 1990.

Reddy, K Venkata & Dhawan, R.K., (Eds.) *Flowering of Indian English Drama: Growth and Development*. New Delhi: Prestige, 2004.

Somalata, Y. "Girish Karnad's *Tale-Danda:* Painful Rite of Passage" *Flowering of Indian English Drama: Growth and Development*. (Eds.) Reddey, Venkata K & Dhawan, R.K. New Delhi: Prestige, 2004.

Soni, J.D. "Girish Karnad's *Naga-Mandala*: An Experiment in Technique" *Indian Writing in the New Millenium*. Ed.Dhawan, R.K. New Delhi: Indian Association for English Studies, 2000.

Suneel Seema. "Karnad's *Yayati* Reconsidered" *Contemporary Indian Drama.* (Eds.) Pandey, Sudhaker & Taraporewala, Freya. New Delhi: Prestige, 1990.

Tripathi, Vanashree. *Three plays of Girish Karnad: A Study in Poetics and Culture: Hayavadana, Tale-Danda, The Fire and the Rain.* New Delhi: Prestige Books, 2004.

5

Existential Dilemma

One of the leading philosophical movements of the twentieth century, existentialism has had more impact on literature and the arts than any other school of thought. Prominent figures of existentialism Sartre, Nietzsche, Heidegger, Kierkegaard, Simon de Beauvoir, Menlieau-Ponty and Camus deal with individuality, free will and personal responsibility, which marked the movement as a way of life, not just a way of thinking.

Among the Western playwrights, Karnad acknowledged "the Greeks, Shakespeare, Shaw, O'Neill, Anouilh, Brecht, Sartre and Camus ... influenced me" (Mukherjee.34-35). Existential element is a natural feature of Karnad's mode of thinking refined by existentialism and its concerns. The chapter endeavours to explore the fundamental thoughts of existential philosophy embedded in Karnad's plays with their modern relevance. Man's existence and transcendence occupied the creative mind of Karnad which is apparently manifested in his plays. Existentialism is a mode of thinking or attitude that manifested itself after World War I. It is actually a revival of Soren Kierkegaard's philosophical postulate that 'the individual must be saved as an individual'. He felt that man's existence is in danger from the orthodox religious system and from the industrial and technological age, and, also from the forces of nature that treat him like an object of scientific investigation. It is essentially a protest against those forces that tend to reduce human beings and the inner realities of the mind to insignificant proportions.

As a dramatist Karnad is an existentialist which implies consciousness of the self in the world of lived experience. It is an attempt to reaffirm the power of the self to deal with experience. It also implies the problems of selfhood, search for identity, isolation and frustration. Existentilism vindicates the individual despite his limitations and failures by insisting that he can transcend reality in his own consciousness. It affirms the dignity of man. Existentialism is humanism.

In the plays of Karnad characters feel alienated in an empty and meaningless universe. Alienation, despair and sense of nothingness haunt them. Yayati, Tughlaq, Devadatta, Kapil, Hayavadana, Rani, King Bijjala and Yavakri endorse Karnad's dexterous handling of existential dilemma and offer ways of transcendence. *Yayati, Tughlaq, Hayavadana, Naga- Mandala, Tale-Danda, The Fire and the Rain* are related with the theme of responsibility and search for identity. *Yayati* is a play on the theme of responsibility, *Tughlaq* deals with the search of identity. First of all, he tries to find his identity in high ideals and imaginative plans and when he doesn't succeed he resorts to murder and blood-shed. In *Hayavadana* Karnad deals with the theme of the search for identity and human relationship. *Naga-Mandala* studies women's struggle for emancipation and search for identity in patriarchcal society. *Tale-Danda* deals with the problem of existence, responsibility and failures. *The Fire and the Rain* advances the notion of identity crisis and search to overcome continues.

Yayati is the first play of Karnad—a self-consciously existentialist drama on the theme of responsibility. The play interprets an ancient myth from the *Adiparva* of the *Mahabharata* in modern context. The story centres round the character of Yayati. "Karnad's interpretation of the familiar old myth on the exchange of ages between father and son", remarked U.R. Ananthmurthy, "baffled and angered many conventional critics but, for others, who were trying to root their contemporary concerns in old myths, Karnad's unheroic hero, Puru, was a great experience" ("Introduction" *Tughlaq.* vii). The interpretation of myth no doubt irritated the orthodox viewers but the more enlightened critics appreciated the new approach of the play. What impressed the modern spectators of the play was the reinterpretation of the ancient myth in the light of the contemporary context. Existential dilemma inherent in the play makes it a complex and didactic. Karnad himself commented on the theme of the play:

> The story of King Yayati that I used occurs in the *Mahabharata*. The king, for a moral transgression he has committed, is cursed to old age in the prime of life. Distraught at losing his youth, he approaches his son, pleading with him to lend him his youth in exchange for old age. The son accepts the exchange and the curse, and thus becomes old, older than his father. But the old age brings no knowledge, no self-realization, only the senselessness of a punishment meted out for an act in which he had not even participated. The father is left to face the consequences of shirking responsibility for his own actions.
>
> ("Author's Introduction" 3)

It was written on the way to England and Karnad was only 23 years old. He was under stressful situation and engagement with the play escaped him from it. Karnad noted: "the myth enabled me to articulate to myself a set of values that I had been unable to arrive at rationally" (Ibid.3). Anouilh, Sartre, O'Neill and Greeks provided Karnada dramatic structure for *Yayati*. He couldn't find appropriate structure in our dramatic tradition to relate his anxieties. Aparna Bhargava Dharwadker observes: "The play itself resolved, as a literary work, the existential crisis that had generated and shaped it" ("Introduction" *Collected Plays*. Volume One. xv). Karnad restructures the story as an ironic drama of discontent, futility, and death. Yayati is a self-centred epicurean who invites the curse because he can't overcome his desire for Sharmishtha (the Asura Princess who is rival and slave of his wife, sage Shukracharya's daughter Devayani) although Devayani has warned him about the destructive consequences of his choice. Puru is a philosopher but self-hating 'outsider' who feels unsettled by the questionable legitimacy of his birth, and oppressed by the weight of dynastic tradition. Puru accepts the curse of his father. Puru ends the play on a note of stark bewilderment, unable to comprehend the point of what he has endured. Devayani the Brahman

Queen, Sharmishtha the slave Princess, Chitrlekha, Puru's new bride succeed in subverting the male world through an assertion of their rights and privileges. Women's centrality also reinforces existentialism that is the way of self-assertion.

Tughlaq, the second play which proved a great success on the stage is a history play. Karnad was told by someone that there is no good history plays in India, so he decided to write one. For this purpose he delved deep into history following the lines of Ishwari Prasad who explored positivism in Tughlaq. Historical perception and existentialism helped Karnad to crate new personality to dramatize it. He acknowledged:

> ...and when I came to Tughlaq I said Oh! Marvellous! That's what I wanted. In those days existentialism was very much in air. To be considered mad was very much fashionable. Everything about Tughlaq seemed to fit into what I had read was the correct thing to do, which was to be mad and do impossible things and so on. So I started reading about Tughlaq...reading what a fantastic character I had hit upon.
>
> ("Author's Introduction" 7)

An interesting story, a complex plot, scope for spectacle, reflection of the political mood of disillusionment which followed the Nehru era of idealism in the country attracted the applause of Indian audiences. *Tughlaq*'s "...elusive and haunting quality which it gets from the character of Tughlaq who has been realized in great philosophical depth...philosophical questions on the nature of man and the destiny of a whole kingdom which a dreamer like him controls" (Murthy. "Introduction" viii-ix). The play brought new laurels to Karnad and he successfully applied existential philosophy. *Tughlaq* has been portrayed with great psychological truth and depth. The dramatist deftly projects the paradoxes in the complex personality of Tughlaq who is at once a dreamer and a man of action, benevolent and cruel, devout and godless. He himself reveals his idealism, scholarship, and secularism in his various speeches. When his idealism and administrative reforms are frustrated a psychological change comes over him. In order to realize his plans and administrative reforms he resorts to murder and bloodshed; gets frustrated and disillusioned: "I am teetering on the brink of madness, Barani, but the madness of God still eludes me. (*Shouting*) And why should I deserve that madness? I have condemned my mother to death and I'm not even sure she was guilty of the crime..." (68). Barani, the scholarly historian, and Najib, the shrewd politician represent the two opposite selves of Sultan. Tughlaq's experiments and administrative reforms are just means to assert and prove his identity. The play has an irreducible, puzzling quality, which comes from the ambiguities of Tughlaq's character. All other characters are dramatized aspects of the personality of Tughlaq, yet they also exist in their own right. Intrigues baffle the mind of Tughlaq; he succeeds to cope with them. He is seen sleeping on the throne exhausted, confused and bewildered at the end of the play.

Hayavadana deals with "mad dance of incompleteness" (126) and search for completeness. In the play almost all the characters suffer from alienation. Devadatta, Kapil, Hayavadana are haunted by their incomplete existence, selves. Kirtinath Kurtkoti rightly observes: "Karnad's play poses a different problem, that of human identity in a world of tangled relationship" ("Introduction" v-vi). When the play opens, Devadatta and Kapil are shown the closest friends—'one mind, one heart'. Devadatta is a man of intellect and Kapil 'a man of the body'. Their friendship is based on the fact that they depend on each other for what each lacks, and both suffer from self-alienation. Thus they need each other for completeness. Their relationship is complicated when Devadatta is married to Padmini. Kapil falls in love with Padmini and she too diverts her mind towards him. Both kill each other and Padmini transposes their heads, giving Devadatta Kapil's body and Kapil Devadatta's. Hence their incompleteness is doubled. The result is a confusion of identities, which reveals the ambiguous nature of human personality. The transposition creates an awkward development—Devadatta stops writing poetry while Kapil is haunted by the memories in Devadatta's body. Padmini, who, after the exchange of heads, had felt that she had the best of both the men, gets slowly disillusioned. Of the three, she has the capacity for complete experience. She understands but cannot control the situation in which she is placed.

Right from the beginning, Devadatta and Kapil are the closest friends and love each other. But Devadatta's infatuation with Padmini implies "that the friendship of Kapil fail to provide him the feeling of completeness he is hungry of. His pledge to sacrifice his arms and head to gods if he succeeds in marrying her, explains the emptiness within him" (Gill. 89). But the marriage brings despair and confrontation between the two friends. Devadatta is disgusted and feels jealous of Kapil though he tries to show that he is very happy, and his inner burning comes out. His suicide in the temple is an attempt on his part to escape disgust and agony. But it haunts him even after his death when life is restored to him with the help of Kali. He is happy after winning back Padmini with a new body but this happiness does not last as she again threatens his existence. Once again she leaves him alienated and melancholic when she sets out to meet Kapil. Again he tries to find the solution of his problem in death when he challenges Kapil to a duel. The sub-plot of *Hayavadana*, the horse-man, deepens the significance of the main theme of incompleteness by treating it on a different plane. The horse-man's search for completeness ends comically, with his becoming a complete horse. The animal body triumphs over the human head. Hayavadana is the embodiment of meaninglessness in human life. His absurd appearance suggests the absurdity of human life. The idea of irrationality initiated with the image of Ganesha is carried forward to the end of the play with the help of Hayavadana. From his parental background to his personal life, nothing happens in any logical order. His figure, bodily movements, his encounter with life, everything is marked by absurdity. Kirtinath Kurtkoti judiciously remarked:

> Karnad uses the conventions and motifs of folk tales and folk theatre—masks, curtains, dolls, the story-within-a story to create a bizarre world. It is a world of incomplete individuals, indifferent gods, dolls that speak and children who cannot, a world indifferent to the desires and frustrations, joys and sorrows of human beings. What is

> real is only the tremendous, irrational energy of the horse and its rider who move round the stage symbolizing the powerful but monotonous rhythm of life.
>
> ("Introduction" vi-vii)

Hayavadana thus presents a typical existentialist despair. The play suggests a strategy for the achievement of integrity in the world inevitably cursed with absurdity and irrationality.

Rani, the female protagonist of *Naga-Mandala,* epitomizes the existentialist characteristics, i.e., alienation, despair, struggle for freedom and individuality, constant fight against social forces which exert perennial pressure to annihilate her existence. Though the play is a richly textured dramatic transmutation of two folk tales of Karnataka, Karnad delves deep to explore contemporary socio-cultural and philosophical concerns giving them modern validity. Rani is placed in a world where orthodox social conventions, cultural taboos and coercive forces work; patriarchy is established which proves greatest blow to the existence of Rani. Apart from overt patriarchy, she is socialized to internalize the male superiority—an invisible conspiracy to derogate and marginalize her position in the society. Unlike G.B.Shaw's Candida she adopts new ways to transcend age-old subjection of woman. Liberation of woman, a fight for woman's emancipation, which characterizes feminism, and is closely aligned with existentialism. Rani is surrounded by evil social forces where she finds herself helpless; tortured by alienation and despair but she never surrenders and she continues her struggle for identity –as a woman, as a wife and as a mother. Karnad's solution appears, at the first observation odd, unconvincing and unconventional, violating traditional mode of treatment. The message is clear: despite alienation, despair and antithetical conditions a woman must continue her struggle for her existence and transcend "nothingness" in life and manipulate co-existence as a means for self-existence. Patriarchy, socio-cultural practices, parents of Rani, Appanna, Village Elders, Naga, Dog, Mongoose etc are the tools to perpetuate exploitation of Rani. Like Kate Millet's *Sexual Politics* (1969), Karnad's *Naga- Mandala* (1990) exposes the mechanisms that express and enforce the relations of power in society and further analyses the social arrangements and institutions as covert ways of manipulating power so as to establish and perpetuate the dominance of man and the subordination of woman.

Prologue introduces Four Flames, which are animated, symbolic representations employed to report the sufferings of women; they also comment on their mental conflicts as Dolls do in *Hayavadana* (1975). Man and Story are identical to Greek Chorus, throughout the play they go on commenting and supplying important information and remain on the stage. Act I unfolds Rani, well known for her tresses; married to a man who was "rich and his parents were both dead" (27); Rani's parents are least concerned about the character and wrong doings of Appanna, they are equally responsible for her atrocities, after marriage they never visit to Rani. No welcome ceremony, nor bridal song is there. Rani is nonplused to hear: " Well ,then, I will be back tomorrow at noon . Keep my lunch ready. I shall eat and go." (27) He pays no attention to her, goes out, shuts the door, and locks it from outside and goes away. She runs to the door, finds it locked. She doesn't know what are happening, stands perplexed. She can't even weep. She goes and sits in a corner of her room, talks to herself indistinctly; tired and exhausted goes into sleep; sees nightmares, cries for parents. Next morning when Appanna comes, Rani tries to explain the pains of loneliness, and tries to win the sympathy of Appanna, he very coldly rebukes: "What is there to be scared of .... Look, I don't like idle chatter. Do as you are told, you understand." (28) He finishes his meal and goes out, locks her. Thus the days rolled by. Rani, mechanically, goes into the kitchen, starts cooking and talks to herself. She becomes a caged bird whereas Appanna is a philanderer; regularly visits to his concubine. When Kurudavva, a blind woman calls at her, and asks about Appanna's treatment to her:

> KURUDAVVA: Does he...talk to you
>
> RANI: Oh that he does. But not a syllable more than required 'Do this', 'Do that', 'Serve the food'. Apart from him, you are the first person I have seen since coming here. I am bored to death. There is no one to talk to. (31)

Rani wants to go back to her parents and requests Kurudavva to send the message to her parents but to no avail. Her mental conflicts bring tears in the eyes of audience, but Appanna remains untouched. Rani is treated in a slavish manner, imprisoned like a caged bird. She is neither allowed to talk to outsiders nor any outsider is allowed to do the same. Despite her chastity and fidelity, she is forced to face the Naga Ordeal. In course of time, Rani becomes pregnant. It is a news of joy for her as a fulfillment of a woman's dream. But her search for identity as a mother is not fulfilled; on the contrary, Appanna reacts violently knowing her pregnant that he has never made love with her. He is out of himself, calls her a strumpet, a whore, drags her out of the house, threatens to give her extreme punishment for cheating him:

> Aren't you ashamed to admit it, you harlot? I locked you in, and yet you managed to find a lover! ....I swear to you I am not my father's son, if I don't abort that bastard! smash it into dust !....I will go to the Village Elders .If they don't throw that child into boiling oil and you along with it , my name is not Appanna ? (52-53).

This is how Rani is greeted for her first pregnancy. Appanna publicly questions Rani's chastity and registers a case in the village court where Village Elders sit to judge. Rani is forced to face an Ordeal to prove her chastity. The traditional test in the village court has been to take the oath while holding a red-hot iron rod in the hand. Occasionally, the accused has chosen to plunge the hand in boiling oil. But Rani insists on swearing by the King Cobra—holding it in her hand. Viewing it as an equally convincing proof the elders agree to her proposal. On the appointed day:

> she plunges her hand in the ant hill and pulls out the cobra. The cobra slides up her shoulder and spreads its hood like an umbrella over her head. The crowd gasps. The cobra sways its hood gently for a while, then becomes docile and moves her shoulder like a garland. (58)

The crowd is enchanted by this miracle and elevates Rani to the position of a Goddess—the crowd surges forward to prostrate itself before her. Appanna is seated next to her in a palanquin, and the couple is taken in a procession to their house. Appanna is admonished: "Appanna, your wife is not an ordinary woman. She is a goddess incarnate. Don't grieve that you judged her wrongly and treated her badly. This is how goddesses reveal themselves to the world. You were the chosen instrument for revealing her divinity" (59). The Elder 2 exhorts him: "Spend the rest of your life in her service. You need merit in ten past lives to be chosen for such a holy duty" (59).

Thus Rani gets everything she wished for: a devoted husband, a life long servant (concubine realiz her sinful life and volunteers to serve Rani), and a child. But how long? Soon Rani discovers that Appanna is different from the one that visits her every night. She is shocked by the fraud done on her for so many nights:

> No two men make love alike. And that night of the village court, when her true husband climbed into bed with her, how could she fail to realize it was someone new? Even if she hadn't known earlier! When did the split take place? Every night this conundrum must have spread its hood out at her. Don't you think she must have cried out in anguish to know the answer? (60)

Rani finally accepts the Cobra who gave her love and motherhood: "You don't know how heavy you are. Let me get used to you....This hair is the symbol of my wedded bliss. Live in there happily, for ever" (64). Rani's acceptance of Naga as her own is a way of co-existence.

King Bijjala of *Tale- Danda* is another instance of existential dilemma whose struggle to establish himself in the upper hierarchy in Hindu brahminical society, facing tough resentment from Basavanna and his *Lingayat* faith, his disgust and anguish due to indecision, alienation and frustration caused by the uprising of subalterns, Sovideva, his son's revolt against him, conspiracy and counter conspiracy for power make him helpless and he fails to overcome adverse socio-religious and political forces and finally killed. *Tale-Danda* draws its story from the life of Kannada saint, Basavanna, who resisted ideologically against the prevailing evils of caste hierarchy. Explosive situations after the official endorsement of Mandal Commission Report and Mandir issue in 1989 motivated Karnad to concentrate on subaltern issue. And the historical context, deeply implanted in his mind, which proved catalyst to the plays of Karnad was predominated with, Karnad himself explains: "...tensions between the cultural past of the country and its colonial past, between the attractions of Western modes of thought and our own traditions, and finally between the various visions of the future that opened up once the common cause of the political freedom was achieved" ("Introduction" 1). Caste politics and its socio-cultural impact on the whole society since earliest times have endangered the existence of lower caste people. The play reveals in the name of Varnashrama Dharma, lower caste people are socialized to internalize the reigning superiority of upper caste. Though Mallibomma adopts *Lingayat* faith, he can't think to enter a brahmin Jagdeva's, house. Bijjala, the king of Kalyan during his reign witnesses a big revolution in the city. A man called Basavanna assembles a congregation of poets, mystics, social revolutionaries and philosophers and condemned idolatry, caste system and sexual discrimination, and rejected anything static in favour of the principle of movement and progress in human enterprise posing great threat to the established brahminical canons. King Bijjala finds himself surrounded by conflicting ideas, challenging socio-religious practices, secret alliances among various warring factions. He is also a victim of inferiority complex. For his superior existence and social status he manipulates a lot but fails. His life is full of frustration and anxiety; he finds himself inferior and alienated in the world dominated by brahmins and other high caste people. He appreciates Basavanna and his *Lingayat* faith professing new ideology for fraternity and progress in the society but he can't acknowledge it openly because he senses tough resistance from orthodox brahmins. He is constantly haunted by antithetical ideas creating mental crisis and indecision. He is swayed by Damodar Bhatta and Manchanna Kramita, the royal priests, who instigate him against the new rising and bolster to perpetuate brahminical ideology where caste distinction places subalterns at the lowest level in social hierarchy annihilating their existence altogether. King Bijjala, like Hamlet, fails to initiate any positive and fruitful action. He is apprehend by *pratiloma* (hypergamous) marriage—mingling of upper caste and lower caste via Sheelavanta, a low caste boy and Kalavati, a Brahmin: "You (Basavanna) know perfectly well the higher castes will not take this lying down. The wedding pandal will turn into a slaughter-house. The streets of Kalyan will reek of human entrails" (48). He is a mere puppet in the hands of brahmins even his own son Sovideva defies his authority and traps him. Sovideva, "kicks Bijjala, who, taken unawares, rolls to the ground" (63) "Tears well up in his eyes" (63). He begs for his life; Sovideva declares himself the King of Kalyan and Bijjala in utter frustration abuses him but can't do anything. Sovideva leads a violent reaction against the *Sharanas* for inter-caste marriage, while Bijjala mutely watches whatever goes before his eyes. In retaliation Jagadeva stabs Bijjala who dies pathetically. Bijjala fails to fulfil his responsibility to bring confronting parties on the negotiating table and usher an era of peace and prosperity. Though he is the King, the supreme authority of Kalyan, yet he finds himself alienated. Finally when he senses his existence in danger, he grasps the *linga* in utter frustration but to no avail. Sovideva continues to gesticulate violently.

Yavakri figures in *The Fire and the Rain*, which is primarily based on the myth of Yavakri described in the Chapters 135-8 of the *Vana Parva* of the *Mahabharata*. Karnad has derived the story from it and filled with modern sensibility suggesting deeper philosophical import and meaning. Yavakri's grievance against the world for non-recognization of his father Bharadwaj's ascetic experience, passion for knowledge, tough penance for ten years to establish his existence in the society dominated by Raibhya, a learned man and his two sons Parvasu and Arvasu, his search for identity, individuality and strong will power lead him to make his own destiny. He revolts against prevailing malpractices and goes into ten years' rigorous penance to obtain knowledge of the *Vedas* from the gods directly to prove his worth. Yavakri's search for completeness, exceptional will power, frustration in love, hostile reactions from Raibhya, severe punishment for his wrong doings followed by his ghastly death endorses existentialists' hypothesis of a man. He endures the conflict between Apollonian and Dionysian tendencies he possesses—he remains in a fix, haunted by contradictory traits of the personality he imbibes further confirm this notion. The ascetic practice was so rigorous that Indra, the lord of gods, appeared to him, but only to persuade him that there were no shortcuts to knowledge. But due to his strong will power and determination he denies to yield:

> ANDHAKA: Ten years of rigorous penance. And still Lord Indra would not oblige. Finally, Yavakri stood in the middle of a circle of fire and started offering his limbs to the fire—first his fingers, then his eyes, then his entrails, his tongue, and at last, his heart—that's when the god appeared to him, restored him limbs, and granted him the boon. (115)

Ultimately Indra relents and lets him have his wish. Thus Yavakri succeeds in proving his existence in the society. Bharadwaj, being a wise man, cautions Yavakri against delusions of omnipotence but Dionysian Yavakri ignores the advice and corners Raibha's daughter-in-law, Vishakha, and molests her. Thus he violates the moral code of conduct and challenges the authority of Raibhya for which he is justly punished. Though he obtain knowledge and power directly from Indra, he remains alienated and melancholic for he cannot get the love of Vishakha whom he cannot forget. The dialogue between Yavakri and Vishakha throws light on his reminiscences and sensual desires:

> YAVAKRI: ....Ten years ago I had come to your house to bid you goodbye. And you let me quickly to the jack-fruit grove behind your house. You opened the knot of your blouse, pressed my face to your breasts, then turned and fled. I stood there stunned....The smell of your body. Ten years later I opened my eyes and I knew, I was hungry for that moment.
>
> VISHAKHA: I can't believe it! The whole world may be singing your praises. But you haven't grown up! These ten years have not made any difference to your teenage fantasies. That's all gone, Yavakri, Indra may be immortal. But...my breasts hang loose now. (121)

His ascetic experience can't transform his sexual desires as he is ruled and overwhelmed by the passion of love, purely physical, and he indulges in romantic gratification. His misdemeanour brings him death. Though he is restored to life by the sun-god because of Arvasu's penance, he is reprimanded for his folly and asked to pursue knowledge in the right manner.

Karnad's handling of existentialism is thought-provoking. It is not only major characters and their socio-psychological conditions but also minor characters, often placed under hostile situations, and suggestions are offered to overcome them. Existentialists contributed a lot to restructure plot and design of his plays. Though the philosophical concept of existentialism was popularized by the Western philosophers and Karnad's mind was very much shaped by its ideology, yet he applied the concept when he created characters in his plays that are more or less feel alienated due to their social, cultural, political or intellectual backdrop.

Works Cited

Dharwadker, Aparna Bhargava. (Ed.) With an Introduction *Collected Plays.*Vol. One: *Tughlaq, Hayavadana, Bali: The Sacrifice, Naga-Mandala.* New Delhi: O.U.P., Fourth Impression, 2008.

________. (Ed.) With an Introduction Collected Plays. Vol. Two: *Tale-Danda, The Fire and the Rain, The Dreams of Tipu sultan, Two Monologues, Flowers, Broken Images.* New Delhi: O.U.P., 2005.

Gill, L.S. Girish Karnad's Hayavadana: A Critical Study. New Delhi: Asia Book Club, 2005.

Karnad, Girish. "Inroduction" *Three Plays: Naga-Mandala, Hayavadana, Tughlaq.* New Delhi:O.U.P., 2002. *Naga-Mandala* has been extensively used and referred from this edition.

________, *Tale-Danada.* Delhi: Ravi Dayal, 1993.

Kurtkoti, Kirtinath. "Introduction" *Hayavadana.* Chennai: O.U.P. (Fourteenth Impression), 1998.

Mukherjee, Tutun. (Ed.) Girish Karnad's Plays: Performance and Critical Perspectives. Delhi: Pencraft International, 2006.

Murthy, U.R. Anantha. "Introduction" *Tughlaq.* Delhi: O.U.P. (Twenty Second Impression), 1998.

Pandey, Sudhaker & Barua, Freya. Eds. *New Directions in Indian Drama.* New Delhi: Prestige, 1994.

Tripathi, Vanashree. *Three plays of Girish Karnad: A Study in Poetics and Culture—Hayavadana, Tale-Danda, the fire and the Rain.*New Delhi: Prestige Books, 2004.

6

Subaltern Issues

I

In the postcolonial theory subaltern studies occupy a significant place; it derives its force from Marxism and Post-Structuralism. Subaltern studies is primarily concerned with socio-cultural and historical aspects of the society, incorporating the entire people that is subordinate in terms of class, caste, age, gender and office, or in any other way. It is the subject position that defines subalternity. Even when it operates in terms of class, age and gender, it is more psychological than physical. The lack and deprivation, loneliness and alienation, subjugation and subordination, the resignation and silence, the resilence and neglect mark the lives of the subalterns. Even when they resist and rise up, they feel bound and defeated by their subject positions. They have no representatives or spokespersons in the society they live in, and so helplessly suffer and get marginal place or no place at all in the history and culture of which they are the essential part as human beings. The subaltern has become, as M.H. Abrams remarks "a standard way to designate the colonial subject that has been constructed by European discourse and internalized by colonial peoples who employ this discourse" (237). Subaltern is a British word for someone of inferior in rank, and combines the Latin terms for "under" (*sub*) and "other" (*alter*). A recurrent topic of debate is how, and to what extent a subaltern subject, writing in a European language, can manage to serve as an agent of resistance against, rather than compliance with, the very discourse that has created its subordinate identity.

Antonio Gramsci used the term first to denote the subordinate position in terms of class, gender, caste, race and culture. And it was popularized by Gayatri Chakravarty Spivak's essay entitled "Can a Subaltern Speak?" (1985). She has used the term for the colonized / the oppressed subject; working class, blacks and the women whose voices have been silenced. Spivak has, observes B.K. Das, "laid stress on 'gendered subaltern—that, women, who are doubly oppressed by colonialism and patriarchy in the Third World countries" (143). G.N. Devy considers that the most important issue she has raised is the "Subalternization of Third World literature" (221). "Worldling" of the "Third World" in Spivak, observes Pramod K Nayar, "is the process through which the local population was persuaded to accept the European version of reality for its modes of understanding and structuring its social world" (192). In the 1970s subaltern studies began in England and subsequently English and Indian historians collectively worked on the subject.

Oxford University Press, New Delhi brought out *Subaltern Studies: Writings on South Asian History and Society* (in three volumes) edited by Ranjit Guha and eight volumes were added later. In 1888, *Selected Subaltern Studies* was published by OUP, New York and Oxford edited by Ranjit Guha and Spivak with a foreword note by Edward Said. In the early 1980s a group of intellectuals known as Subaltern Studies group successfully attempted to write a historiography that was different from the colonial one. The theories of nationalism, identity and ethnicity came in for close scrutiny. Asian colonial history owed much to Spivak and Ranjit Guha's energy. Lodge and Wood acknowledge, "in deconstructing imperial accounts of 'native' rebellion and customs to allow other voices freer play" (414). Gyan Prakash explicitly links the subaltern studies project with postcolonial studies in its combination of post-structuralism, Marxism and archival research. The focus is on the general attribute of subordination in South Asian society whether this is expressed in terms of class, caste, age, gender and office. It looks at "history from below", that is, the history of those common people (tribals, lower classes /castes and women) that have been silenced in accepted histories of the nationalist movements which is elitist, dictated by the dominant groups, foreign as well as indigenous. Leela Gandhi explores the mechanism of the Subaltern Studies group which:

> Sketched out its wide- ranging concern both with the visible 'history, politics, economics and sociology of subalternity' and with the occuled 'attitudes, ideologies and belief system...Subaltern Studies defined itself as an attempt to allow the people finally to speak within the jealous pages of elitist historiography and in so doing, to speak for, or to sound the muted voices of the truly oppressed (1-2).

Time has changed. Both the colonized and the women have now spoken. B.K. Das rightly remarks in this regard:

> The subaltern in the colonial era have become intellectuals in the postcolonial period...thanks to the writers of the Third World countries who write in English today. And literatures in English by the Third world writers have gained acceptance among the Anglo-American intellectuals today. It is in this subaltern studies have acquired a new dimension (146-147).

II

Karnad's deep-rooted humanism allowed him to give voice to the silenced majority through his plays. His plays abound in subalterns, especially women and lower caste people subjected since ancient times by patriarchy or upper hierarchy of the society. Karnad has not only exposed their subalternity but also fused energy in their lives so that they can speak; shifted their position from "margin" to "centre". *Yayati, Tughlaq, Hayavadana, Naga-Mandala, Tale-Danda, The Fire and the Rain* etc. amply exemplify the above notion. Devayani, Sharmishtha and Chitralekha in *Yayati,* Kapil and Padmini in *Hayavadana,* Rani and Kurudavva in *Naga-Mandala,* lower caste people in *Tale-Danda,* tribals, nittilai and Vishakha in *The Fire and the Rain,* Mahout in *Bali: The* Sacrifice, Chandrawati in *Flowers*, Malini in *Broken* Images and Rahabai in *Wedding Album* display subalternity of the class they represent. Karnad as a cultural administrator goes beyond this and attempts to provide them their due space, and to defy the traditional hierarchies prevalent in Indian society. The chapter endeavours to analyse Karnad's handling of the subaltern issue and remedial measures suggested in his plays.

Yayati, the first play of Karnad which is based on the myth of Yayati in the *Mahabharata,* is highly relevant as far as the socio-psychological study of women is concerned. Devayani, Sharmishtha, Swarnalata and Chitralekha are generic; represent the subalternity of woman in a masculinist society where she is identified as the "other", "non-man", or "second sex" despite her high position in society. Karnad doesn't adhere to traditional glorification of the son's 'self-sacrifice', but rather raises the question against this. Devayani, the Queen, has to endure every sort of humiliation and becomes insane; Swarnalata is tortured by her husband's unfounded doubts of infidelity, insults and finally deserted; Sharmishtha is an easy prey of Yayati's filthy sexual gratification.

Though Chitralekha also faces similar conditions, she emerges as a new woman who boldly challenges the decision of Pooru and false rhetoric of Yayati. She doesn't allow Pooru to enter into her bedroom—who accepts the curse of his father for his moral transgression and becomes old: "I will not let my husband step back into my bedroom unless he returns a young man" (61) and frankly elaborates the reason of her marriage to Pooru: "I married him for his youth. For his potential to plant the seed of the Bharatas in my womb. He has lost that potency now. He doesn't possess any of the qualities for which I married him. But you do" (65-66). Yayati abuses her for these piercing words, "whore" (66). She defies everything, i.e., kingdom and high reputation of Bharat dynasty and wants "room" for herself. She smiles defiantly and swallows the poison and dies. She prefers to die rather than yield before old conventions and assigned roles set for woman. Her death endorses new woman's quest for emancipation. Sharmishtha precisely explains the condition of women, "A woman dead (Chitrlekha), another gone mad (Devayani), and a third in danger of her life (Sharmishtha)" (68). Jealousy and racial conflict also weaken their lot. The play reinforces the centrality of women. Aparna Bhargava Dharwadker rightly comments: "The most remarkable feature of *Yayati*...is its quartet of sentient, articulate, embittered women, all of whom are subject in varying degrees to the whims of men, but succeed in subverting the male world through an assertion of their rights and privileges" ("Introduction" Vol. One. xvii).

Padmini and Kapila define subalternity in *Hayavadana.* Padmini is unlike Rani of *Naga-Mandala.* She belongs to a family of leading merchant of Pavana Veethi of Dharampura. Though, in the play she enjoys a commanding position, she is close to the spirit of Cleopatra of Shakespeare, succumbs to Dionysian tendency and indulges in cuckoldry. She camouflages the love of Devadatta, his poetry gets new charm and vitality. She is so fascinating that Devadatta finds her "beyond my wildest dreams" (14) and swears "if I ever get her as my wife, I will sacrifice my two arms to the goddess Kali, I'll sacrifice my head to Lord Rudra..." (14). Even Kapila finds "Yakshini, Shakuntala, Urvashi, Indumati—all rolled into one" (16) and warns Devadatta, "She is not for the likes of you. What she needs is a man of steel" (19). While talking to Padmini Kapila rightly says: "I know what you want, Padmini. Devadatta's clever head and Kapil's strong body" (38). The fact is soon discovered—her temptation to Kapila's muscular body; she is the real Padmini of Vatasyayana:

> PADMINI: [*Watching him, to herself*]. How he climbs—like an ape. Before I could even say 'yes', he had taken off his shirt, pulled his *dhoti* up and swung up the branch. And what an ethereal shape! Such a broad back—like an ocean with muscles rippling across it—and then that small, feminine waist which looks so helpless.... He is like a Celestial Being reborn as a hunter.... How his body sways, his limbs curve—it's dance almost.... No woman could resist him. (25-26)

Devadatta senses her leaning towards Kapila but he feels helpless.

Devadatta and Kapila represent Apollonian and Dionysian tendencies respectively, hence Padmini's hunger for Kapila is the very outcome of her own nature. But in the temple of Kali, after Devadatta and Kapila's sacrifice, she is very much embarrassed to see the melodramatic scene and frightened to sense the sarcasm of people, anticipating people would blame her for both deaths. She instantly decides to kill herself. Transposition, no doubt, is a very frightening experience to her, yet she feels she has the best of both the man: "My Devadatta comes like a bridegroom with the ornament of a new body.... It's my duty to go with Devadatta. But, remember I'm going with your [Kapil's] body" (41), "fabulous body—fabulous brain" (43) and "male smell" (43) which express her nymphomaniac ecstasy and lust for sexual gratification. Even Doll I and Doll II comment on her psychic reactions—dreams, phantasies and reveries in which Kapila figures "climbing a tree!", "dived into a river" (50) symbolically let loose Padmini's suppressed sexual desire and hunger for Kapila.

Soon she is disillusioned and finds herself, like Devadatta, Kapila and Hayavadana a victim of "mad dance of incompleteness" (57). Even after marriage, she can't resist herself and goes to the forest with her son and enjoys extramarital sexual relation with Kapila cuckolding her husband for four or five days. In a duel Devadatta and Kapila kill each other. Subsequently, Padmini finds herself nowhere. She suffers from alienation and a perplexing situation erupts. She is abetted to perform *sati*—for the sake of the glory of her son or she cannot live without Devadatta and Kapila: "Kali, Mother of all Nature, you must have your joke even now. Other women can die praying that they should get the same husband in all lives to come. You haven't left me even that little consolation" (63). Padmini's practice of *sati,* comments Bhagavatta, "it would not be an exaggeration to say that no *pativrata* went the way Padmini did" (63). Female Chorus justifies Padmini's misdemeanour: "Why should love stick to the sap of a single body? When the stem is drunk with the thick yearning of the many-petalled, many-flowered lantana, why should it be tied down to the relation of a single flower?.... I have neither regret nor shame" (64). Karnad attempts to give due space to women in human society where they have been marginalized since time immemorial. His plays present the evolution of women and their quest for a better position in the world.

Kapila, the son of the iron smith Lohita, is "dark and plain look at, yet in deeds which require drive and daring, in dancing, in strength and in physical skills he has no equals" (92). His physical features and traits of the personality mark off his social identity and inferior position in society contrasted with Devadatta's "comely appearance, fair colour, unrivalled in intelligence.... Only son of the Revered Brahmin Vidhysagara... felled the mightiest pundits of the kingdom in debates on logic and love, having blinded the greatest poets of the world with his poetry and wit... apple of every eye in Dharampura" (2). Devadatta and Kapila represent two opposite extremes—one soul, another body. Their friendship is exceptional, "One mind, one heart" (2).

Despite his closeness with Devadatta, there is always a deep-rooted feeling in Kapila's mind that he belongs to a lower caste. He doesn't dare to sit on a chair with Devadatta, rather, he sits down on the ground happily. Even Devadatta satires his profession: "What do you know of poetry and literature? Go back to your smithy—that's where you belong," (13) which reminds the subalternity of Kapila. He is an easy target of Padmini's lust. His arguments in favour of body, after exchange of heads, are declined instantly in *Brihadkathasaritasagara*, but Karnad doesn't accept the solution offered by Vikram; rather he ridicules such an easy answer to a serious problem. Kapila's arguments too get a place in the play. Here, the playwright has shifted the subalterns to the central position. The passing reference of Hayavadana's mother and Hayavadana's anxiety enlarge the subaltern world.

Karnad's *Naga-Mandala* is a sociological study of Indian women; richly textured dramatic transmutation of two folk tales of Karnataka usually narrated by women while feeding children in the kitchen. It exposes the ugliness of a society where women are considered "second sex", "other", "subject", "non-man"—— women are taught in the process of being socialized, to internalize the reigning patriarchal ideology, e.g., male superiority; and so conditioned to derogate their own sex and to cooperate in their own subordination. Patriarchal dominance has prevented women from realizing their productive and creative possibility.

The play also suggests remedial measures and slaps the orthodox society by an act of reconciliation between Rani and Naga. Karnad was well acquainted with feminist ideologies and the havoc wrought by patriarchal ideologies in Indian society. *Naga-Mandala* appears to be a battleground where ideological conflicts, power relations, and the struggle for identity have been dramatized effectively.

In *Naga-Mandala* Rani, the female protagonist, and Kurudavva, the other female character, are both generic, and represent the extreme physical torture and mental trauma, struggle for their identity as women, as wives, and as mothers. Four Flames, Story, and the Man also reflect the sufferings and exploitations of women.

Rani is treated in a slavish manner, imprisoned like a caged bird, neither is she allowed to talk to outsider nor outsider is allowed to do the same. Despite her chastity and fidelity, she is forced to face the Naga Ordeal. Appanna (Rani's husband), Naga (Cobra), Dog, Mongoose, Three Village Elders and the orthodox society have been used as the forces of subjection. Karnad has treated 'eternal—triangle' unlike of G.B.Shaw. Shaw in Candida gave a different twist to 'eternal—triangle' where Candida is a New Woman and finale brings the impression that conjugal love must be fostered and glorified whereas Karnad exposes the hollowness of male- chauvinism. Rani's acceptance of Naga as her own is a curt reply to the question of extra-marital relation in which only males are allowed to go freely. Prologue introduces Four Flames, which are animated, symbolic representations employed to report the sufferings of women. The tragic sufferings of women are extended to other female character—e.g. Kurudavva, who is an example of wisdom and philanthropy. Nobody in the society has eyes to see Rani's laceration at the hands of her philandering husband, but blind Kurudavva alone can see the truth. She extends motherly love and care to Appanna as well as to Rani. She is also the victim of orthodox society where the role of a woman is subservient and marginalized. Except her son Kappanna, there is none to look after her. Even the Village Elders treat her cruelly and unsympathetically while she has lost her only son.

The play *Tale-Danda* endeavours to highlight the subjection, role, upsurge, and revolution of the subalterns (i.e. lower caste), and how and why their revolution failed. Under Basavanna, a social reformer of the twelfth century assembled a congregation of poets, mystics and social revolutionaries and philosophers formed the *Lingayat* faith, giving impetus to courageous questioning and social commitment. The abolition of caste, equality of sexes, rejection of idol worship, repudiation of Brahaminism, and of Sanskrit in favour of the mother tongue i.e. Kannad; were the main tenets of subaltern revolution. The resentment reaches its climax when Madhuvarsa, a Brahmin gives his daughter Kalavati in a marriage to an untouchable— Sheelvanta. This last act opposing caste hierarchy, not just in theory but in practice also, brought down upon the wrath of orthodox; the movement ended in terror and bloodshed. The playwright wants to suggest whenever such important issues are not considered seriously and solutions offered by these thinkers go unheeded, disastrous results would follow again. *Tale- Danda* draws its story from the life of Kannada saint Basavanna who resisted ideologically against the prevailing evils of caste hierarchy. Explosive situations after the official endorsement of Mandal Commission Report and Mandir issue in 1989 motivated Karnad to concentrate on subaltern issue. And the historical context, deeply implanted in his mind, which proved catalyst to the plays of Karnad. It was the impact of humanism, which has nurtured in Karnad a dominant will for social justice, a sincere compassion for the socially oppressed and subaltern. Vanashree Tripathi rightly comments, "playwright's understanding of a long tradition of humanism in India...since the earliest periods" (25) has moulded his mind and attitude. The play explores how lower caste people are socialized to internalize the reigning superiority of upper caste. Mallibomma though adopts *Lingayat* faith, can't think to enter Jagdeva, a Brahmin's house. King Bijjala tried to ascend to higher Varna from barber to Kshatriya but failed and remains a subaltern though politically the supreme authority of Kalyan but socially suppressed and deeply realizes: "One's caste is like the skin on one's body. You can peel it off top to toe, but when the new skin forms, there you are again; a barber –a shepherd. (14-15)

Among subalterns tribals, shepherds, cowherds and low caste untouchables figure. Resistance of subalterns has two forms: ideological and physical. They rejected anything "static in favour of the principle of movement and progress in human enterprise" ("Preface"). They tried to come out of caste venom and religious fanaticism. The devotee of the faith was called *Sharana*. Mallibomma (a tanner by birth), Kakkaya (skinner), Haralayya (cobbler), Kalayani (Haralayya's wife), Sheelvanta and King Bijjala are *Sharanas* from lower caste. Jagdeva, Basavanna, Madhuvarsa and Gundamma are *Sharanas* from higher castes. This ideological resistance touches climax when Sheelavanta, a cobbler is married to Kalavati, a Brahmin; and immediately violent reaction starts. Antagonistic forces are *vis-à-vis* to gain power – hence hegemonic war begins. Physical resistance of *Sharanas* comes to dismal end. *Sharanas* lost their drive, mutual differences and in-fights, prompt reaction from orthodox Brahmins against *Sharanas* led by young Sovideva; Basavanna's resignation from the movement and power politics brings failure to the subalterns' resistance. Vanashree Tripathi comments:

> play that intends to revive upon the Indian stage the age old debate on the virtues and vices of casteism ...an endeavour to do justice to history—a stark reminder of our past, of the struggles and movements that bestowed upon us the freedom to think and question. The play is an invitation to look at ourselves—our empty present and our futurelessness. (91-92)

Sharanas lived a life of contradiction because of their mixed identity. Basvanna's vision of egalitarian society and spiritualized politics was the vision of Karnad himself. The subaltern issue was one of the most important thematic concerns in the plays of Karnad, and he has exposed the the hollowness of the caste hierarchy and its harmful implications on Indian society.

Vishakha and Nittilai belong to two different socio-cultural backgrounds in *The Fire and the Rain*. Vishakha is the wife of Paravasu, a brahmin, and daughter-in-law of Raibhya, a learned ascetic whereas Nittilai hails from a tribal community. Despite cultural polarities, both experience similar socio-psychological taboos and restrictions and feel bounded. For Nittilai, subjection is more intense—apart from patriarchy her inferior position in social hierarchy deteriorates her standing in the society. Though the play is based on C. Rajgopalachari's prose retelling of the *Mahabharata* especially the myth of Yavakri in Vana Parva, Karnad constructs a story of passion, loss, and sacrifice in the contexts of Vedic rituals, spiritual discipline, social and ethical differences between human agents, and interrelated forms of performance still close to their moments of origin, yet the treatment of the feminine world, images of women, their subjection and changing status is not less remarkable. Vishakha, an archetypal character, and Nittilai, Karnad's invention, symbolize the subalternity of women that has been highlighted by the playwright exposing the ugliness in our society restricting their place and creativity in human society.

Vishakha loves Yavakri but his decision to get knowledge directly from gods initiates him into ten years' penance that leaves Vishakha helpless, alienated "sick of silence" (141) and deeply frustrated. Subsequently, she is married to Paravasu who offers up Vishakha's life, first to his sensual appetite and then to his lust for fame:

> VISHAKHA: The night of the wedding, my husband said to me: 'I know you didn't want to marry me. But don't worry. I'll make you happy for a year.' And he did. Exactly for one year.... Then on the first day of the second year of our marriage, he said: 'Enough of that. We now start on our search'.... He used my body, and his own body, like an experimenter, an explorer. As instruments in a search. Search for what? I never knew. To be the Chief Priest of the fire sacrifice... in all seven years he hasn't come back... I have become dry like tinder. Ready to burst into flames at a breath. (123)

The meeting of Vishakha with her former lover Yavakri infuriates Raibhya who grabs her by her hair and starts beating and kicking her. She is condemned as a "whore" (127) and "bitch" (138) thereafter left to be handled by her husband. She is an easy prey to Raibhya's anger over his rejection as the Chief

Priest by the king. He creates *Brahma Raksha* to kill Yavakri. Vishakha is bold and acknowledges her meeting with Yavakri before her husband candidly. Nittilai, a tribal girl of 14, loves Arvasu, a brammin of 18. Both work in a troupe. She is exposed to face the world and knows how cruel and ruthless it can be. Only Andhak appreciates their love; the elders of Nittilai's tribe are anxious to interrogate Arvasu. Hers is a romantic love, a world of teenage phantasies, ignorant of caste and cultural distinctions. On the contrary, Raibhya condemns her as "savage" (126). When Arvasu fails to appear before the Council of Tribal Elders, they decree, "Nitilai will marry another boy—of our own tribe" (135). She is handed over to a tribal boy and married against her wishes. She has no say. Her protest touches the climax when she runs away from her husband, family and everything for the sake of love. But, as an Indian married woman, she doesn't want to cuckold her husband. She transcends from petty sexual gratification and romantic love, and develops a pious relationship with Arvasu:

> NITTILAI: Arvasu, when I say we should go together—I don't mean we have to live together—like lovers, or like husband and wife. I have been vicious enough to my husband. I don't want to disgrace him further. Let's be together like brother and sister. You marry any girl you like. Only please, Arvasu—spare a corner for me. (153)

Nittilai's brother and husband chase her like hounds. She is frightened of their evil designs. She is offered a ghastly death despite her innocence: "the husband pulls out a knife, grabs Nittilai by her hair and slashes her throat in one swift motion. He then lets her drop.... She lies there, her eyes open, bleeding, dying like a sacrificial animal" (172). The killing of Nittilai, endorses still today that patriarchy and long established social conventions are strong enough to crush women's liberty or any kind of adventurism. But the quest by women for emancipation has started. The play also presents shudras and tribals as subalterns in Varna hierarchy.

In *Bali: The Sacrifice* the Mahout, a low-caste, elephant keeper of the King is always haunted by his inferior birth and ugly looks, hence he feels alienated in the world. His reaction is a natural outcome of his long subjugation and humiliation: "People mock at Mahouts. Call us 'low-bor. But where would all your princes and kings be without us, I want to know. What would happen to their elephants? No elephants. No army. No pomp and splendor. No processions. No kings! Ha!" (80). He, like Kapil, is dark-complexioned but muscular that tempts women to mate with him. He is a good singer. He has plenty of women to seduce. Even the Queen succumbs to this temptation and cuckolds her husband.

Flowers exposes the social mentality against womenfolk—the body of the woman is always a target of man's hungry, lustful eyes; and plots to exploit her sexually and make her an easy prey. Even the holy Priest, unnamed in the play, feasts his eyes on and indulges in filthy sensual gratification with Chandrawati, a courtesan. His wife knows everything, but she has to tolerate passively. Malini of *Broken Images* brings home the idea that subalternity emanates at home when Manjula Nayak, the only character of the play writes stories in Kannada, but for the sake "fame, publicity, glamour...power" (265) prefers writing novel in English. She indulges in plagiarism and secretly publishes a novel out of Malini's fragments. Radhabai of *Wedding Album* represents subalternity of the maid.

Karnad has great concern for the caste or gendered subalterns in his plays, and he has brought them from the margin to the centre through his plays. His plays are the medium where he raises socio-political and cultural problems prevalent in Indian society and calls upon us to discuss and evolve a common consensus rather than provide a ready-made answer to the problem. The subalterns in Indian society are particularly lower caste people and women who have been assigned an inferior position in the Hindu orthodox society as well as patriarchy. But Karnad, through his plays, has given due space and attempted to bring them in the mainstream.

Works Cited

Abrams, M.H. *A Glossary of Literary Terms.* (Seventh Edition), Singapore: Thomason Asia Pvt. Ltd., 2003.

Das, B.K. *Twentieth Century Literary Criticism.* (Fifth Edition), New Delhi: Atlantic Publishers and Distributors, Pvt. Ltd. 2007.

Devy, G.N. Ed. *Indian Literary Criticism.* Hyderabad: Orient Longman, Pvt. Ltd., 2007.

Dharwadker, Aparna Bhargava, (Ed.) With an Introduction *Collected Plays.* Vol. One: *Tughlaq, Hayavadana, Bali: The Sacrifice, Naga-Mandala.* New Delhi: O.U.P., (Fourth Impression), 2008.

________. (Ed.) With an Introduction Collected Plays. Vol. Two: *Tale-Danda, The Fire and the Rain,The Dreams of Tipu sultan, Two Monologues, Flowers, Broken Images*. New Delhi: O.U.P., 2005. The Fire and the Rain has been quoted from this edition.

Gandhi, Leela. *Postcolonial Theory: A Critical Introduction.* (Sixth Edition), New Delhi: OUP, 2005.

Karnad, Girish. *Two Plays: Dream of Tipu Sultan, Bali: The Sacrifice.* New Delhi: O.U.P., (Fourth Impression), 2005. References are from this edition.

________. "Inroduction" to *Three Plays: Naga-Mandala, Hayavadana, Tughlaq.* New Delhi: O.U.P., 2002. *Naga-Mandala* has been extensively used and referred from this edition.

________. *Tale-Danada.* Delhi: Ravi Dayal, 1993. This edition has been extensively used and referred in.

________. *Yayati.* New Delhi: O.U.P., 2008.

________, *Hayavadana.* (Fourteenth Impression), Chennai: OUP, 1998. This edition has been used and subsequent references are from this edition.

________, "Interview" *Flowering of Indian English Drama: Growth and Development.* (Eds.) Reddy, K Venkata & Dhawan, R.K. New Delhi: Prestige, 2004.

Lodge, David and Wood, Nigel. Eds. *Modern Criticism and Theory.* New Delhi: Dorling Kinderslay (India) Pvt. Ltd., 2007.

Mukherjee, Tutun, ed. Girish Karnad's Plays: Performance and Critical Perspectives. Delhi: Pencraft International, 2006.

Nayar, Pramod K. *Literary Theory Today.* New Delhi: Prestige / Asia Book Club, 2002.

Tripathi, Vanashree. *Three Plays of Girish Karnad: A Study in Poetics and Culture: Hayavadana, Tale-Danda, The Fire and the Rain.* New Delhi: Prestige Books, 2004.

7

Feminism and the Quest for Women's Emancipation

I

Feminist literary criticism is essentially linked to the political movement for equality of the sexes and end to discrimination against women. Feminist criticism seeks to uncover the ideology of patriarchal structure of society in the works of art. It reads literary texts for their representation of women, and argues that these representations mark socio-political oppression of the category of women by justifying this oppression and naturalizing it. For feminists, the text is a battleground where actual power relations between men and women are played out. Feminist criticism is a distinctive and concerted approach to literature; it was not inaugurated until late in the 1960s. Behind it, however, lie two centuries of struggle for the recognition of women's cultural roles and achievements, and for women's social and political rights, marked by such books as Mary Wollstonecraft's *A Vindication of the Rights of Women* (1792), J.S. Mill's *The Subjection of Women* (1869), and the American Margaret Fuller's *Women in the Nineteenth Century* (1845). Much of feminist literary criticism continues in our time to be interrelated with the movement by political feminists for social, legal, and cultural freedom and equality.

An important precursor in feminist criticism was Virginia Woolf who wrote *A Room of One's Own* (1929) and numerous other essays on women authors and on the cultural, economic and educational disabilities within what she called a "patriarchal" society that have prevented women for realizing their productive and creative possibilities. A much more radical critical mode was launched in France by Simon de Beauvoir's *The Second Sex* (1949), a wide ranging critique of the cultural identification of the women as merely the negative object, or "other", to man as the dominating "subject" who is assumed to represent humanity in general. The book also dealt with "the great collective myths" of women in the works of many male writers.

In America, modern feminist criticism was inaugurated by Mary Ellman's deft and witty discussion in *Thinking about Women* (1968), about the derogatory stereotypes of women in literature written by men, and also about alternative and subversive points of view in some writings of women. Even more influential was Kate Millett's hard-hitting *Sexual Politics* (1969). By "politics" Millett signifies the mechanisms that express and enforce the relations of power in society; she analyses Western social arrangements and institutions as covert ways of manipulating power so as to establish and perpetuate the dominance of men and the subordination of women. In her book she attacks the male bias in Freud's psychoanalytic theory and also analyses the selected passages by D.H.Lawrence, Henry Miller, Norman Mailer and Jean Genet as revealing the ways in which the authors, in their fictional fantasies, aggrandize their aggressive phallic selves and degrade women as submissive sexual objects.

Since 1969 there has been an explosion of feminist writings without parallel in previous critical innovations, in a movement that, as Elaine Showalter has remarked, "Displays the urgency and excitement of a religious awakening" (Abrams 89). This current criticism, in America, England, France and other countries, is not a unitary theory or procedure. It manifests, among those who practise it, a great variety of critical vantage points and procedures, including adaptations of psychoanalytic, Marxist, and diverse poststructuralist theories, and its vigour is reflected in the debates within the ranks of professed feminists themselves. Yet various versions of feminism share certain assumptions and concepts that underline the diverse ways that individual critics explore the factor of sexual difference and privilege in the production, the form and content, the reception, and the critical analysis and evaluation of works of literature. Anglo-American feminism maintains a major interest in traditional critical concepts like "theme, motif, and characterization" whereas French Feminists are particularly concerned with "language and psychology" (Barry 124-126). Within feminism there is a strong emphasis on the 'constructedness' of feminity, that is, conditioning and socialization, and the influence of images and representations of feminity in literature and culture.

The basic view is that Western Civilization is pervasively "Patriarchal" (ruled by father), that is, male-centred and controlled, and is organized and conducted in such a way as to subordinate women to men in all cultural domains: familial, religious, political, economic, social, legal and artistic. From the Hebrew *Bible* and Greek philosophical writings to the present, the female tends to be defined by negative reference to the male as the human norm, hence as an "other", or kind of "non-man", by her lack of the identifying male organ, of male powers, and of male character traits that are presumed, in the patriarchal view, to have achieved the most important scientific and technical inventions and the major works of civilization and culture. Women themselves are taught, in the process of being socialized, to internalize the reigning patriarchal ideology (that is, the conscious or unconscious presuppositions about male superiority), and so are conditioned to derogate their own sex and to cooperate in their own subordination.

It is widely held that one's sex is determined by anatomy, the prevailing concepts of "gender"—of the traits that are conceived to constitute what is masculine and what is feminine in identity and behaviour—are largely, if not entirely, cultural constructs that were generated by the pervasive patriarchal biases of our civilization. As Simon de Beauvoir puts it, "One is not born, but rather becomes a woman....It is civilization as a whole that produces this creature ....which is described as feminine" (Qtd. in Pramod K Nayar 88). By this cultural process, the masculine in our culture has come to be widely identified as active, dominating, adventurous, rational, and creative; the feminine, by systematic opposition to such traits, has come to be identified as passive, timid, emotional andconventional. Further claim is that this patriarchal (or "masculinist", "androcentric") ideology pervades those writings which have been written mainly by men for men.

Typically, the most highly regarded literary works focus on male protagonists—Oedipus, Ulysses, Hamlet, Tom Jones, Faust, The Three Musketeers, Captain Ahab, Huck Finn, Leopold Bloom—who embody masculine interests and ways of feeling and pursue masculine interests in masculine fields of actions. To these males, the female characters, when they play a role, are marginal and subordinate, and are represented either as complementary to or in opposition to masculine desires and enterprises. Such works, lacking autonomous female role models, and implicitly, addressed to male readers, either leave the women reader an alien outsider, or else solicit her to identify against herself by taking up the position of the male subject and so assuming male values and ways of perceiving, feeling, and acting. It is often held, in addition, that the traditional aesthetic categories and criteria for analyzing and appraising literary works, although represented in standard critical theory as objective, disinterested, and universal, are in fact infused with masculine assumptions, interests, and ways of reasoning, so that the standard selections and rankings, and also the critical treatments, of literary works have in fact been tacitly but thoroughly gender-biased.

A major interest of feminist critics in English-speaking countries has been to reconstitute the ways we deal with literature in order to do justice to female points of view, concerns and values. One emphasis has been to alter the way a woman reads the literature of the past so as to make her not an acquiescent, but (is the title of Judith Fetterlay's book published in 1978) "The Resisting Reader", that is, one, who resists the author's intentions and design in order to, by a "revisionary rereading", to bring to light and to counter the covert sexual biases written into a literary work. Another prominent procedure has been to identify recurrent and distinctively "images of women", especially in novels and poems written by men. These images are often represented as tending to fall into two antithetic patterns.

On the one side we find idealized projection of man's desires; on the other side are demoniac projections of man's sexual resentments and terrors (Eve and Pandora as the sources of all evil, destructive sensual temptresses as Delilah and Circe, the malign witch, the castrating mother). While many feminist critics have decried the literature written by man for its depiction of women as marginal, docile and subservient to men's interests and emotional needs and fears, some of them have also identified male writers who, in their view, have managed to rise above the sexual prejudices of their time sufficiently to understand and represented the cultural pressures that have shaped the characters of women, and forced upon them their negative or subsidiary social roles. The latter class is said to include, in selected works, such authors as Chaucer, Shakespeare, Samuel Richardson, Henrik Ibsen, and G.B. Shaw.

A number of feminists have concentrated, not on the women as a reader, but on what Elaine Showalter calls "gynocriticism", that is, a criticism which concerns itself with developing a specifically female framework for dealing with works written by women, in all aspects of their production, motivation, analysis, and interpretation, in all literary forms, including journals and letters. Notable books in this mode include Patricia Meyer Specks' *The Female Imagination* (1975), on English and American novels of the past three hundred years; Ellen Mores' *Literary Women* (1976) on major women novelists and poets in England, America and France; Elaine Showalter's *A Literature of Their Own: British Women Novelists from Bronte to Lessing* (1977); and Sandra Gilbert and Susan Gubar's *The Mad Woman in the Attic* (1979). The last book stresses especially on the psychodynamics of women writers in the nineteenth century.

One concern of gynocritics is to identify what are taken to be distinctly feminine subject matters in literature written by women—the world of domesticity, for example, or the special experiences of gestation, giving birth, and nurturing, or mother-daughter and woman-woman relations, in which personal and affectional issues, and not external activism, are the primary interests. Another concern is to uncover in literary history a female tradition, incorporated in sub communities of women writers who were aware of; emulated, and found support in earlier women writers, and who in turn provide models and emotional support to their own readers and successors. A third undertaking is to show that there is a distinctive feminine mode of experience, or "subjectivity" in thinking, feeling, valuing and perceiving oneself and the outer world. Related to this is the attempt to specify the traits of a "woman's language", or distinctively feminine style of speech and writing, in sentence structure, types of relations between the elements of a discourse, and a characteristic figures and imagery.

Some feminists have turned their critical attention to the great number of women's domestic and sentimental novels, which are noted in derogatory fashion in standard literary histories, yet which dominated the market for fiction in the nineteenth century and produced most of the best-sellers of the time; instances of this last critical enterprise are Elaine Showalter's *A Literature of Their Own* (1977) on British writers and Nina Baym's *Woman's Fiction: A Guide to the Novels by and about Women in America,1840-1870* (1978). Sandra Gilbert and Susan Gubar have described the later history of women's writings in *No Man's Land: The Place of the Woman Writer in the Twentieth Century* (2 Vols; 1988-89).

The often asserted goal of feminist critics has been to enlarge and reorder, or in radical instances entirely to displace, the literary "canon", that is, the set of works which, by a cumulative consensus, have come to be considered "major" and to serve as the chief subjects of literary history, criticism, scholarship and teaching. Feminist studies have serve to raise the status of many female authors (including Anne Finch, George Sand, Elizabeth Barrett Browning, Elizabeth Gaskell, Christina Rossetti; Hariet Beacher Stone, Aphra Behn, Lady Mary Wontley Montagu, and a number of African- American writers such as Zora Neale). Some feminists devoted their critical attention, especially to the literature written by lesbian writers, or that deals with lesbian relationships in a heterosexual culture.

American and English critics have for the most part engaged in empirical and thematic studies of writings by and about women. The most prominent critics in France, however, have been occupied with the theory of the role of gender in writing, conceptualized within various "post structural" frames of reference, and above all Jacques Lacan's reworkings of Freudian psychoanalysis in terms of Saussure's linguistic theory. English-speaking feminists have drawn attention to demonstratable and specific evidences that a male-bias is called in our linguistic conventions; instances include the use of "man" or "mankind" for human beings in general; of "chairman" and "spokesman" for the people of either sex, and of the pronouns "he" and "his" to refer back to ostensibly gender-neutral nouns such as "God", "human being", "child", "inventor", "author", "poet". The radical claim of some French theorists, on the other hand, whatever their differences, is that all Western languages, in all their features, are utterly and irredeemably male-engendered, male-constituted, and male-dominated. Discourse, it is asserted, is a term proposed by Lacan, is "Phallogocentric". A basic problem for French theorists is to establish the very possibility of a woman's language. To evade this dilemma Helene Cixous posits the existence of an incipient "feminine writing" which has its source in the mother, in the stage of the mother-child relation before the child acquires the male-centred verbal language.

Feminists in the 1980s and 1990s also move beyond the essentialising tendencies of early feminism by delineating local, racial, and region specific gender oppression. While the early feminists sought a common platform for all women irrespective of racial or regional differences, the later feminists argued for different approaches to built these specific conditions. Here feminism moves away from the Eurocentric and heterosexual biases of early feminism and develops into Black Feminism, "Third World" or Post-Colonial Feminism, and Lesbian Critical Theory. Feminist thought developed in the twentieth century in various forms, i.e., early feminism (Woolf, Beauvoir, Kate Millett), psychoanalytical feminism (Juliet Mitchell, Luce Irigaray, Helene Cixous), political feminism (Pauline Johnson, Carole Pateman), socialist and Marxist feminism (Eli Zarestsky, Michele Barreth) and post-structuralist feminism (Irigaray,

Cixous) and lesbian as well as eco-feminism. Feminism is perhaps the most interdisciplinary and plural of approaches studied in colleges, universities and various periodicals, anthologies and conferences are focused on the writings by and about women. Of the many critical and theoretical innovations of the past several decades they concern with the effects of sexual differences in the writing, interpretation, analysis, and assessment of literature seems to destined to have the most prominent and enduring effects on literary history, criticism, and academic instruction, when conducted by men as well as by women.

Feminism is a concept Anglo-American in origin. Despite its Western origin, it's highly relevant to the Indian context. Assumptions, methods and procedures of the feminists can be applied, dexterously, as a tool to evaluate the status, role, image, and socio-cultural recognition of women in Indian society represented through literary texts – classical, regional, standard Hindi or Indian English literature. Whether it is the work of Premchand, Sharat Chandra, Mahasweta Devi, Kamala Das, Shobha De, Taslima Nasreen, Arundhati Roy, Kiran Desai, Girish Karnad or the Classical Indian literature—all can be evaluated from a new perspective, i.e., feminist which will definitely enlighten our understanding of feminine psyche. Patriarchal structure of Indian society, socio- cultural practices and conventions and canonical writings still perpetuate the subordination of Indian women. Few women in India, often quoted to extol as model, is a fallacious proposition because that group of women does not represent the spirit of average Indian women. To dismiss feminism as an imported concept is an eccentricity of Indian mind; failing to recognize its validity in Indian context, whereas the condition of women is more or less the same globally. Hence the significance and application of the feminist approach is global.

II

Karnad championed the cause of silenced womenfolk in Indian orthodox society through his plays. Karnad was well acquainted with feminist ideologies and the havoc wrought by patriarchal ideologies in Indian society. His plays abound with subalterns especially women and lower caste people subjected since ancient time by patriarchy or upper hierarchy of the society. Karnad has not only exposed their subalternity but also fused energy in their lives so that they can speak; shifted their position from "margin" to "centre". *Yayati, Tughlaq, Hayavadana, Naga-Mandala, Tale-Danda, The Fire and the Rain, Flowers, Broken Images* and *Wedding Album* illustrate the above proposition. The chapter endeavours to analyse the plays of Girish Karnad from a feminist perspective. Theme/motif, characterization, image and psychology of the women have been targeted with the purpose to evaluate Karnad's vision, attitude, concern and treatment of the feminine issue. His deep-rooted humanism and concern for the upliftment of Indian women have produced two sets of characters—one the traditional representing the gendered subalternity; another progressive which mark the evolution of womenfolk. Devayani, Sharmistha and Chitralekha in *Yayati,* Padmini in *Hayavadana,* Rani and Kurudavva in *Naga-Mandala*, Vishakha and Nittilai in *The Fire and the Rain*, Mother and Queen Mother in *Bali: The Sacrifice*, Chandravati in *Flowers*, Manjula Nayak and Malini in *The Broken Images*, Vidula Nadkarni, Pratibha Khan and Hema, Radhabai, Mira, Vatsala and Yamuna in *Wedding Album* define the feminine world of Karnad which embodies several aspects possessing modern relevance.

Yayati, the first play of Karnad which is based on the myth of Yayati in the *Mahabharata* is highly relevant as far as the socio-psychological study of women is concerned. Devayani, Sharmishtha, Swarnlata and Chitralekha are generic; they represent the subalternity of woman in masculinist society where she is identified as the "other", "non-man", or "second sex" despite her high position in the society. Karnad doesn't adhere to traditional glorification of the son's 'self-sacrifice', rather he raises the question against this. Devayani, the Queen has to endure every sort of humiliation and becomes insane; Swarnalata is tortured by her husband's unfounded doubts of infidelity, insults and finally deserted; Sharmishtha is sexually exploited by King Yayati. Though Chitralekha faces similar conditions, she emerges as a new woman who boldly challenges the decision of Pooru and false rhetoric of Yayati. She doesn't allow Pooru to enter into her bedroom—who accepts the curse of his father for his moral transgression and becomes old: "I will not let my husband step back into my bedroom unless he returns a young man" (61) and frankly elaborates the reason of her marriage to Pooru: "I married him for his youth. For his potential to plant the seed of the Bharatas in my womb. He has lost that potency now. He doesn't possess any of the qualities for which I married him. But you do" (65-66). Yayati abuses her for these piercing words, "whore" (66). She defies everything i.e. kingdom and high reputation of Bharat dynasty. She smiles defiantly and swallows the poison and dies. She prefers to die rather than yield before old conventions and assigned roles set for woman. She "succeeds in subverting the male world through an assertion of their rights and privileges" (Dharwadker. "Introduction" *Collected Plays,* Vol.One, xvii). Her death endorses new woman's quest for emancipation. Sharmishtha precisely explains the condition of women, "A woman dead (Chitralekha), another gone mad (Devayani), and a third in danger of her life (Sharmishtha)" (68). Jealously and racial conflict also weakens their lot. The play reinforces the centrality of women.

Padmini in *Hayavadana* is unlike of Rani of *Naga-Mandala.* She belongs to a family of leading merchant of Pavana Veethi of Dharampura. Though, in the play she enjoys commanding position, she is nowhere depicted as a weak character. She succumbs to Dionysian tendency and indulges into cuckoldry. She camouflages love of Devadatta, his poetry gets new charm and vitality. She is so fascinating that Devadatta finds her "beyond my wildest dreams" (14) and swears "if I ever get her as my wife, I will sacrifice my two arms to the goddess Kali; I'll sacrifice my head to Lord Rudra..." (14). Even Kapila finds "Yakshini, Shakuntala, Urvashi, Indumati—all rolled into one" (16) and warns Devadatta, "She is not for the likes of you. What she needs is a man of steel" (19). While talking to Padmini Kapila rightly says: "I know what you want, Padmini. Devadatta's clever head and Kapil's strong body" (38). The fact is soon discovered—her temptation to Kapila's muscular body; she is real Padmini of Vatasayana:

> PADMINI: [*Watching him, to herself*]. How he climbs—like an ape. Before I could even say 'yes', he had taken off his shirt, pulled his *dhoti* up and swung up the branch. And what an ethereal shape! Such a broad back—like an ocean with muscles rippling across it—and then that small, feminine waist which looks so helpless.... He is like a Celestial Being reborn as a hunter.... How his body sways, his limbs curve—it's dance almost.... No woman could resist him. (25-26)

Devadatta senses her leaning towards Kapila but he feels helpless. Devadatta and Kapila represent Apollonian and Dionysian tendencies respectively hence Padmini's hunger for Kapila is very outcome of her own nature. But in the temple of Kali, after Devadatta and Kapila's sacrifice, she is so much embarrassed to see the melodramatic scene and frightened to sense the sarcasm of people, anticipating people would blame her for both deaths. She instantly decides to kill herself. Transposition, no doubt, was a very frightening experience to her, yet she felt she had the best of both the man: "My Devadatta comes like a bridegroom with the ornament of a new body.... It's my duty to go with Devadatta. But, remember I'm going with your [Kapil's] body" (41), "fabulous body—fabulous brain" (43) and "male smell" (43) express her nymphomaniac ecstasy and lust for sexual gratification. Even Doll I and Doll II comment on her psychic reactions—dreams, phantasies and reveries in which Kapila figures "climbing a tree!", "dived into a river" (50) symbolically let loose Padmini's suppressed sexual desire and hunger for Kapila. Soon she is disillusioned and finds herself, like Devadatta, Kapila and Hayavadana a victim of "mad dance of incompleteness" (57). Even after marriage, she can't resist herself and goes to the forest with her son and enjoys extramarital sexual relation with Kapila cuckolding her husband for four or five days. In a duel Devadatta and Kapila exchange forgiveness and kill each other. Subsequently, Padmini finds herself nowhere. She suffers from alienation and perplexing situation erupts. She is abetted to perform *sati*—for the sake of the glory of her son or she couldn't live without Devadatta and Kapila: "Kali, Mother of all Nature, you must have your joke even now. Other women can die praying that they should get the same husband in all lives to come. You haven't left me even that little consolation" (63). Padmini's practice of *sati,* comments Bhagavatta, "it would not be an exaggeration to say that no *pativrata* went the way Padmini did" (63). Female Chorus justifies Padmini's misdemeanor: "Why should love stick to the sap of a single body? When the stem is drunk with the thick yearning of the many-petalled, many-flowered lantana, why should it be tied down to the relation of a single flower?.... I have neither regret nor shame" (64). Karnad attempts to give due space to women in human society where she is marginalized since time immemorial. His plays present evolution of women and quest for better position in the world.

Karnad's *Naga-Mandala* is a close study of Indian women; richly textured dramatic transmutation of two folk tales of Karnataka usually narrated by women while feeding children in the kitchen. It not only exposes the ugliness of a society where woman is considered "second sex", "other", "subject", "non-man"—women are taught in the process of being socialized, to internalize the reigning patriarchal ideology—e.g. male superiority; and so conditioned to derogate their own sex and to cooperate in their own subordination. Patriarchal dominance has prevented women from realizing their productive and creative possibility. The play also suggests remedial measures and slaps the orthodox society by an act of reconciliation between Rani and Naga. *Naga-Mandala* appears to be a battleground where ideological conflicts, power relations, and the struggle for identity have been dramatized effectively. In *Naga-Mandala* Rani—the female protagonist, and Kurudavva—the other female character, both are generic, represent the extreme physical torture and mental trauma, struggle for their identity as a woman, as a wife, and as a mother. Four Flames, Story, and the Man also reflect the sufferings and exploitations of women. Rani is treated in a slavish manner, imprisoned like a caged bird, neither is she allowed to talk to outsider nor outsider is allowed to do the same. Despite her chastity and fidelity, she is forced to face the Naga Ordeal. Appanna (Rani's husband), Naga (Cobra), Dog, Mongoose, Three Village Elders and the orthodox society have been used as the forces of subjection. Karnad has treated 'eternal—triangle' unlike of G.B.Shaw.

Shaw in Candida gave a different twist to 'eternal—triangle' where Candida is a New Woman and finale brings the impression that conjugal love must be fostered and glorified whereas Karnad exposes the hollowness of male- chauvinism. Rani's acceptance of Naga as her own is a curt reply to the question of extra-marital relation in which only males are allowed to go freely, even after getting married, to concubine (as Appanna does) whereas the yardstick of morality is imposed upon women. J.D.Soni judiciously comments that Karnad in the play tries to "fuse artistically dialectical relationship between tradition and modernity" (76). Prologue introduces Four Flames, which are animated, symbolic representations employed to report the sufferings of women. The tragic sufferings of women are extended to other female character—e.g. Kurudavva, who is an example of wisdom and philanthropy. Nobody in the society has eyes to see Rani's laceration at the hands of her philandering husband, but blind Kurudavva alone can see the truth. She extends motherly love and care to Appanna as well as to Rani. She is also the victim of orthodox society where the role of a woman is subservient and marginalized. Except her son Kappanna, there is none to look after her. Even the Village Elders treat her cruelly and unsympathetically while she has lost her only son.

Vishakha and Nittilai belong to two different socio-cultural backgrounds in *The Fire and the Rain.* Vishakha is the wife of Paravasu, a Brahmin, and daughter-in-law of Raibhya, a learned ascetic whereas Nittilai hails from a tribal community. Despite cultural polarities, both experience similar socio-psychological taboos and restrictions and feel bounded. For Nittilai, subjection is more intense—apart from patriarchy her inferior position in social hierarchy deteriorates her standing in the society. Though the play is based on C. Rajgopalachari's prose retelling of the *Mahabharata* especially the myth of Yavakri in Vana Parva, Karnad constructs a story of passion, loss, and sacrifice in the contexts of Vedic rituals, spiritual discipline, social and ethical differences between human agents, and interrelated forms of performance still close to their moments of origin, yet the treatment of feminine world, images of women, their subjection and changing status is not less remarkable. Vishakha, an archetypal character and Nittilai, Karnad's invention symbolize the subalternity of women that has been highlighted by the playwright exposing the ugliness in our society restricting their place and creativity in human society.

Vishakha loves Yavakri but his decision to get knowledge directly from gods initiates him into ten years' penance leaves Vishakha helpless, alienated—"sick of silence" (141) and deeply frustrated. Subsequently, she is married to Paravasu who offers up Vishakha's life, first to his sensual appetite and then to his lust for fame:

> VISHAKHA: The night of the wedding, my husband said to me: 'I know you didn't want to marry me. But don't worry. I'll make you happy for a year.' And he did. Exactly for one year.... Then on the first day of the second year of our marriage, he said: 'Enough of that. We now start on our search'.... He used my body, and his own body, like an experimenter, an explorer. As instruments in a search. Search for what? I never knew. To be the Chief Priest of the fire sacrifice... in all seven years he hasn't come back... I have become dry like tinder. Ready to burst into flames at a breath. (123)

The meeting of Vishakha with her former lover Yavakri infuriates Raibhya who grabs her by her hair and start beating and kicking her. She is condemned as "whore" (127) and "bitch" (138) thereafter left to be handled by her husband. She is an easy prey to Raibhya's anger over his rejection as the Chief Priest by the king. He creates *Brahma Raksha* to kill Yavakri. Vishakha is bold and acknowledges her meeting with Yavakri before her husband candidly. Nittilai, a tribal girl of 14 loves Arvasu, a Brammin of 18. Both work in a troupe. She is exposed to face the world and know how cruel and ruthless it can be. Only Andhak appreciates their love; the elders of Nittilai's tribe are anxious to interrogate Arvasu. Hers is a romantic love, a world of teenage phantasies ignorant from caste and cultural distinctions. On the contrary, Raibhya condemns her as "savage" (126). When Arvasu fails to appear before Council of tribal Elders; they decreed, "Nitilai will marry another boy—of our own tribe" (135). She is handed over to a tribal boy and married against her wishes. She has no say. Her protest touches climax when she runs away from her husband, family and everything for the sake of love. But, as an Indian married woman, she doesn't want to cuckold her husband. She transcends from petty sexual gratification and romantic love and develops pious relationship with Arvasu:

> NITTILAI: Arvasu, when I say we should go together—I don't mean we have to live together—like lovers, or like husband and wife. I have been vicious enough to my husband. I don't want to disgrace him further. Let's be together like brother and sister. You marry any girl you like. Only please, Arvasu—spare a corner for me. (153)

Nittilai's brother and husband chase her like hounds. She is frightened of their evil designs. She is offered a ghastly death despite her innocence: "the husband pulls out a knife, grabs Nittilai by her hair and slashes her throat in one swift motion. He then lets her drop.... She lies there, her eyes open, bleeding, dying like a sacrificial animal" (172). The killing of Nittilai endorses still today patriarchy and long established social conventions are strong enough to crush women's liberty or any kind of adventurism. But the quest of the woman for emancipation has started. The play also presents sudras and tribals as subalterns in Varna hierarchy.

The Queen Mother and Queen in *Bali: The Sacrifice* represent two conflicting ideologies, i.e., one is static, traditional and deeply rooted in age-old social conventions while the second is progressive, sensitive, open-minded and rebellious in spirit. The Queen is a Jain who follows the path of non-violence; on the contrary, Queen Mother is a Hindu who frequently indulges in blood sacrifice. Karnad has developed two sets of women folk to demonstrate their socio-psychological evolution. The Queen, despite her high position in the society, feels alienated and desperate. Though she is witty and eloquent in speech and rebellious in spirit she falls a prey to filthy sexual gratification. She is haunted by libidinous compulsions and alienation, hence, swayed by the enchanting song of the Mahout she fails to resist herself. Like Padmini of *Hayavadana,* she is tempted by the muscular body, in spite of the ugly complexion of the Mahout.

She freely violates the social norms and spends one night with him "nameless" (88) hiding her real identity to satisfy her erotic urge. She indulges in extra-marital relationship and redefines conjugal relationship. She is bold enough and candidly acknowledges what she has done with the Mahout before her husband:

> QUEEN: I do not regret anything that has happened. I will not disown him or anything he gave me.
>
> KING: How can you be so crass? So brazen? You—
>
> QUEEN: Because it just happened. Without my willing it. It just happened. That's all.
>
> And what happened was beautiful.
>
> I want to come back to you. I feel fuller. Richer. Warmer. But not ashamed. Because I didn't plan it. It happened. And it was beautiful.
>
> I am yours. I'll never betray you again. (118-119)

The Queen changes the King's mind by her strong ideology of non-violence. Any kind of violence vexes her; even the killing of birds or dough hurts her profoundly. Her involvement with the Mahout is an alarming signal to patriarchal society where any man can enjoy coquetry while the yardstick of morality is imposed on woman and if she goes beyond it ordeals are there to punish her in the name of infidelity. Karnad has responded and attacked such discriminatory social behaviour in his plays especially in *Yayati, Hayavadana, Naga-Mandala, The Fire and the Rain* and *Bali: the Sacrifice* and the *Wedding Album* where the female protagonists pose a challenge to the whole society.

The Queen has undergone through the bitter experience of miscar; again she is pregnant and the Queen Mother who blesses her for "a son whose glory blinds the eight directions" (94) and endorses patriarchy that has socialized her to internalize male superiority. She perpetuates, though unconsciously, the subjection of woman. Karnad had juxtaposed the Queen and the Queen Mother vis-à-vis to symbolize two different images of women, one indulging in sacrifice for the well-being of the family and to celebrate auspicious occasions, the other at the extreme end condemns any kind of violence. One conforms to traditional conventions, taboos and practices and the other ready to show their futility. They have developed a relationship based on hatred. She abuses the Queen as a "harlot", "whore" (107) possessing a "fickle womb" (115), and instigates the King to "cut her to pieces...feed her to the wolves and vultures" (107) for cuckoldry. The Queen Mother knowing the Queen to be pregnant decides to celebrate the occasion which means blood sacrifice: "QUEEN: The animals are graded according to occasion. Poultry is offered at daily rites. Sheep, goats for more important rituals. Then buffalo" (96). The Queen thwarts any kind of sacrifice in honour of her child. Even the morality of substitution is not acceptable to her, she rather sacrifices herself.

The two monologues, *Flowers* and *Broken Images,* also throw light on the feminine issues. *Flowers* shows that a woman's body is always a target of man's lustful eyes. Man conspires as a predator to exploit her sexually and make her an easy prey. Even the holy man, the unnamed priest in the play feasts his eyes and indulges in sensual pleasures with Chandrawati, a courtesan, and develops an extra-marital relationship with her. The priest's wife knows his advances but tolerates everything silently. Later, with the disappearance of Chandrawati, the priest devotes his full time to Lord Shiva and hopes his wife would assist him, as Paravasu does in *The Fire and the Rain* and leaves his wife Vishakha desperate: " I was among the chosen of the Lord and she could not possibly think of herself as a wife now, only as a slave and guardian, all shades of the marital bond expunged in favour of her devotion to me, her good fortune in having me for her husband" (259). The priest fails to understand the feminine sensibility. A woman is used the way man desires—i.e. sex item, slave, and guardian or bound to carry out whatever role has been assigned to her.

Broken Images highlights the changing role, status and transformation in feminine psyche in the modern world. Manjula Nayak, the only character in the play, a teacher of English in Bangalore writes short stories in Kannada. But for the sake of "fame, publicity, glmour...power" (265) prefers writing novel in English. She leads a typical literary life. She endeavours, by hook or crook, to earn name, fame and money out of writing. She publishes, unexpectedly, a novel titled *The River Has No Memories*, that fetches wide admiration but resentment too for she has betrayed Kannada for the sake of fame, fortune and a larger audience. However her conversation with her own television image reveals that she is an imposter who has passed off her dead sister Malini's novel as her own. Opportunism, plagiarism and her justification for a larger audience and money making and acknowledging them as not illegitimate pursuits for a writer epitomizes modern Indian writers' dilemma and frustration writing in regional languages.

Aparna Bhargava Dharwadker has rightly observed the position of Manjula Nayak: "The switch to English, hailed as an inspired act of self-fashioning on the author's part, turns out in reality to be an act of dishonesty, desperation, and cowardice, the implication being that the material lure of English as a medium can only lead the Indian-language author to prostitute herself" ("Introduction" Vol. Two. xxvii). Karnad deals with literary politics in the play and thereafter relates language to genre. This was hitherto unexplored area for women erstwhile, but Manjula Nayak has refuted it and proved that a woman writer can also succeed either by opportunism or plagiarism. She has realized how to manipulate the things for bestseller and accrue immediate success. She can challenge the authority of male writers. She has learnt and taught us how to "survive" (283) in the changed world order.

The *Wedding Album* which is structured into nine scenes is a gyno-text that deals primarily with women and their two different worlds, i.e., traditional and modern cyber world. But both of them merge into each other. Even the traditional elder gynes are fused with energy, hope and modern sensibility. Younger sorts enjoy liberty in education, love, courtship via 'distance' technology; and marriage. The play marks the highest evolution of feminine psyche. The backdrop of the play is unlike that of *Yayati, Hayavadana, Naga-Mandala,* and *The Fire and the Rain.* It deals with middle class Saraswat Brahmin family—an epitome of multiculturalism and cosmopolitan ideology. The play also examines the growing fundamentalism of the Hindu middle class family weakening. The family comprises Father Nadkarni, a doctor, a Mother, an intelligent housewife, progressive in her ideas who sacrificed her talent for the sake of the family, conscious of children's career. Hema, the eldest daughter married and living in Australia; Vidula, younger daughter has done BA in Geography, Rohit, son who writes stories and script for teleplays, is seeking better future prospects and Radhabai, a cook in Nadkarni's family is antitype of rest of the women. Vidula Nadkarni is exposed to modern education, social culture and science and technology. She is twenty two and half; has done BA in Geography and presently doing nothing. She is the product of modern cyber world. She regularly visits to Internet Café to find her life partner. On the surprise of Pratibha Khan she, "agrees to consider marrying a man whom she has never met…in this day and age?" (8). Like Westernized Indian youths, she is facilitated by video tapes, SMSs, phone calls and webcam to decide her husband. Aswin Panje, a Sarswat Brahmin is her choice, finally their marriage is materialized. Though she suffers due to miscarriage, yet waits for next chance. Amrit Srinivasan comments about Vidula:

> Vidula is not exactly as he [Karnad] pictures her and that like any other modern, mixed up, unhappy, Hindu gal, she leads a secret life. Whether willingly submitting herself as Kulcha the Jezebel to the disembodied randy voice of Swami Ananga Nath the Bodyless, in a darkened Cyber Café, or transmuting her guilt at being found out into hysterical rage, screaming 'sexual harassment' to make her moral tormentors run away—she is resourceful enough to find herself a surrogate swami, a flesh and blood stranger to help her work her way through desire. The subjugation she seeks in her secret, erotic world can after all be served as well through man and marriage and to higher purpose.
>
> ("Forward" xi)

Unlike Vidula, Pratibha Khan is a modern self-made Oriya woman of forty who develops her own business in Bangalore and takes tough decision to marry a Khan. And for being successful producer of television serials, she understands the psychology and emotional appetite of the audience and rejects out rightly the story of Vidula as a possible theme for future episode. She has a practical approach to life. She wonders over Vidula's decision to marry a man without meeting him. Pratibha is an important figure in modern corporate world symbolizing modern Indian woman's emerging role and image. Hema, though born in modern age, educated and married and lives in Australia, is rooted in conservative practices and customs of Sarswat Brahmin family. She disapproves Rohit's advances to Isabel, a Christian girl. She is satisfied as a housewife. As a fair sex, she has bitter experience of how, first, her father-in-law observes her body; secondly, Vivan, a young boy, younger to her son feels crazy for her: "VIVAN: The moment I saw you the other day, I fell desperately in love. I want to die kissing you. I want to die with my hand inside your blouse..." (45). She feels humiliated and slaps on his cheek. These two instances prove a woman is always a prey to male sexual desire irrespective of age or relation. Mother is a fusion of tradition and modernity. She maintains age-old social conventions prevalent in Saraswat Brahmins. The most remarkable feature of her character is that she understands the need of the time and proper human resource development. Despite limitations of middle class family, she has "skill at management" (91). She is talented who sacrificed it for the sake of the family. She has learnt a lot from life. Consequently, she insists on, especially to Vidula, to make sound career and become self-reliant: "MOTHER: ...so many opportunities in today's world. We couldn't even dream of such world...there are lots of openings in America....Don't throw away your talents in just bearing children" (90). Mother has developed a cosmopolitan vision which refutes any caste or religious distinction: "I don't see any difference between Christian girls and Hindu girls these days" (43). Radhabai, Mira and Vatsala have been characterized to depict first set of woman in Indian society. Mira and Vatsala regiser their presence in Scene Three. They are generic and typed characters. Radhabai, a widow, is a cook in Nadkarni's family who takes personal care of the family and serves delicious dishes to children and is reminded of her own daughter Yamuna she has shamelessly left, naked and abused on the road. At the end of the Scene Nine she finds her daughter in the street below in a very pitiable condition: "RADHABAI: ...There she was—this mad woman—stark raving mad. Shouting foul abuses at the kids who were throwing stones at her....Yamuna! She was shouting and screaming: 'Where is Amma? Where is Amma's house," (92-93). Radhabai is paralyzed to see her and avoids from her eyes apprehending the loss of job; and engages in kitchen menials. The gloomy image of the widow and her mad daughter figure in the last page of the wedding album leaves us to think over their lot seriously.

Karnad has a deep and comprehensive understanding of subalterns in his plays and he has brought them from the margin to the centre through his plays. His plays are the platform where through he raises the socio-political and cultural problems prevalent in Indian society and calls upon us to discuss and evolve a common consensus rather than provide a solution to the problem. The evolution of Karnad's dramatic genius from *Yayati* to *Wedding Album* parallels the evolution of his vision of feminine issues. Myths, legends and folktales which were used in the early plays to discuss feminine issues were dropped, and he takes everthing from actual life and treats them in a realistic manner.

Works Cited

Abrams, M.H. *A Glossary of Literary Terms.* (Seventh Edition), Singapore: Thomason Asia Pvt. Ltd., 2003.

Barry, Peter. Beginning Theory: An Introduction to Literary and Cultural Theory. (Second Edition). Chennai: T.R. Publications, 2004.

Dharwadker, Aparna Bhargava. (Ed.) With an Introduction *Collected Plays.*Vol. One: *Tughlaq, Hayavadana, Bali: The Sacrifice, Naga-Mandala.* New Delhi: O.U.P., Fourth Impression, 2008.

________. (Ed.) With an Introduction Collected Plays. Vol. Two: *Tale-Danda, The Fire and the Rain, The Dreams of Tipu sultan, Two Monologues, Flowers, Broken Images.* New Delhi: O.U.P., 2005. The Fire and the Rain, Flowers and Broken Images have been quoted from this edition.

Karnad, Girish. *Two Plays: Dream of Tipu Sultan, Bali: The Sacrifice.* New Delhi: O.U.P., Fourth Impression, 2005. *Bali: The Sacrifice* has been quoted from this edition

________. "Inroduction" to *Three Plays: Naga-Mandala, Hayavadana, Tughlaq.* New Delhi: O.U.P., 2002. *Naga-Mandala* has been extensively used and referred from this edition.

________. *Yayati.* New Delhi: O.U.P., 2008.

________, *Hayavadana.* (Fourteenth Impression), Chennai: OUP, 1998. This edition has been used and subsequent references are from this edition.

________. *Wedding Album.* New Delhi: Oxford Uiversity Press, 2009.

Nayar, Pramod K. *Literary Theory Today.* New Delhi: Prestige / Asia Book Club, 2002.

Srinivisan, Amrit. "Forward" *Wedding Album.* New Delhi: Oxford University Press, 2009.

8

Characterization

Karnad is an exponent of problem or thesis play which explores a particular social problem, raising several questions about it and provoking the audience into finding answers. The ideas in the play "constitute some issue of deep concern to the dramatist with which he wishes to engage the minds and consciences of audiences. The power of a problem play presented in well-made format, is the contrast between the apparent logical simplicity of the form and the real complexity of the issue with which the play deals" (Pickering 79). Ibsen, Shaw, Galsworthy, David Mamat, Steve Gooch, David Edger, Shirley Gee, and Caryl Churchill superbly and successfully handled this genre. In a problem or thesis play, there is always a manifest danger of characters reduced to 'mouth pieces' or mere 'puppets' in the hands of the playwright. Characters, especially the protagonists, are used as a tool or a medium to express the philosophy, vision or ideas of the playwright sacrificing the individuality of the characters. Such plays often develop 'type' or 'flat' or 'stereotyped' characters which hardly add beauty and power to the play and its performance on the stage.

Karnad is well aware of the limitations of the the problem play, and he pays close attention to the art of characterization. Though his characters are from Indian myths, legends, history and folk-tales, they are not devoid of life and energy. They are livng and moving characters; despite their mythical or historical background they are very close to us and bear modern sensibility. They are puffed with Indian imagination and cultural ethos. They are "true to life" and possess "consistency" (Aristotle 53) and develop naturally. It's Karnad's skill that both incident and situation are correlated with characters. Karnad employs the devices of dialogue, contrast, parallelism and irony for characterization. Only those points of character are emphasized, which develop the plot. It would be unjust to evaluate his art of characterization in the light of Romantic cannons or classical rigid formalism. If we focus on its format, genre and objectives of the playwright to create dramatis personae, we can do justice to it. Plot and characters are closely interwoven. Chitralekha, Padmini, Tughlaq, Rani, Manjula Nayak and Vidula Nadkarni have been portrayed with great psychological depth. Often Karnad himself provides a brief biography of the characters which subsequently figure in the play. This facilitates the audience to understand the entire personality of the characters. There are obviously two sets of characters, i.e., major and minor. Major characters through dialogue, mental and emotional reactions, and contrasting features with the rest of the characters highlight the central concern and the problems the playwright intends to raise. Minor characters are supportive, and their actions help to develop the personality of the protagonist. Though Karnad's primary concern is not 'soul-dissection' in his plays, there are great psychological explorations which refute the charge levelled against the problem playwright.

Yayati deals with an ancient myth and Sutradhara in his maiden address to the audience, giving basic information about the plot as well as major characters: "The King's son, Prince Pooru, is returning home today after many years of absence. He has successfully completed his education in the hermitage under renowned gurus, and is bringing home with him his bride, Chitralekha, the Princess of Anga" ("Prologue" 6). He is antithetical to his father King Yayati who is cursed for his moral transgression by Sukracharya, and he is reduced to old age. His sexual urge compils him to ask his son to exchange his youth in lieu of his old age. Pooru readily accepts the plea and assumes the old age of his father. He emerges as an obedient son and is glorified. Karnad has developed Chitrlekha to defy this glorification and raise a practical question on it by the reaction of the newly wed bride. She condemns the decision of Pooru as well as the exhortations of King Yayati who is an unheroic hero. She possesses a rebellious spirit; she is very much a New

Woman who fights for her identity and status in the society. She is depicted as being a great intellectual. She moves from a mythical world of obedience to the modern world of interrogation. The dialogue between Yayati and Chitralekha reflect two different point of views, i.e., one traditional and another anti-traditional and progressive. Both are given due space to present their point of view. The dialogues are precise and crispy, and suit the personality of the characters. Instances of verbal and retrospective irony are skilfully handled—King Yayati himself indulges in sexual transgression and expects Chitralekha to follow the path of virtue and morality rather than condemn the decision of Pooru and Yayati:

> YAYATI: This is no time for recriminations. My heart goes out to you. But you are an educated woman, versed in the arts, trained in warfare. You could have displayed more self-control. Now act in a manner worthy of an Anga princess and Bharata queen. Act so that generations to come may sing your glory and Pooru's. (61)

Women characters. Devayani, Sharmishtha, Chitralekha and Swarnalata represent the feminine world. They have been dexterously treated by the playwright. Their jealously, hatred, racial conflict and anger come out natuarally. Devayani is profoundly hurt by her husband Yayati's involvement with Sharmishtha, a rakshasi whom she abuses as "bitch" and "whore" (13). Swarnalata is a royal maid who keeps the company of Devayani and goes on feeding her mind against Sharmishtha. Devayani, Sharmishtha, Swarnalata and Chitralekha all are constrasted with one another; they have specific traits of their personality. Despite being generic, they develop independently and help to move forward the plot. Karnad, like Aristotle, gives the second highest place to character next only to plot. It is the character who is the source of action—physical, mental and spiritual. All the dramatis personae in *Yayati* contribute to highlight the core issue which has baffled the mind of the playwright: "glimpses of the fears and desires sleepless within us" ("Prologue" 6).

Tughlaq, the second play of Karnad, is based on the history of Mohamad-bin-Tughlaq who is known as the mad emperor of the Delhi Sultanat. Complex plot, character of Tughlaq and dramatic conventions used in the play arrested the attention of the audiences. It closely reflects the political mood of disillusionment which followed the Nehru era of idealism in the country. What struck Karnad about Tughlaq was its history and contemporaneity. That was a striking parallel: "TUGHLAQ: I have hopes of building a new future for India" (40) which exactly reflects Karnad's vision for the future of India. But, according to U.R. Ananthamurthy, "the play is more than a political allegory. It has an irreducible, puzzling quality which comes from the ambiguities of Tughlaq's character, the dominating figure in the play. All other characters are dramatized aspects of his personality, yet they also exist in their own right" ("Introduction" viii). Tughlaq has been portrayed with great psychological thruth and depth. The dramatist deftly projects the paradoxes in the complex personality of Tughlaq who is a dreamer and a man of action, benevolent and cruel, devout and Godless. He is the only unifying character of the play. All important actions and events which constitute the plot of the play issue from his character. Tughlaq himself reveals his idealism, scholarship, secularalism in his various speeches:

> My empire is large now and embraces the South and I need a capital which is at its heart. Delhi is too near the border and as you well know its peace is never free from the fear of invaders. But for me the most important factor is that Daulatabad is a city of the Hindus and as the capital it will symbolize the bond between Muslims and Hindus which I wish to develop and strengthen in my kingdom. I invite you all to accompany me to Daulatabad. This is only an invitation and not an order. Only those who have faith in me may come with me. With their help I shall build an empire which shall be the envy of the world. (3-4)

When his idealism and administrative reforms are frustrated a psychological change comes over him. In order to realize his plans and administrative reforms he resorts to murder and bloodshed, gets frustrated and disillusioned:

> BARANI: Your Majesty, there was a time when you believed in love, in peae, in God. What has happened to those ideals? You won't let your subjects pray. You torture them for the smallest offence. Hang them on suspicion. Why this bloodshed? Please stop it, and I promise Your Majesty something better will emerge out of it. (56)
>
> MUHAMMAD: I am tethering on the brink of madness, Barani, but the madness of God still eludes me, (*shouting*). And why should I deserve that madness? I have condemned my mother to death and I'm not even sure she was guilty of the crime... (68)

The intrigue in the play is a dramatized projection of Tughlaq's tortured, divided self. The external action throughout the play parallels the inner drama of Tughlaq's conflict. The whole play is structured on the opposites—Tughlaq as well as his enemies initially appear to be idealists; yet, in the pursuit of the ideal, they perpetrate its opposites. Ideal versus real, divine aspiration versus deft intrigue are the marked features of the characters. Tughlaq is what he is in spite of his self-knowledge and an intense desire for divine grace. He is aware of the irony of his life when Aziz, the only character in the play who has skilfully used all the schemes of Tughlaq for his own designs, kills Ghiya-ud-din and comes in his guise as a holy messenger of peace to purify the land and revive the banned prayer. The irony is deeply tragic. In the end Tughlaq and his kingdom are one in their chaos, and he knows it. Other characters too throw light on Tughlaq's wilfulness and callousness as Ratan Singh says: "I have never seen an honest scoundrel like your Sultan. He murders a man calmly and then actually enjoys the feeling of guilt" (28). The Step-Mother comments: "But he is so impulsive—and when gets into one of his moods I don't know what he'll do next" (17). Barani, the scholarly historian, and Najib, the shrewd politician, represent the two opposite selves of the Sultan. Aziz, who is shrewd, wise, intelligent, pragmatic and utilitarian, is a notorious cheat who represents all those who take unlawful advantage of Tughlaq's idealism as well as his crafty nature. The dialogues have decorum; they are lucid, pointed and precise. The language used by the characters suit their status and temperament.

In *Hayavadana*, there are two episodes. In the central episode Devadatta, Kapila and Padmini figure, and the sub-plot deals with Hayavadana, a horse-headed man, which deepens the significance of the main theme of incompleteness by treating it on different plane in a parallel way. Karnad has introduced major characters through Bhagvatta:

> This is the city of Dharmpura, ruled by King Dharmasheela whose fame and empire have already reached the ends of the eight directions. Two youths who dwell in this city are our heroes. One is Devadatta. Comely in appearance, fair in colour, unrivalled in intelligence, Devadatta is the only son of the Revered Brahmin Vidyasagar. Having felled the mightiest pundits of the kingdom in debates on logic and love, having blinded the greatest poets of the world with his poetry and wit, Devadatta is as it were the apple of every eye in Dharampura.
>
> The other youth is Kapila. He is the only son of iron-smith, Lohita, who is to the King's armoury as an axle to the chariot-wheel. He is dark and plain to look at, yet in deeds which require drive and daring, in dancing, in strength and in physical skills he has no equal....[both are] One mind, one heart. (2)

Padmini who lives in the Pawan Veethi, is as dreamt by Vatasyayana, beyond the "wildest dreams" (14) of Devadatta who is so much thrilled with her presence that he is prompted to sacrifice his life: "if I ever get her as my wife, I'll sacrifice my two arms to the goddess Kali, I'll sacrifice my head to Lord Rudra" (14). She is extremely beautiful, "she is Yakshini, Shakuntala, Urvashi, Indumati—all rolled into one" (16). Hayavadana is a fantastic, grotesque and awesome character who is born of a union of a horse and a woman. He is an embodiment of incompleteness which haunts not only Hayavadana but also all of us. Both the episodes heighten this existential dilemma and these characters play a vital role to develop it. The main plot of *Hayavadana* is based on Thomas

Mann's *Transposed Heads* which goes back to *Brihadkatha Saritasagar,* an ancient collection of stories in Sanskrit. The sub-plot that deals with Hayavadana is Karnad's invention. Karnad has created a "world of incomplete individuals, indifferent gods, dolls that speak and children who cannot, a world indifferent to the desires and frustrations, joys and sorrows of human beings" (Kurtkoti vii). Devadatta and Kapila are two opposite extremes—one represents Apollonian tendency another Dionysian; Devedatta is a brahmin who keeps on realizing his friend Kapila has an inferior status in the social hieararchy. Devadatta is a poet and man of intellect, and on the contrary, Kapila is a man of muscle who enjoys life like Mahout of *Bali: The Sacrifice* thwarting moral code, and indulges in sexual relationship with his friend's wife. Both the friends after transposition of heads suffer from the burden of identity and finally kill each other. Padmini, who resembles Cleopatra, is the real Padmini of Vatsyayana. She is nymphomaniac, tempted to have sexual intercourse with Kapila's muscular body and cuckolds her husband. She is never embarrassed in the company of Kapila and is lost in her phantasy. Doll I and II report and comment on the psyche of Padmini:

> DOLL I: Behind her eyelids. She is dreaming
>
> DOLL II: I don't see anything.
>
> DOLL I: A Man...
>
> DOLL II: But not her husband.
>
> DOLL I: No, someone else.
>
> DOLL II: Is this the one who came last night?
>
> DOLL I: Yes—the same. (48)

She is least concerned about her libertine disposition and freely indulgences in extra-marital relationship. She neither regrets nor feels shame. After the death of Devadatta and Kapila, like a *pativrata,* she enters the funeral pyre with both. She becomes *sati* that seems a joke to her: "Kali, Mother of all nature, you must have your joke even now. Other women can die praying that they should get the same husband in all the lives to come.

You haven't left me even that little consolation" (63). Her last act highlights her subalternity. She is so much abetted or socialized to internalize the secondariness of women—her existence without a husband is meaningless. She tries to establish her glorious 'heroic image'. She is disillusioned about the 'best of the two' after transposition. Her situation is beautifully summed up by the images of the river and scarecrows in the chorus song. Hayavadana at last becomes a complete horse. All these characters are true to their nature and impart power and beauty to the play. They are instrumental in making us realize the moral question posed by the transposition, and how to overcome the mad dance of incompleteness. Bhagavata is the Sutradhar who remains on the stage, and goes on providing important information and commenting about events and characters. His role is analogous to Greek Chorus. He occupies the status of an ideal spectator as well as a character of the play.

In *Naga-Mandala*, Karnad has shifted his attention from male to female protagonist—Rani. The play is essentially a study of socio-psychological condition of the Indian woman who is a victim of patriarchy and socio-cultural practices of the society. Rani is not a flat or stereotyped character, rather she is a round and multidimensional character. Throughout the play, the playwright has exposed the subjection and cruelty against the women, and his finale is very revolutionary. Rani's act of reconciliation with Naga is Karnad's overt response to traditional Indian society where man has got the licence to do whatever he wants to do whereas the yardstick of morality is strictly imposed upon women. Though Rani is unlike Padmini of *Hayavadana*, she emerges with a new personality and defies the long established conventions. She accepts Naga as her own: "You don't know how heavy you are. Let me get used to you, will...This hair is the symbol of my wedded bliss. Live in there happily, for ever" (64).

Karnad has dealt with the character of a woman very closely. Rani is generic as well as very individual; her characterization never gives the impression that she is merely used as a tool to convey the philosophy of the writer. She has individual traits of the personality, rights and wrongs. Kurudavva is another woman character in the play who extends and intensifies the tragic impression. She is an incarnation of love, affection and philanthrophy. She is blind but she can see the truth of life. Karnad is not very much interested in developing the personaliy of male characters—Appanna and Kappanna. They have been used as supportive and subservient characters. Appanna which literally means 'any man' and Kappanna 'the dark one' prove that kannad is least concerned about the male characters. Rani's character highlights the feminine issue. Karnad was very deeply concerned about it and he wanted to evolve concrete resolution.

Two folk-tales of Karnataka, which contributed to develop the plot of the play, have allegorical significance. Though they belong to the folk-tale world, they enter into our modern social life, and the playwright has skilfully conveyed what he wants to convey. The Man, The Flame, The Story, Three Village Elders and Naga all have been used to further the main action and its consequences.

Naga is also an interesting character that completes the 'eternal triangle' and creates conflict in the mind of Rani and complication in the plot. The atmosphere of awe, wonder and suspense run with the entry of Naga.

Rani and Appanna are contrasted; they are juxtaposed vis-à-vis to represent two etreme realities of life. The play expresses "a distinctly woman's understanding of the reality around her, a lived counterpart to the patriarchal structures of classical texts and institutions" ("Author's Introduction" 17). The Village Elders, Appanna, and the entire social milieu have been used as tools to perpetuate the subordination and exploitation of women. Use of irony is remarkable. In the play the whole society is enthused to punish Rani through an ordeal for her innocent crime. Nobody is there to reprimand Appanna who is a liberatine and goes to a concubine even after marriage. Karnad has punished Appanna so that he will serve Rani for the rest of his life knowing that he never mated with Rani and still she is pregnant. The dialogues are precise, straitforward and suit the personality of the speaker. The speeches of Naga are highly poetic. The Story and the Man goes on commenting about the off-stage developments and make-up, the limitations of the stage and conform to the conventions of the threatre.

Tale-Danda deals with caste politics. The play was written in the backdrop of "Mandir' and 'Mandal' movements which were catalytic to the playwright. These movements try to show again how relevant the questions posed by medieval thinkers were for our age. The horror of subsequent events and the religious fanaticism that has gripped our national life today have only proved how dangerous it is to ignore the solutions they offered. During the twelfth century, in the city of Kalyan, there emerged a man called Basavanna who assembled a congregation of poets, mystics, social revolutionaries and philosophers. In the history of Karnataka, this period is remarkable for their creativity, courageous questioning and social commitment. They rejected anything "static in favour of the principle of movement and progress in human enterprise. They believed in the equality of sexes and celebrated hard, dedicated work. They opposed the caste system, not just in theory but in practice too. This last act brought down upon them the wrath of the orthodox. The movement ended in terror and bloodshed" ("Preface").

Basavanna is the protagonist of the play. He is the voice of subalterns—lower caste people discriminated on various grounds. His entire character and deeds revolve round this theme. He is an epitome of subaltern movement; he taught them to speak against social evils. His whole life is of confrontation; he is a rebellious spirit that schemes to destroy everything that is like a canker to our society. He is a man of courageous thinking, revolutionary zeal and ready to introduce corrective measures in the society. The dream of an egalitarian society motivates him to go forward.

Basavanna dominates the entire action of the play; the rest of the characters either try to carry out his philosophy or condemn it. There are two opposite factions in the play: Basavanna and his followers on the one side, Sovideva and the clerics on the other side who represent the long established sanatana dharma and social conventions. Basavanna's formation of *Lingayat* faith and entry to all was a part of the enactment of his philosophy. *Lingayat* faith was formed on humanitarian grounds and its members were known as *sharanas.* Even King Bijjala appreciates his mission:

> In all my sixty-two years, the only people who have looked me in the eye without a reference to my lowly birth lurking deep in their eyes are the *sharanas*: Basavanna and his men. They treat me as—as what?—*(Almost with a sense of wonder)* as a human being. Basavanna wants to eradicate the caste structure, wipe it off the face of the earth. Annihilate the Varna system. What a vision! And what prodigious courage! And he has the ability. Look at those he has gathered around him: poets, mystics, visionaries. And nothing airy-fairy about them, mind you. All hard-working people from the common stock. They sit together; eat together, ague about God together, indifferent to caste, birth or station. And all this is happening in the city of Kalayan. (15)

Basavanna is a custodian of public treasury. His presence fuses extra energy among people; the hypergamous marriage of Sheelavanta and Kalavati prove fatal to the new faith. There is a nexus among various groups to defy their attempt. The movement goes into the hands of young Jagadeva and his contrary Prince Sovideva. Basavann anticipates dire consequences of the mingling of the castes:

> Until now it was a matter of thereotical speculation. But this—this is real. The orthodox will see this mingling of castes as a blow at the very roots of varnasharma dharma. Bigotry has not faced such a challenge in two thousand years. I need hardly describe what venom will gush out, what hatred will erupt once the news spreads...some day this entire edifice of caste and creed, this poison-house of varnasharama, will come tumbling down. Every person will see himself only as a human being...But we have a long way to go. (38-39)

Basavanna's retirement to a secluded place and the violent reaction from the orthodox society led by Sovideva turns everything to disgust. King Bijjala, Jagadeva, Somideva, Rambhavati, Damodar Bhatta, Manchanna and other characters are set to advance the action of the play and allow space to develop the personality of the protagonist. Dialogues are very apt, suggestive and embody a philosophical touch. Use of parallelism, contrast and irony are, as usual, dominant features of the art of characterization in *Tale-Danda.*

The Fire and the Rain with its theamatic richness is the finest of Karnad's plays. It has a complex plot, accomplished art of characterization, dialogue, parallelism, contrast and ancient atmosphere. The play is based on a myth from the *Mahabharata* which gives a contemporary meaning to it. It stresses the danger of knowledge without wisdom, and power without integrity. Karnad spent 37 years to think over the content of the play. He has expanded the original story and added a sub-plot (Aravasu and Nittilai episode) with a much larger significance.

All the characters are learned brahmins but that doesn't eschew them from immoral conduct. Yavakri falls a prey to lust, Raibhya and Bhardwaj to anger and jealousy, Paravasu to dishonesty.

A variety of characters from several sections of the society enhance the dramatic effect. The character of Yavakri takes us to the world of rigorous penance, spirituality and pastoral romance. His character illustrates the thematic concern of the play. He is a young man of strong determination and spends 10 years in penance to get power from Indra. He succeeds in his plan but his divine knowledge remains devoid of wisdom. He doesn't attain maturity; remains or comes back to what he was: "VISHAKHA: I can't believe it! The whole world may be singing your praises. But you haven't grown up! These ten years have not made any difference to your teenage fantasies" (121).

Vishakha is married to Paravasu, hence unethical to seduce her for his sexual desires. Yavakri molests her which brings his ruin. Raibhya creates Brahmarakshasa that kills Yavakri. Paravasu, the chief priest in the play, is a man 28 years old. He is a traditional brahmin who follows the socio-cultural practices; his engagement in fire sacrifice for the last seven years, his ambition to maintain a high position in the royal court, subtlelty of mind, rude and indifferent attitude towards Vishakha and Aravasu, shifting blame of brahminicide and fratricide to younger brother make him a mixture of opposites. He sneaks stealthily from the sacrifice. He is hypocritical and contrasted with Aravasu.

The sub-plot in which Aravasu and Nittilai figure, develops an antithetical world to Raibhya, Paravasu and Yavakri. As an actor and Nittilai's lover, Aravasu counterpoints brahminism and asceticism of the other male characters, and enables Karnad to systematically contrast the life of discipline and sacrifice with the life of instinct and emotion.

Aravsu and Nittilai come from a different caste and cultural background. But the love of Arvasu is very earnest: "ARAVASU: I can't give up Nittilai. She is my life. I couldn't live without her—I would rather be an outcaste" (113). Aravasu's character shows, comments Dharwadker, an

> explicit opposition between Brahmin and shudra, with Aravasu functioning as the connective link between the two worlds. As ascetic males Yavakri, Raibhya, and Paravasu have a will to power that empties their spirituality of moral value, and Paravasu's patricide and his false denunciation of Aravasu are of course acts of deliberate evil. Aravasu, in contrast, has committed himself to love and community, and is prepared to renounce his twice-born status for the sake of Nittilai.
>
> ("Introduction" Vol, Two. xviii)

Vishakha and Nittilai are victims of patriarchy and social stratification. First, Vishakha is left for seven years by her husband Paravasu who prefers fire sacrifice for fame to her company: "VISHAKHA: He used my body, and his own body like an experimentor, an explorer. As instruments in a search. Search for what? I never knew". (123) Second, for her transgression she is not only condemned but also abused and kicked by Raibhya: "You whore —you roving whore! I could reduce you to ahes—turn you into a fistful of dust—with a simple curse" (127). Among brahmins, Karnad points out the transgressive woman (Vishakha) is chastised but not punished, whereas among the tribals Nittilai pays with her life for choosing Aravasu over her husband. Ironically, Aravasu loses Nittilai because of his inability to give up orthodoxy at a crucial juncture. Even as he lags behind to perform the last rites for Yavakri, Nittilai is given away to another man.

The Dreams of Tipu Sultan continues the tradition of history plays which Karnad started with *Tughlaq* and extended in *Tale-Danda*. Initially, it was written as a radio play for BBC to celebrate the Fiftieth Anniversary of India's Independence; later rewritten for the stage. The plot deals with some aspect of Indo-British relations and Karnad for the present purpose chose Tipu Sultan, "one of the most politically perceptive and tragic figures in modern Indian history" ("Preface"). Karnad's aim is to establish Tipu Sultan as a major figure in the history of Karnataka. The dreams of Tipu Sultan, which were recorded by Tipu Sultan himself in a diary, enthuzed Karnad to find them out and explore the inner world of Tipu Sultan, hithereto unknown to the world. A copy of the diary Karnad located in 1987 at Chicago Regenstein Library. The valour, political acumenship, innovative ideas and their implementation, anti-colonial resistance, political crisis and its handling, internal dissensions and the presence of a powerful alien adversary embody potential for application to contemporary problems that have also made the history of *Tughlaq* and *Tale-Danda* relevant to modern India. It is the character of Tipu Sultan, the protagonist—his actions, deeds, dreams and reactions the highlight—the above aspects, and the playwright is successful to carry out this purpose using modern theatre techniques.

Major characters of the play have been cast in the light of historical evidence. The character of Tipu Sultan has two contradictory personalities: heroic figure that fought and checked the expansion of British imperialism; and a treacherous and fallible adversary in another. This amalgam makes him complex and highly entertaining.

The play has forward-backward movements; Hussain Ali Kirmani, among the dramatis personae, enables Karnad to show the process of history writing. The major characters such as Tipu, Haider Ali, Nana Phadnavis, Lord Cornwallis, Arthur and

Richard Wellesley are cast vis-à-vis Kirmani, Tipu's Queen and sons, courtiers and military officials, senior citizens and soldiers. Karnad has successfully developed them as products of their culture and transitional phase in Indian history and politics. Aparna Bhargava Dharwadker has closely observed the character of Tipu Sultan who has been an amlgam of numerous personalities:

> Karnad also casts his protagonist in multiple and contradictory roles—as a beloved ruler, legendary warrior, loving father, and visionary dreamer, but also as the Machiavellian schemer who plots with the French against the English, the defeated soldier who enters into humiliating treaties with the enemy, and the guillible commander who is eventually betrayed by his own side. The perceptions of Tipu that have the greatest energy, however, are those with Brechtian-materiliast overtones: they underscore Tipu's excitement over the 'new ideas' of Europe, his understanding of political economy, his interest in the link between commerce and empire, and his desire for an up-to-date army. In this analysis, the tragedy of Tipu's fall is not only that it made way for a full-scale takeover, but that it destroyed a visionary who shared the modernizing impulses of the European Enlightenment, and could meet the English on their own terms.
>
> ("Introduction" Vol.Two. xiv)

The dreams of Tipu Sultan reflect his deep-rooted ambitions. Even the image of Haider Ali shows his excited imagination. "Dilapidated temple" (18) of the first dream, "white elephant" (20), "fair-skinned and light-eyed young man" (28), "white plague depart" of the subsequent dreams are mental projections of the unfulfilled desires accumulated in his unconscious. Karnad has very deftly explored the inner psyche of the protagonist.

Tipu is a man with practical vision of life; he goes on learning new things: "TIPU: I've had two teachers in my life. My father, who taught me war, and the English who taught me trade" (35). He consolidates Marathas and Nizam, and uses them against the English. Though he fails, he gives tough resistance to British colonialism. His dreams are shattered but his predictions for the future of Marathas and Nizam come true.

Tipu is defeated due to internal dissensions and lack of diplomacy. But his characterization establishes him as a heroic figure with a complex personality. Kirmani and Mackenzie act as choric characters and go on commenting on the action. Poornia, Nadeem Khan, Mark Wilks, Cornwallis, Arthur Wellesley are juxtaposed as strong foils to Tipu Sultan. Dialogues, imagery, metaphors, symbols, constrasted personalities enrich the texture of the story and the art of characterization.

Bali: The Sacrifice is a tribute to the "astuteness and sensitivity of Mahtama Gandhi that he saw so clearly the importance of non-violence to the cultural and political survival of India" ("Preface"). Jains, Buddhists and even Hindus have renounced any kind of violence but brahmins substituted miniature figurines, made of dough for live animals. But the instinct of violence continued and Karnad has successfully endeavoured to expose the instinct of violence and morality of substitution. The Queen, the Mother Queen and the King contribute to advance this central point in the play. The Queen and Mother Queen are contrasted due to their ideological differences and socio-cultural practices regarding animal sacrifices. The Queen is a Jain while the Mother Queen is a Hindu. Both of them represent two different cultural backgrounds. Vedic fire sacrifices conducted by a brahmin priest, involve the slaughter of animals as offerings to the gods, which the Jain's consider repugnant. To them, indulging in any kind of violence means forefeighting one's moral status as a human being.

Queen Amritamati is a character with "too much imagination", "sensitive" and "wrapped up in herself" (100). She is haunted by alienation, libidinous compulsion and swayed by the "heavenly voice" (78) of the Mahout and spends one night with him "nameless" (88). Thus she cuckolds her husband yet she is unlike Padmini *Hayavadana*, who is tempted by the muscular body of Kapila. She is close to Rani of *Naga-Mandala* who, unknowingly, out of passion, enters into extra-marital relationship with Naga. The Queen is honest and candid who acknowledges whatever happened:

> I do not regret anything that has happened. I will not disown him or anything he gave me...Because it just happened. Without my willing it. It just happened. That's all...I want to come to you. I feel fuller. Richer. Warmer. But not ashamed. Because I didn't plan it. And it was beautiful...I am yours. I'll never betray you again (118-119).

The relationship between the Queen and the Mother Queen is based on hatred; it's because of polarity in their vision of life. When the Queen becomes pregnant, the Mother Queen plans to celebrate according to family tradition which implies animal sacrifice, "QUEEN: The animals are graded according to the occasion. Poultry is offered at daily rites. Sheep, goats for the more important rituals. Then buffalo" (96). The Queen strongly condemns this practice: "I don't want it. Not in the name of our child" (97). The King adopts her faith because he finds truth in it and compassion for the world in pain. The Queen Mother knowing the Queen's ompany with the Mahout infuriates her: "She has fallen so low? The whore—And you. How can you stand here like this? I should cut her to pieces...feed her to wolves and vultures. Do it, son, now!" (107). The King also supports the cause of non-violence. He is meek and friendly. The Mahout is a subaltern voice, a womanizer and a drunkard. He is haunted by his low birth and ugly appearance but he is a melodious singer that fetches the Queen to the ruined temple. The singer works as a Greek Chorus, and goes on commenting on the development in the story. Dialogues are crisp, precise and argumentative, sometimes broken and criptic to suit the personality of the characters and situation.

Flowers and *Broken Images* introduce new subjects and forms. Characters through their deeds, actions, dialogues or voices connect themselves with the subjets. *Flowers* which is based on the legend of Veeranna of Chitradurga region was successfully used by T.R. Subbanna in his novel *Hamsageete.* Karnad has highlighted the conflict between religious devotion and erotic love. It is the only work of Karnad that studies male rather than female desire, and develops a triangle unlike that of *Hayavadana, Bali: The Sacrifice* and *Naga-mandala.* Here, it is a man and two women. The unnamed priest of the temple is the protagonist who is known for his devotion to the *linga*. He narrates:

> I am the priest here. I have lived here all my life and discouraged all friendly attentions from the world outside. And in the isolationof this place, I spend most of my time with the *linga*—talking to it, singing to it, even discussing recent political developments and most of all, decorating it with flowers... 'The *linga* is my step-wife', grumbles my wife. (243-244)

His obsession with the *linga* has fetched him recognition. On the contrary, with the entry of Chandravati, a courtesan conflict begins: "I wanted her. I had never lusted for a woman before and so felt emasculated by this sudden weaknes. Yet I could not control the fire raging in my loins. During the rest of the week, I started the day impatient for a glimpse of hers" (245). The priest regularly visits Chandravati. One day the chieftain of the region finds a hair in the *prasad*, so he wants an explanation from the priest. The chieftain intends to humiliate him publicly; but due to the priests devotion to the *linga*, it grows a tuft of hair. A brahmin who dares to pluck it out is shocked to see the oozing of blood from the *linga*. He feels extremely sorry. The chieftain and the rest of the people fall at the feet of the priest and begs forgiveness. The priest realizes deeply the meaning of this act. His wife reports to him that Chandravati and her old woman left the town the very next day. The priest devotes his all his time to God: "The courtesan was gone and had been replaced by Lord Shiva. I was among the chosen of the Lord" (259). The wife of the priest tolerates everything. She is the victim of patriarchy. Chandravati too is a target of lustful eyes of man; even the religious man doesn't spare the body of a woman. His whole life is full of irony and contradictons. The character of the priest elaborates the theme that the playwright has conceived.

Broken Images deals with the modern debate on language politics, i.e., modern Indian languages versus English as well as genre in literary writing. Manjula Nayak, the only character of the play, extends and illustrates this debate graphically. She is a writer of short and long fiction in Kannada, and works as a teacher of English in Bangalore. She leads a rather typical literary life. The publication of her very novel in English connotes two things: first, for fame, recognition, larger audience and to "survive" (283) betrayed Kannada; second, it is revealed soon that she has used the manuscript of her invalid sister Malini's novel as her own and accrued everything that she has dreamt of. Thus she has indulged in plagiarism. She is truly crazy and represents the dilemma of modern Indian writers writng in regional languages; she is exposed to modern technology like Vidula of *Wedding Album*. In her television image she admits: "My response to the charge that I write in English for money would be: Why not? Isn't that a good enough reason? Would you like to see what royalties I earned when I wrote in Kannadda?" (264). She justifies her action for "fame, publicity, glamour…power" (265). Her television image reflects her psyche which is quite new and innovative in technique.

Soon Manjula and her image (psychic reaction) react to each other, throughout the play exactly as though they were both live characters. Every action and reaction of hers is directly linked with the debate which constitutes the content of the monologue. Manjula is contrasted with her invalid sibling Malini. Ironically, it is hoped that she will take care of Malini, but rather reversely, she exploits her talent for her own selfish motifs and doubts the illicit relationship between Malini and her husband. Karnad has portrayed Manjula very closely and minutely which helps to objectify his thematic intent.

Wedding Album, the latest play of Karnad, is a wonderful comedy on marriage and the various facets of it, especially of middle class. The play is a result of his personal experience he gained during his sister's marriage that was full of celebration as well as anxiety; hence to a great extent the play is autobiographical. But its large canvas and art of characterization give it universal acknowledgement. It is the urban middle class Saraswat Brahmin family—its wedding culture, pros and cons which constitute the very substance of the play. The family comprises father Dr. Nadkarni, Mother, a housewife, Hema, the eldest daughter, married and living in Australia, Rohit, son, writing stories and scripts for teleplays, Vidula, the youngest daughter and the protagonist of the play, Radhabai, a cook in Nadkarni's family. All these characters have been developed with the view to vindicate the argument of the play and the playwright is quite successful in his endeavour. All these characters create a world close to us; we hardly feel we are different from them. It's essentially a family drama.

The role of Gopal, Vatsala, Mohan and Mira supplement the role of the Nadkarnis. Pratibha Khan is an instance of modern woman with cosmopolitan attitude in marriage and entrepeunership. She is constrasted with traditional Nadkarni and Sirur families. She also objects to Vidula's decision to marry a man whom she has never met. Vidula is the product of modern cyber world; it is 'distance' technology she has easy access to choose a suitable boy through SMSes, Internet, Video Call, Telephony and Mobile. She is an individual as well as type character. She embodies the changing characteristics of modern world and mode of selection. She lives for eight days with Aswinand on a later date both agree to marry. She is a moody and very complex personality who enjoys porno video chats.

Vidula is new in her ideas, timid in her efforts. She is constrasted with Hema: "FATHER: It's Hema. She was always so confident and Vidu has developed this self-image, contrary to hers. Children define themselves against each other" (73). Hema is married to a Saraswat Brahmin who works in Austrialia. She is conservative in family relations and condemns Rohit's love for Isabel, a Christian. She is satisfied as a housewife and follows the traditional values of the family. Vidula's and Her's would-be husbands are finest examples of modern youths who don't believe in dowry or any kind of demand. Both of them are well settled abroad.

Though Mother, conforms to traditional values of the family, she is at once very progressive and modern in her outlook: "I achieved nothing in my life…so many opportunities in today's world. We couldn't even dream of such a world…Don't throw away your talents in just bearing children" (90). She is very affectionate and caring and expert in household affairs. She believes in pomp and shows in marriage and spends lavishly during Hema's marriage; now she is anxious about Vidula's marriage. She dismisses caste barrier as requisite for a marriage.

For Dr. Nadkarni marriage is a "gamble" (89). It is Vidula's wedding that's awaited, and in the family we witness mixed reactions of celebration and anxiety. Celebration of the occasion and anxiety for marriage preparations and Vidula's pending marriage are not decided till the last moment.

Rohit is a young, smart and modern man with high aspirations; he is very close to his family, especially Vidula, and consoles her in every way: "We live in a modern world. A divorce is okay. It's no shame...if at any moment you wish to divorce Ashwin and come back, don't hesitate to do so" (86). He loves a Christian girl Isabel but due to certain complications their marriage cannot materialize. Radhabai is a typical cook who has a painful story of her life: husband dead and daughter mad and lost. She makes the family of Saraswat complete.

The family of Sirurs—Gopal, Vatsala, Mohan and Mira—also help to elaborate the marriage culture of the concerned society. They come to Nadkarni with a marriage proposal of their daughter Tapasaya to Rohit, and make every effort to grab the boy. Their dialogues, reactions and pleadings are very natural and give the story beauty and power. All the characters, according to Amrit Srinivasan form: "The constellation of sexual, conjugal, caste, class, and age-related behviours and attitudes of selfishness and sacrifice, chastity and commerce, obedience and authority, all integral to modern Hindu marriage...But it is in enabling us to see these cultural blind spots for what they really are..." ("Foreward" viii-ix).

Works Cited

Aristotle. *Poetics.* Translated by Butcher, S.C. New Delhi/Ludhiana: Kalyani Publishers, 1998.

Dharwadker, Aparna Bhargava. "Introduction" *Collected Plays.* Volume Two. New Delhi: Oxford University Press, 2005.

Pickering, Kenneth. *Studying Modern Drama.* (Second Edition) New York: Palgrave/ Macmillan, 2003.

Karnad, Girish. *Yayati.* New Delhi: Oxford University Press, 2008.

________. *Tughlaq.* (Twenty Second Impression) Delhi: Oxford University Press, 1998.

_________. *Hayavadana.* (Fourteenth Impression) Chennai: Oxford University Press, 1998. This impression has been used and referred in.

_________. "Author's Introduction" *Three Plays: Naga-Mandala, Hayavadana, Tughlaq.* (Eighth Impression) New Delhi: Oxford University Press, 2002. For *Naga-Mandala* present edition has been extensively used and reffered in.

_________. "Preface" *Tale-Danda.* New Delhi: Ravi Dayal, 1993. Subsequent references are from this edition.

_________, "Preface" *Bali: The Sacrifice* in *Two Plays by Girish Karnad: The Dreams of Tipu Sultan, Bali: The Sacrifice.* (Fourth Impression) New Delhi: Oxford University Press, 2005. Both the playtexts of this editon have been consuled and refered in.

_________. "Preface" *The Dreams of Tipu Sultan* in *Two Plays by Girish Karnad: The Dreams of Tipu Sultan, Bali: The Sacrifice.* (Fourth Impression) New Delhi: Oxford University Press, 2005. Both the playtexts of this editon have been consutled and refered in.

_________, *The Fire and the Rain* in *Collected Plays.*Volume Two. (Ed.) Dharwadker, Aparna Bhargava. New Delhi: Oxford University Press, 2005. References are from this edition.

_________. *Flowers* and *Broken Images* in *Collected Plays.* Volume Two. (Ed.) Dharwadker, Aparna Bhargava. New Delhi: Oxford University Press, 2005. References of both the monologues are from this edition.

_________. *Wedding Album.* New Delhi: Oxford Uiversity Press, 2009.

Murthy. A.R. Ananth. "Introduction", *Tughlaq.* (Twenty Second Impression) Delhi: Oxford University Press, 1998.

Srinivasan, Amrit. "Foreward", *Wedding Album.* New Delhi: Oxford Uiversity Press, 2009.

9

Techniques

Dramatic techniques or dramatic conventions are those devices which are employed by the playwright in his playtext (work) and in its representation on the stage before the lively audience to make both (i.e. text and performance) more effective to attain the desired objectives. Theatre techniques are procedures that facilitate a successful presentation of a play. They also include any practices that advance and enhance the understanding that the audience brings to the action and acting by the cast on stage. Theatre techniques are part of the playwright's creative writing of drama, as a kind of mimesis rather than mere illusion or imitation of life, in that the playwright is able to present a reality to the audience that is different, yet recognizable to that which they usually identify with their everyday lives. The playwright's art also includes the ability to convey to the audience the ideas that give essence to the drama within the frame of its structure. Finally, the feeling for the natural divisions of a play—including acts, scenes, and changes of places, its entries and exists, and the positioning of the cast—are integral to playwriting technique. Una Ellis-Fermor considers that "Imagery and prosody, together with certain bold conventions and even devices of setting" (77) serve to overcome the limitations of the drama. Drama being a composite work of art in which drama, dramatist and the producer/ director involve can't be complete with literary composition, Karnad in an interview to Tutun Mukherjee responded:

> Play lives on the stage and its dynamism derives from its interaction with he audience. It belongs to the moment when it is being watched. The playwright, the actors, the

> technicians, the director, the spectators create that experience together; they can determine or even modify that experience. (47)

Drama is unlike poetry, novel and other forms of literature; but as a performing art, a collaborative art form, it is "Lyricism+Mime. If 'lyricism' refers to the words on the printed page of a text, 'mime' refers to the action on the stage" (Ramaswamy 272). It is written to be staged, hence, apart from compositional accomplishments; technical requirements of the stage and the understanding of the psychology of the audience deserve equal attention and incorporation in its performance. Playtext, according to Kenneth Pickering is "the blueprint for performance" (10). Drama is "a social art. No one can produce a play by himself. The words of the text are not the play, nor is the theatre in which it will eventually be produced. Even a dress rehearsal can hardly be called a performance. A play is the cumulative product of many relationships" (Whitfield 4). Both the text and performance contribute to create a cathartic effect, i.e., entertainment, instruction, enlightenment, happiness, peace and moral upliftment. The success of a play is to be tested only on the stage as, comments M.K. Naik: "drama is a composite art in which the written word of the playwright attains complete artistic realization only when it becomes the spoken word of the actor on the stage, and through that medium reacts on the mind of the audience" (Qtd. in S.K. Bhatt 2). Technique can be studied broadly under two heads:

(a) Compositional Techniques and

(b) Theatrical Techniques.

Compositional Techniques or Conventions include:

(i) *Plot*: source of the plot, structural design, i.e., Acts and scenes, setting, time, space, action and its development, prologue and epilogue, choric characters (i.e. sutradhar, announcer, flames, story, man or song), supernatural and their specific use.

(ii) *Characterization*: flat or round, deeds—physical, mental and spiritual—and their correlation with the plot. Personal traits and personality development through dialogues or introductory remarks by the playwright himself or through Chorus figure etc.

(iii) *Thought*: aside, soliloquisies, mimes, body gestures, Chorus, song, symbols, metaphors etc. express mental and emotional make-up of the characters, especially the protagonist in a specific way.

(iv) *Language*: language or diction is equally important in a playtext. The choice of words and phrases, structure of sentences, compound words—traditional or newly coined—allusions, references, symbols, metaphors, similes, irony, satire, humour, use of verse or prose and other artistic embellishments. Unless the composition is dignified, it can't produce the desired effects.

Compositional or textual accomplishments with numerous techniques that the playwright uses are closely linked with the theatrical techniques. Though drama can be enjoyed in isolation, in our private reading, its real spirit and degree of perfection can be enjoyed and understood when it is performed on the stage. Hence textual perfection and technical innovations collectively work to make it a successful one. Theatrical techniques or conventions include the devices which are used by the playwright to transform playtext into a performing art. George Whitfield has defined conventions in a broader sense:

> The things in a theatre or in a play which people are willing to accept as part of the 'Let's pretend...', and which they will come to expect as part of the performance, are called the *conventions* of drama. It is a pity that this word 'conventions' has come to mean only good manners in social behavior, for when it is used of drama the meaning is much bigger. The conventions of drama are not merely rules and methods of the theatre which dramatists have created and followed; they show the angle from which people of different nations and of varying periods have looked out upon life. They point to the popular philosophy and, by showing what it took for granted in interpreting human experience; they form a kind of commentary upon the age which produced them. (9)

It's possible through various forms of theatre and their conventions:

(i) Classical Theatre and its conventions;

(ii) Folk Theatre and its conventions;

(iii) Modern Theatre and its conventions; and the fusion of the classical, folk and modern theatrical conventions.

It was the belief of Aristotle that, in the true performance of a tragedy, the crude emotions of the audience were absorbed into the perfect expression of these emotions in the drama, where they were cleansed and purified of their imperfections. Such a "catharsis" (Aristotle 23) may be possible only when a great play is greatly acted, but every true drama enlarges the bounds of human experience so that actors and audience become newly aware of the significance of human personality, and of the acts by which that personality is expressed.

India has a dramatic tradition of its own, and Indian theatre was entirely independent in its origins, in the ideas which governed it in its development. Indian Classical drama originated from the folk theatre of the country in the forms of pageants, rituals, mimes and other folk forms. In course of centuries both went on borrowing from each other and developed. Similiarly, Greek drama had its origins in fertility rites and frenzied worship of Dionysus. Ancient Greeks formalized theatre as an art and developed the concept of tragedy and comedy as well as other forms, including satyr plays. Greek plays made use of mythological characters and developed the concepts of dramatic ciriticism, acting as a career, and theatre architecture.

Modern Western theatre derives in large measure from Greek drama, from which it borrows technical terminology, classification into genres, and many of its themes, stock characters, and plot developments. The process of evolution of the dramatic art in India, according to S.K. Bhatt, "can be traced right from the ancient period of *Rigveda* which contains some dramatic dialogues. Also there are references to drama in the *Ramayana* and the Mahabharata, and in Panini's works; and traces of its development in Krishna legends" (1).

Classical and folk theatre of India provides a background to the study of modern Indian theatre. The modern Indian theatre is characterized with contrasting colour and variety. Despite rich diversity and infinite variety, it has unity. All the three traditions, that is, the classical Sanskrit, the folk, and the modern are intimately connected with each other. They can be co-existent and complementary to each other. The modern Indian playwrights such as Vijay Tendulkar, Girish Karnad, Badal Sircar, and Mohan Rakesh use them effectively and successfully. Their plays can be, "studied as modern with an awareness of the classical and folk elements in it" (Wadikar 27). The modern Indian theatre is also influenced by the Western theatre, particularly the Euro-American one.

Bharatmuni's *Natyashastra* is considered the foundation of dramatics and dramaturgy. Like Aristotle's *Poetics*, it is accepted as the greatest treatise in the field of drama. The classical theatre is known as the Sanskrit Theatre as most of the plays are written in Sanskrit. *Natyashastra*, apart from the origion and development of drama in India, throws light on the elements of drama, purpose of drama, production, direction, make- up, costume, jewellery, body movements, dance and music. The drama is called 'Drishyakavya' or 'Rupaka' which has three essential constituents: *Vastu* (plot), *Neta* (hero) and, *Rasa* (sentiment) which collectively work for *Rasotpatti* and *Rasawadana. Vastu* or plot refers to the story which develops throught the play, is primarily of two kinds: principal and accessory. The first relates to the chief characters and pervades the whole arrangement while the accessory furthers the main topic, and is concerned with characters other than the hero or heroine. *Pataka* or 'Banner' is an episode which refers to the rising action; *Prakari* is also an episodical incidence of limited duration. *Bija, Bindu* and *Karya* are other techniques to develop plot. *Neta* or the hero is required to be modest, decorous, comely, munificent, civil, of sweet address, eloquent, sprung from a noble family. Pithmarda, Vidushaka, and Vita are the supportive characters to develop the personality of the hero. Vidushaka provides comic relief and makes satirical remarks similar to clown of Shakespeare.

Rasa is the lasting impression of feeling produced to his overwhelming delight in a man of poetic susceptibility by the proper action of the *Vibhavas* and the *Anubhavas,* as well as the *Sattvikabhavas* and the *Vyabhicharibhavas. Bhavas, Vibhavas, Anubhavas, Sthayibhava, Vyabhicharibhava,* and

Satvikabhavas are the six types of *Rasas*. The eight *Sthayibhavas*—Rati, Hasya, Shoka, Krodha, Utsaha, Bhaya, Jugupsa and Vismaya are based respctively on the sentiments—erotic, comic, pathetic, furious, heroic, terrible, loathsome and marvellous. Every dramatic piece opens with a Prelude or Prologue introduced by *Nandi*; a Sutradhara may sometimes retire after the recital of the *Nandi*. The Sutradhara suggests the subject the characters and presents song to please the audience.

The play is divided into Acts and Scenes. Death of the hero is never exhibited. As regards the language hero and other majot characters speak in Classical Sanskrit, while female and minor characters use different Prakrit dialects. Kale has observed three characteristic peculiarities of the Indian Drama: "(i) its peculiar structure, (2) the absence of the distinction between Comedy and Tragedy and (3) the diversity of language to be spoken by the characters" (xxi).

The Sanskrit stage declined due to Persian and Mughal regime, and the most popular Islamic Theatre forms were puppet theatre, shadow plays, marionette productions, *ta'ziya*, where actors re-enact episodes from Muslim history. In particular, Shia Islamic plays revolved around *shaheed* (martyrdom) of Ali's sons, Hasan ibn Ali and Husayn ibn Ali.

Secular plays were known as *akhraja,* recorded in medieval *adab* literature, though they were less common than puppetry and *ta'ziya* theatre. The polpular theatre of the mass with well-known themes in local languages went on growing, and even inherited many of the conventions of Sanskrit theatre like the *Sutradhara* and the *Vidushaka*, who appear under different names in different regional forms. Thus the classical Sanskrit drama survived in some crystallized folk-theatre forms like *Ramlila, Raslila*, and *Nautanki* of North, *Bhavai* of Gujarat, *Tamasha* of Maharashtra, *Jatra* of Bengal, *Akia-nat* of Assam, *Yakshagana* of Karnataka, *Veedhinatakamu* of Andhra and *Therukoothu* of Tamil Nadu. These folk forms use music, dance, mimic action, simplicity of language, staging and costumes. The modern Indian theatre in its process of evolution has absorbed, "the cultural richness of the classical drama, the folk traditions of the medieval times and above all the influence of the West" ("Development of Theatre in India").

In its earlier decade, the modern Indian theatre was known as *Amateur Theatre* since it was used as a pastime without any exploitation of income. The popularity of the *Amateur Theatre* is challenged by the experimental theatre that came into being with the establishment of the National Centre for the Performing Arts in 1985. It is characterized with realism in the theme, structure, dialogues, setting and performance of the play. The presentation of the contemporary daily life is its main purpose. Utpal Dutt, Badal Sircar, Girish Karnad, C.T. Khanolkar, Sadanand Rege, Amol Paleker, Vijay Tendulker, Satish Alekar and Mahesh Elkunchwar have contributed a lot to the growth and development of the modern Indian theatre by their innovative works and techniques of presentation on the stage. The birth of several dramatic organisations like the Indian People's Theatre, the Indian National Theatre (established by Kamaladevi Chattopadhyaya), Ebrahim Alkazi's Theatre Unit, the Bharatiya Natya Sangha (affiliated to the World Theatre Centre of UNESCO) and several regional amateur theatres followed by Post-Independence period, led to the performing arts being given further impetus by the establishment of the Sangita-Natak Akademi, the National School of Drama, training centres like Adyar Kalakshetra in Channai and Darpana in Ahmedabad, and drama departments in some universities in the country.

Karnad's dramatic technique is superb and flawless. His plays have the tone and expression of great drama. The plots in his plays are well-knit, the devices of parallelism and contrast, suspense and surprise help in the logical development of plot. His characters are vivid. Both the plot and character are correlated and promote the unity of effect or impression. His English is simple, his vocabulary from different stocks, imagery, symbols, irony and metaphors heighten the dramtic effects. His language is situation modified and vechicle to express typical Indian ethos. Karnad is a progressive dramatist—a pioneer in neo-drama, and all his plays are actable. Earlier it was a mere literary exercise; the new dramatic movement has given a new lease of life to Kannada theatre.

Kirtinath Kurtkoti has rightly commented: "With this new theatre growing around them, [non-professionals] new playwrights like Girish Karnad have been able to bring to drama a first hand knowledge of the practical demands of the stage and a better understanding of dramatic style and technique" ("Introduction" v). The influence of theatre was immense on the making of Karnad as a playwright. He himself has narrated the experience of his making:

> In my childhood, in a small town in Karnataka, I was exposed to two theatre forms that seemed to represent irreconcilably different worlds. Father took the entire family to see plays staged by troupes of professional actors called *natak companies* which toured the countryside throughout the year. The plays were staged in semipermanent structures on proscenium stages, with wings and drop curtains, and were illuminated by petromax lamps.
>
> Once the harvest was over, I went with the servants to sit up nights watching the more traditional *Yakshagana* performances. The stage, a platform with a back curtain, was erected in the open air and lit by torches.
>
> ("Author's Introduction" 1)

Soon both the theatre forms ceased to function, and Karnad was exposed to Strindberg's dimmers in Mumbai. Western theatre techniques and playwrights with realistic theatre (G.B. Shaw was the presiding diety), an improvement over Parsi theatre, was established both as an art and an instrument of social change. The proscenium continued, only now the grand spectacles gave way to the *interior set* with the invisible fourth wall. And that three-walled living room succinctly defined the basic limitations of this school of writing. The influence of Kannada drama was quite profound, and Karnad represents the best traditions of Kannada drama which are immensely rich. Vanashree Tripathi has rightly observed the process of forging a theatre of our own in Karnad:

> Karnad has discovered and reinvented diverse patterns of drama from Indian and the world literature and his drawing on the myths, folktales and histories have

> rejuvenated, expanded and energized the poetics of contemporary drama....Both tradition-seeking and intercultural in innovative acumen, his eclectic adaptation of the Western mode makes it relevant to the Indian experience...the desire to repossess an Indian form of theatre is more than apparent. (9-11)

Karnad's plays from *Yayati* to *Wedding Album* are the testimony of the above features, theamatic as well as theatre techniques. His experiments with folk and classical techniques are highly fruitful to create an effective and successful stage production: the use of Sutradhara, announcer or song, the supernatural elements, play within the play, masks, mime, songs, half-curtains,, dolls, etc blend with modern devices such as sound , light, flashforward, flashback, rigging, conscience corridor, sound-scaping, role-on-the-wall, physical theatre, split focus, cross-cutting, tableaux, and teichoscophy (viewing from the wall).

Tughlaq was moulded on Natak Company, offshoots of Parsi Theatre, conventions in which all the scenes were divided and alternated between deep scenes and shallow scenes. The shallow scenes were usually played in the foreground of the stage with a painted curtain—depicting a street—as a backdrop. These scenes were reserved for 'lower class' characters and kept for comedy. They served as link scenes in the development of the plot, but the main purpose was to keep the audience engaged while the deep scenes, which showed interiors of palaces, royal parks, and other such visually opulent sets, were being changed or decorated. The major characters rarely appeared in the street scenes, and in the deep scenes the lower classes strictly kept their place. Characters of the play were clearly divided into those which came into shallow scenes and those which came into deep scenes. The first half of the play was written on the above conventions, but with the development of the form on its own and in the end Aziz, one of the characters meant to be comical, ended up in the palace, which seemed to be right, given the political chaos that one was writing about. For a history play, Karnad found Natak Company conventions suitable while the Hindus have no tradition of history. The plot of the play developed into thirteen scenes—deep as well shallow. Karnad had chosen the historical figure, Muhammed Tughlaq, as a protagonist that constitutes the main plot:

> The most brilliant individual ever to ascend the throne of Delhi and also one of the biggest failures...ended his career in bloodshed and political chaos. In a sense, the play reflected the slow disillusionment my generation felt with the new politics of independent India: the gradual erosion of the ethical norms that had guided the movement for independence and the coming to terms with cynicism and realpolitik.
>
> ("Author's Introduction" 7)

Tughlaq is one of the best plays of Karnad due to his art and technique. It is a judicious mixture of fact and fiction. The plot of the play is based on history, and most of the characters and events are close to the history but there are certain additions, i.e., Aziz and Aazam are invented by the playwright suited for shallow scenes and comical portrayal. Thus Karnad has added a comic sub-plot to the play. The story of Aziz and Aazam parodies the story of Tughlaq. The play is wanting, according to Tilak, "in catharsis in the true Aristotlean sense. Then denouement is weak and in the end Tughlaq has not been murdered but is seen sleeping confused and bewildered on his throne" (12). The Announcer has been used as a chorus figure who beats his drum and makes important announcement. Use of contraries, symbols (chess game, prayer, and python), metaphors, idioms and phrases and words from Arabic, Urdu, Hindi and Kannada, interesting story, complex plot, make the play highly innovative in technique.

Hayavadana is developed on Yakshagana and other folk-forms. The conventions of the folk-tales and motifs of folk theatre are dexterously fused together: masks, curtains, mime songs, the commentator-narrator, dolls, horse-man, the story-within-a-story, world of human and the non-human create a grotesque world. It is a world of incomplete individuals, indifferent gods, dolls that speak and children who cannot, a world indifferent to the desires and frustrations, joys and sorrows of human beings. Karnad employs poetry, music, a sense of gaiety and celebration linked with theatrical event in the play.

The plot is based on Thomas Mann's *Transposed Heads* which is rooted in Somdeva's *Brihadkatha Saritasagar* and *Vetal Panchavimshati*. Through these borrowings, Karnad has developed the themes of existential dilemma and theme of incompleteness. The play is structured into two acts: the main plot deals with Devadatta, Kapil and Padamini while the sub-plot deals with Hayavadana. Both the plots advance the concern of the play—the mad dance of incompleteness and search for completeness. Karnad introduces the mask of Lord Ganesha, the presisiding deity of traditional theatre on the stage, and pooja is done in his praise like a typical Yakshagana play. Soon Bhagavatta introduces the theme of the play through Ganesha possessing the head of an elephant and human body signifying incompleteness; thereafter Bhagavatta narrates the story with a formalistic expression in the manner of a folk-tale. Savita Goel finds consummate excellence in this technique: "There is a superb technical achievement in the way in which Karnad uses Brechtian type of narrator figure in the role of Bhagavatta. He is primarily intended to draw the audience into the play. He is able to step out of the play, talk to the audience, explaining the action with his insightful comments" (211).

Use of mask is a popular feature of Yakshagana to highlight personalities of dramatis personae. In the beginning of the play, Devadatta enters on the stage putting on a pale-coloured mask and Kapila a dark mask. After transposition, their masks also change to signify change of heads. Lord Ganesh is presented with an elephant-headed mask and Kali, a terrible mask. Hayavadana appears with the mask of a man in the beginning, later with the mask of a horse. Curtains—half- curtains, painted curtains, carried by two stage hands–sort of curtain used in Yakshagana or Kathakali—are used to carry specific meaning. The curtain marks the entry of Hayavadana and the scene of Padmini performing Sati is marked by a curtain that has a blazing fire painted on it and as it is lifted, the flames seem to leap up. Kali is also represented by the picture of Kali on the curtain. There is no front curtain nor any elaborate stage set up.

Use of dolls is another feature of the popular theatre. They are used to satisfy the emotional appetite of the audience and comment on the psyche of Padmini. While Devadatta, Kapila and Padmini are going to Ujjain in a bullock cart, the action is mimed. Here is no cart on the stage, rather Kapila is followed by Padmini and Devadatta, enter miming a cart ride. Kapila is driving the cart. An image of Kali in the play creates the world of mystery and wonder with frightening image animated: "Behind the curtain one sees the uplifted blood-red palms of the goddess. The curtain is lowered and taken away and one sees a terrifying figure, her arms stretched out, her mouth wide open with the tongue lolling out. The drum stops and as she drops her arms and shuts her mouth, it becomes clear she has been yawning" (31-32). These theatrical techniques are suitable, to deal with the thematic concerns and entertain the audience.

Sutradhara in *Yayati*, Bhagavata in *Hayavadana* and Story in *Naga-Mandala* are derivative of Sutradhara in Clssical Drama in India, and it also moves into folk theatre conventions with different names. Sutradhara plays the role of an actor and stage manager. He introduces the gist of the play in the initial stage, goes on commenting and reporting off-stage developments as well as course of action of the play, and throws light on the characters. He can be equated with Chorus of Greek drama which performs similar functions through its song, and is recognized as an ideal spectator because the concerns, dilemmas and reactions of the spectators are also represented by it. For instance, Sutradhara in *Abhijnanshakuntalam* of Kalidas, the best play on classical model, in the very first act narrates the summer season, and introduces Dushyanta, the protagonist and his undertakings, and the action moves forward and there is a natural sequence of event. *Yayati* begins with a Prologue and Sutradhara enters and addresses the audience and introduces the content of the play:

> Our play this evening deals with an ancient myth....We turn to ancient tale not because it provides fleetng glimpses of the fears and desires sleepless within us....What is represented here on the stage is an inner chamber on the first floor of King Yayati's palace. The King's son, Prince

> Pooru, is returning home today after many years of absence. He has successfully completed his education in the hermitage under renowned gurus, and is bringing home with him his bride, Chitralekha, the Princess of Anga. The crowds have started collecting in the grounds around the palace, eager to see the royal couple. The two must enter this space and on this bed they must create themselves the magic kingdom of love, ambition, and power. He must sow his seed here and then launch forth on a campaign of victory and death....But we must trust the narrative we have chosen for ourselves. Invent bits if necessary, but go on. We must relive, not a saga embedded in books, but a tale orally handed down by our grandmothers in lamplit corners. (5-6)

Thereafter the mythical story of Yayati develops into four acts: Yayati, Devayani, Sharmishtha, Pooru, Chitralekha, Swarnalata, all are portrayed as mythical characters. Karnad has added new dimensions in the personality of Pooru who, unlike the mythical Pooru, at last gathers the courage to ask question on the death of Chitrlekha: "What does all this mean. O God? What does it mean?" (69). Chitrlekha, too, is developed to the stature of a New Woman who doesn't yield but protests against male-chauvinism and succeeds in subverting the male world through an assertion of her rights and privileges.

Karnad's mythical characters embody human depth. Sutradhara reappears at the end of the play and consoles the audience that "conventions of Sanskrit drama require that play have a happy ending. So let's assume that this question led to many more and that finally Pooru found the question he was seeking. For we have it on the authority of the epics that Pooru ruled long and wisely and was hailed as a philosopher King" and bids "Namaskara" (70) to mark a formal end to the play. The tone and temperament of Sutadhara in the second appearance is that of an epilogue—that concludes the play and expresses gratitude to the audience.

Bhagavata in *Hayavadana* first sings verses in praise of Ganesha, and immediately thereafter he, like a Sutradhara, introduces the scene, setting, characters and the theme of the play to the audience. The play is formally structured into two acts—the first deals with the story of love, sacrifice and transposition and Act Two ponders on the question raised by transposition about human identity. Bhagavata is not merely an introducer and commentor in the play but a character who makes lively talks to rest of the characters and represents the reactions of the audience through his songs which are symbolic in meaning but connected with the theme of the play. First, like a Sutradhara of classical drama of India, he fulfils the obligations attached to him, i.e., introduction and commentation on the action, characters and events of the play:

> This is the city of Dharmpura, ruled by King Dharmasheela whose fame and empire have already reached the ends of the eight directions. Two youths who dwell in this city are our heroes. One is Devadatta. Comely in appearance, fair in colour, unrivalled in intelligence, Devadatta is the only son of the Revered Brahmin Vidyasagar. Having felled the mightiest pundits of the kingdom in debates on logic and love, having blinded the greatest poets of the world with his poetry and wit, Devadatta is as it were the apple of every eye in Dharampura.
>
> The other youth is Kapila. He is the only son of iron-smith, Lohita, who is to the King's armoury as an axle to the chariot-wheel. He is dark and plain to look at, yet in deeds which require drive and daring, in dancing, in strength and in physical skills he has no equal....[both are] One mind, one heart. (2)

Padmini is the daughter of the leading merchant in Dharampura. In her house, the very floor is swept by the Goddess of Wealth. In Devadatta's house, they've the Goddess of Learning for a maid "....Padmini became the better half of Devadatta and settled in his house. (19)

After transposition, an intricate development complicates the story due to identity of Devadatta and Kapila; hence relations are entangled that concerns the "future of these three unfortune beings..." (39). Bhagavata invites the audience for an answer. Act Two begins with Bhagavata who reminds the answer of King Vikram to demon Vetal whose answer was backed by Sacred Texts and endorsed by a *rishi* on logical ground. But Karnad through Bhagavata raises doubts on the validity of the solution in a real-life situation. The transposition creates a dilemma of "mad dance of incompleteness" (57) and Padmini is soon disillusioned with the "good mix" (56). Finally Bhagavata reports, off-stage development, Padmini's performance of *Sati*, Hayavadana transformed into a complete horse, the grandson of Vidyasagar's homecoming, and pays thanks to Ganesha for having ensured completion and success of the play.

The story in *Naga-Mandala* appears in the form of a woman dressed in a new colourful sari. This is very much identical to Sutradhara of Sanskrit theatre. In the very first act the Story introduces the female protagonist, Rani, whose life is the nucleus of the play and salient features of her personality:

> A youg girl. Her name...it doesn't matter. But she was an only daughter, so her parents called her Rani. Queen. Queen of the whole wide world. Queen of the long tresses. For when her hair was tied up in a knot, it was as though a black King Cobra lay curled on the nape of her neck, coil upon glistening coil. When it hung loose, the tresses flowed, a torrent of black, along her young limbs, and got entangled in her silver anklets. Her fond father found her a suitable husband. The young man was rich and his parents were both dead. Rani continued to live with her parents until she reached womanhood. Soon, her husband came and took her with him to his village. His name was ...Appanna. (27)

Rani's suffering and cruelty of her husband Appanna, an epitome of patriarchy in the orthodox society, her loneliness and frustration make her hysteric. The Cobra by the magical paste becomes crazy for Rani and a cobra "can assume", the Story narrates,"any form it likes" (38). The Cobra takes the shape of Appanna, and introduced as Naga that enters the house during the night through the bathroom drain makes love to Rani. In Act II, the Story reports the killing of the dog and mongoose, and the operation of the Cobra that is also wounded. For next fifteen days he doesn't visit Rani. Rani spends her nights "crying, wailing, and pining for him" (49). After Naga Ordeal Rani is raised to the status of a Goddess—"a Divine Being" (59) and her husband is instructed by the Elders to serve her. Once again the Story comments:

> So Rani got everything she wished for, a devoted husband, a happy life...life-long servant....For Appanna's concubine was present at the trial...she felt ashamed of her sinful life and volunteered to do menial work in Rani's house. In due course, Rani gave birth to a beautiful child. A son. Rani lived happily ever after with her husband, child and servant. (59)

The Story further elaborates the agony of Rani when she meets with her husband during night for the first time: "No two men make love alike. And that night of the Village Court, when her true husband climbed into bed with her, how could she fail to realize it was someone new?...Don't you think she must have cried out in anguish to know theanswer ?" (60). The Cobra is also haunted by the old memories, visits Rani and dies in her tresses. Rani's eyes are filled with tears as she picks up the dead snake and presses it to her cheeks. The Story disappears from the play. Rani, once again finds the Cobra and she allows it to live in her "hair...the symbol of ...weddd bliss. Live in there happily, for ever" (64). The last act proves her revolutionary, who symbolizes the quest for women's liberty and Karnad has worked it with the help of the folk-tale. The role of the Story is highly useful to develop the plot, and the characters and make-up limitations of the stage.

Yayati, Hayavadana and *Naga-Mandala* conform to the conventions of classical theatre. Apart from the use of Sutradhara, they have a happy ending, use of song, music, arouse different sentiments—*rasotpatti,* and the audience is amply entertained, instructed and enlightened.

In the modern theatre, the director is responsible for the actual production of a play, as opposed to earlier days when it was the producer, the author, an actor-manager, or a leading actor with whom the responsibilities of staging a drama were invested. The director produces the play in the way he envisages, how it ought to be seen as he interprets, what the playwright intended within the drama. He takes care of the effictiveness of the rehearsals of the actors, and coordinates the work of designers and technicians in the production. However, the playwright's work is still reflected in the director's *prompt copy*, a separate form of stage instructions worked out in detail by the director, in which each actor is given details as to what is happening onstage, where exactly he has to be in relation to the back, front, left, or right of the stage, and what he is to do at any one time during the play. The *stage manager* has to work with the director, and ascertain whether both the director's objectives, and the perceptions of the *stage designers* are compatible and realistic. *Stagecraft* overall has to address the various shortcomings of the stage's spatial and physical limitations. Karnad had used the following modern theatre techniques: use of prologue, epilogue, music, light and sound effect, miming, freezing, quick shift of scenes, use of spectacular, silence and pauses, use of supernatural, irony, humour, story-within-the-story, shape-shifting technique, flahforward and flashback etc to heighten the dramatic effects.

The use of Prologue in *Yayati* is akin to the modern theatre technique to introduce basic information about the play, theme, and dramatis personae, stage-setting; here the Epilogue has done it through the Sutradhara. There is a direct address, to the audience, thereafter the action develops through four acts. In *Naga-Mandala* the Prologue introduces a man who is sitting lonely in a ruined temple; moonlit night is there, he is anxious of his life and death; the first sentence he uses is: "I may be dead within the next few hours" (22). Thereafter he narrates that he was a playwright and was cursed to death for not writing play to entertin the audience properly. A mendicant advised, if he could keep awake one whole night, he would succeed in warding off the curse.

Flames join him. They are the symbolic representation of women's pitiable condition and they report the subjugation of their mistress. The Story in the form of a woman, dressed in a new saree, joins their company and agrees to narrate the story to please the audience. Thus whatever the Story narrates develops the plot of the play, characters and suggestions for women's emancipation. The Prologue in *The Fire and the Rain* similiarly introduces the main action of the play along with the characters—Paravasu, Arvasu, Nittilai, the King, the Actor-Manager of the play-within-the-play, supernatural element is also introduced in the Prologue—Brahma Rakshasa, a brahmin soul trapped in the limbo between death and rebirth, is moving around the sacrificial precincts and none can see him. The fire sacrifice is being held for the last seven years to please Indra, altar, oblations to fire, gathering of priests create a proper supportive background to the play and its plot. Fire sacrifice versus theatre is also highlighted. The Prologue prepares the ground for the mythic story of Yavakri and Epilogue presents a play-within-the-play on the myth of Vritri to propitiate Indra, the god of rains.

Music, light and sound effect technique have been effectively used by Karnad in *Yayati, Naga-Mandala, The Dreams of Tipu Sultan, The Fire and the Rain, Broken Images* and *Wedding Album*. *Yayati* begins with the slow lighting up of the stage, music with Hindustani Classical, *Khayal in Darabari Kannada* raga, in low pitch is heard from the background and it becomes louder with light that marks the day. A congenial atmosphere is created to introduce the Sutradhara who addresses the audience and provides important information about plot and its significance, characters and the mythical background of the play to prepare the audience to watch and enjoy the performance. When he concludes the speech, once again the stage becomes dark gradually. At the end of Act One the stage darkens and immediately in the next act the scene is changed; music is played outside the door to welecome Yayati, Pooru and Chitralekha (33) and finally, the stage once again darkens.

Act Four begins with "a few clay lamps burning; the room is therefore very dimly lit" (51). And "a thunderous eruption of the drums and conch shells" (54), mark the welcome of Pooru who agrees to take on his father's old age; with old age Pooru enters his room where Chitralekha is waiting for him. Again it is "dark" and "his face cannot be seen...bent double...voice is feeble and quivers with exhaustion" (56). Change of light and music not only suggests the change of scene but also makes the presentation aesthetically satisfying by creating atmosphere that suits the context.

Naga-Mandala is a remarkable play for the use of light, miming, freezing, music, and shape-shifting techniques. The

Prologue begins with the image of a dilapidated temple; it is night and "Moonlight seeps in through the cracks in the roof and the walls" (22). The play ends as "Sunlight pours in through the cracks in the temple roof" (65). The time of dramatic action is confined to a single night. Appanna leaves Rani when it is daytime and she is left alone for night, her "words become distinct as the lights dim" (27) on the stage. It is in the dark that the Cobra assumes human form identified as Naga who enters in her room and makes love; the Flames emerge on the stage. When Rani is declared a Divine Being, "Music fills the skies. The lights change into a soft luminous glow" (58). When Naga decides to withraw from the happy life of Rani and enters her room, "A beam of light on him. The rest is plunged into darkness. Long dark hair appear to descend and cover him. He covers himself and dances. Finally ties a tress into a noose and places it around his neck, the stage slowly becomes dark. Long silence" (62). On the death of the Cobra "music" is played out and Rani picks up the Cobra and presses to her cheeks; it gets "brighter" (63) and the Flames disappear. Appanna's taking bath is shown through miming.

About the staging of *The Dreams of Tipu Sultan*, Karnad has warned to

> Resist the temptation of using masks, special lighting or costumes for dream scenes. It is essential for the total impact of the play that the dreams are staged absolutely realiastically, and that the scenes follow each other in rapid succession. As this rapidity can best be achieved by shifts of location on stage and of lighting, exists and entrances of characters have not always been indicated in the text in the traditional fashion.
>
> ("Note" to *The Dreams of Tipu Sultan*)

The technique of flashback and flashforward is perfectly used to highlight the exploits of Tipu Sultan. Kirmani and Mackenzie, while discussing about writing the history of Tipu Sultan, focuses on his dreams he has recoreded in his diary. The play is divided into two acts. There is, R.B. Changule observes, "costant flux in between dream and reality. Though technically

Karnad has not divided the play into scenes there are various scenes in the play. The scenes shift from one place to other and from one time to another. The time moves from the present to the past and vice-vera" ("cyberliterature.net"). Through flashback he takes us to the night of the fourth of May 1799, "Ramparts of the Seringapatana fort. Midnight. There has been savage fighting and the ground is thick with the bodies of the dead and the dying. British soldiers are searching through the piles of bodies for Tipu's corpse" (9). The stage darkens, the scences in quick succession change. Tipu enters, accompanied by Poornaiya, and lively talks go on, "roar of tigers is heard in the background" (23). There is use of dark and light to bring quick shift of scenes in the play.

The Fire and the Rain is characteristic for the use of play-within–the–play, named *The Triumph of Lord Indra,* quite similar to *Murder of Gonzalo* in *Hamlet*. It is presented as a parallel contradiction to the fire sacrifice to bring rain. In the Epilogue, among "roar of drums" and "sudden silence" (166), the myth if Vritri is performed that has deeper connotations. Darkness is used to mark the end of an act as well as night.

Act Three begins with "Night" (149). Oblations to the fire is mimed, the image of Brahma Raksha compels all to "freeze" (169); Raibhya pulls out a "strand of hair from his head and throws it on the ground. The Brahma Rakshasa apeerears" (128). This is highly specutacular; at the end "lightning. Thunder" (176) bring rainfall.

Broken Images and *Wedding Album* use modern theatrical convention to a great extent. In contrast to Yakshagana and Natak Company using lantern and petromax, *Broken Images* uses "New technology" (261) i.e. "the interior of a television studio. A big plasma screen...several television sets... red bulbs...lapel mike...Elephantine lights, Headphones, Cameras...the yellow light" (261-262). The Announcer appears on the big plasma screen, a modern avatar of Sutradhara, and introduces the only character of the play, Manjula Nayak, and disappears. Thereafter she addresses the audience through television image. Her address is self-exploratory—how she became a bestseller writer in English and earned wide recognisation and money. When the address is over still the image of Manjula is there on the screen and "From now on, throughout the play, Manjul and her image react to each other exactly as though they were both live characters" (267). The image is Manjula's inner self and Karnad has explored her psycho-biography in an entirely new way on the stage. Finally, "all the screens start speaking loudly, some in Kannada, the others in English. The cacophony is deafening. The revolving stage moves out into the dark. Then one by one, the sets switch off, leaving the studio, dark and empty" (284).

Wedding Album was first produced by the Primetime Theatre Company at the Tata Auditorium, National Centre for the Performing Arts, Mumbai on 10 May, 2008, and it was directed by Lillete Dubey. The play is structured into nine scenes and "Scene One and Five take place about three years after the rest of the play" (5). The forward-backward movement technique is highly effective to develop the plot. The action of the play is confined to Nandkarni's living room, Software Production Office of Pratibha Khan, Internet Café and Restaurant. Modern technology and gadgets have been used to dramatise the most important issue of the play: marriage, a moment of celebration and anxiety. A detailed description of the stage setting by the playwright is similar to G.B. Shaw's technique. The story-within-the-story is another characteristic feature. Rohit and Praibha Khan are busy in making a story in video cassette for the twenty-first century young viewers.

Scene One starts with "a screen on which we see Vidula in close-up, speaking directly to the camera. She is extremely self-conscious and ill at ease" and introduces herself like Manjula Nayak of *Broken Images*: "I am Vidula. Vidula Nadkarni. I am twenty-two and a half, actually. I have done my BA in Geography. Passed my exams last year. I am not doing anything at the moment. Worked for a travel agency for six months" (5). Vidula's self-introduction is a modern version of Suradhara. Plenty of humour and satire have been used to expose the traditional Indian marriage culture. Camera, screen, SMS, Internet Café, video chatting, laptop, mobile phones, etc. have been frequently used to suit the subject and young cyber-generation. The play ends with the darkening of the stage.

The myths and legends used with, "imagination and creativity resulting in stageworthy plays is Girish Karnad. The technique of bringing together myth and legend to folk narrative style is the way in which he succeeds where many others have not. He creates a bridge between the elite and the folk which has proved to be his strength" (Ramaswamy 278). M.K. Naik has rightly judged the contribution of Karnad to drama: "...his technical experiment with an indigenous dramatic form...is a triumph which has opened up fresh lines of fruitful exploration for the Indian English Playwrights" (275). Khatri and Arora observe that Karnad's originality as a dramatist lies in his "extraordinary skill of using myth, history, and folktale to make the drama lively, thought provoking and gripping. In the wake of globalization where drama is gasping for breath, it is the dramatic genius of Karnad who has provided it not only oxygen for its life but also energized it by Indianising it for further maturation" ("Preface" v-vi). Asked about the lasting legacy of Karnad, he replied embarrassingly: "I see a legacy of my generation. I am happy to belong to a generation that had a Dharamveer Bharati, a Mohan Rakesh, a Vijay Tendulker and I. Together we can claim that we did create a national theatre for modern India" (Kalidas and Merchant 2). A.K. Sinha explores identical dramatic techniques in Karand and Brecht. Like Brecht, Karnad strives to:

> Break the "illusion" of the theatre by which the spectators become so engrossed in a play that they forget, for the time being what they are. Therefore, like Brecht, Karnad leaves the stage apparatus visible, presents synoptic announcements, has narrators directly talking to the audience. All this compels the audience to respond intellectually to the action of the play and to question it instead of responding emotionally and merely accepting it. (55)

Karnad endeavours to explore theatrical vision, form and language which can embody the consciousness of Indian masses, deeply rooted in Indian cultural heritage. The fusion of content and form governed by the strong sense of Indianness and Indian imagination is highly entertaining and aesthetically gratifying. The consistency with "our rich cultural heritage" (Jain 82) and indigeneous folk conventions make him a de-colonizer of Indian English drama.

Works Cited

Aristotle. *Poetics.* Translated by Butcher, S.C. New Delhi/Ludhiana: Kalyani Publishers, 1998.

Bhatt, S.K. "Indo-Anglian Drama: A Critical Study" <yabaluri.org/TRIVENI/CDWEB> 12.02.2011.

Changule, R.B. "Girish Karnad's *The Dreams of Tipu Sultan*: A Critical Introduction" <englishcyberliterature.net> 18.01.2011.

"Development of Theatre in India" <*www.Indianetzone.com*> 12.02.2011.

Ellis-Fermor, Una. *The Frontiers of Drama.* (Second Edition) New Fetter Lane: Meuthen & Co. Ltd. 1964.

Goel, Savita. "Folk Theatre Strategies in *Hayavadana*" *The Plays of Girish Karnad.* New Delhi: Prestige, 2009.

Jain, Nemichandra. *Indian Theatre.* New Delhi: Vikas Publishing House Pvt. Ltd., 1992.

Kale, M.R. "Introduction: The Sanskrit Drama" *The Abhjnasakuntalam of Kalidas.* Delhi: Motilal Banarsidas Publishers, 2005.

Kalidas, S and Merchant, Rehmat. "Renaissance Man" <india-today.com/itoday/.../arts.html> 20.08.2010.

Karnad, Girish. "Author's Introduction" *Three Plays: Naga-Mandala, Hayavadana, Tughlaq.* (Eighth Impression) New Delhi: Oxford University Press, 2002.

______. *Yayati.* New Delhi: Oxford University Press, 2008.

______. Tughlaq. (Fourteenth Impression) Chennai: Oxford University Press, 1998.

______. *Hayavadana.* (Fourteenth Impression) Chennai: Oxford Univerity Press, 1998.

______. *Naga-Mandala. Three Plays: Naga-Mandala, Hayavadana, Tughlaq.* (Eighth Impression) New Delhi: Oxford University Press, 2002.

______. *The Fire and the Rain* in *Collected Plays.*Volume Two. (Ed.) Dharwadker, Aparna Bhargava. New Delhi: Oxford University Press, 2005. References are from this edition.

______. *Broken Images* in *Collected Plays.* Volume Two. (Ed.) Dharwadker, Aparna Bhargava. New Delhi: Oxford University Press, 2005.

______. *Wedding Album.* New Delhi: Oxford Uiversity Press, 2009.

Khatri, C.L. and Arora, Sudhir K. (Eds) *Thunder on Stage: A Study of Girish Karnad's Plays.* Jaipur: Book Enclave, 2008.

Kurtkoti, Kirtinath. "Introduction" *Hayavadana.* (Fourteenth Impression) Chennai: Oxford University Press, 1998.

Mukherjee, Tutun. Interview with Kanrand "In His Own Voice: A Conversation with Girish Karnad" (Ed) *Girish Karnad's Plays: Performance and Critical Perspectives.* Delhi: Pencraft International, 2006.

Naik, M.K. *A History of Indian English Literature.* New Delhi: Sahitya Akademi, 2009.

Pickering, Kenneth. *Studying Modern Drama.* (Second Edition) New York: Palgrave Macmillan, 2003.

Ramaswamy, S. "Indian Drama in English: A Tentative Reflection" *Makers of Indian English Literature.* (Ed) Narasimhaih, C.D., Delhi: Pencraft International, 2000.

Sinha, A.K. "Thematic Concerns and Technical Features in Girish Karnad's Plays" *The Plays of Girish Karnad.* (Ed) Dodiya, J. New Delhi: Prestige, 2009.

Tilak, Raghukul. *Tughlaq: A Critical Study.* (Third Edition) New Delhi: Rama Brothers, 1998.

Tripathi, Vanashree. Three Plays of Girish Karnad: A Study in Poetics and Culture. New Delhi: Prestige, 2004.

Wadikar, Shailaja B. "Background of Indian Theatre" *Flowering of Indian Drama: Growth and Development.* (Ed) Reddy, Venakata K. & Dhawan, R.K. New Delhi: Prestige, 2004.

Whitfield, George. *An Introduction to Drama.* Oxford: Oxford University Press, n.d.

10

Language

Language in Karnad is a social tool, and it is simultaneously shaped by socio-cultural factors. The plays of Karnad adhere to Indianized version of standard English defying the notion of superiority of King's English, freely indulges and incorporates the popular Indian slangs, dialectic words,words from various Indian languages, metaphors, symbols, irony, imagery, idioms and pharases, specific sentence structures which are pregnant with Indianness. Karnad is a master of rich vocabulary. Though, for him, English was a language of adulthood, not his mother tongue, he has perfectly used English to discuss certain important socio-cultural and political issues of the contemporary India through his plays. He never hesitates or feels an inferiority complex to use English in the Indianized twist. English, in his hand, has become a tool to make people conscious of the evils which have beset our whole society.

His translation or transcreation of his earlier plays as well as the plays, i.e., *The Dreams of Tipu Sultan, Two Monologues: Flowers, Broken Images* and *Wedding Album* of the later phase of his dramatic career show marked distinction and accomplishment in linguistic expression. We notice the evolution of themes, techniques and language in his plays. He chooses apt and suitable words from a rich treasury of vocabulary. His words are suggestive and reveal both character and situation. He writes dialogues in lucid, pointed and precise language which possess decency and decorum. His plays are in prose, the use of poetic rendering is not excepted. Either he or Prof. A.K. Ramanujanhas translated original Kannada verses into English.

Karnad's characters use language which suit their status and temperament. Frequent use of Indian vocabulary, idioms and phrases, symbols, images, metaphors and irony facitilate to create an Indian atmosphere and lend his style the charm of familiarity. Grace in his style is hardly sacrificed for social cause or idea. His style is, however, straightforward and idiomatic. There is a typical Indianness about his style in his plays. His style is not loose but periodic—a complete whole or a part of a bigger whole. It has specific form that cannot be easily tempered.

Aristotle has laid down two essentials of good writing: "clearness and propriety" (46). Clarity or intelligibility and propeiety or suitability are necessary to convey the writer's menaing to the audience; and these can be attained by the use of current words. Unfamiliar words—archaic words, foreign words, dialect words, newly-coined words, metaphors and all kinds of words—are used in a judicious combination to make the work a dignified composition. Karnad has dexterously handled all these rhetorical techniques. Karnad makes use of traditional as well as personal symbols which are employed to highlight his concern for the psychological problems of the protagonists and their revolutionary outlook towards old values.

Karnad's plays from *Yayati* to *Wedding Album* present a variety of themes, characters, techniques and situations which require a specific language to suit the context. For instance, *Yayati* draws its plot from the myth of *Mahabharata*, characters, situations, atmosphere, and socio-cultural practices. Different status of characters cannot be presented in a natural way without the congenial vocabulary, structure of sentences, idioms and phrases, symbols and metaphorical representation of certain aspects of life, compound words, poetic expression to yield charm and beauty to the dialogues suiting the personality and status of the speaker. Above all the air of ancient mythical culture would flow due to the corresponding language. Even the names of the characters of the play immediately takes us to the nostalgic cultural past of India—Yayati, Pooru, Devayani, Chitralekha, Sharmishtha. In the Prologue of the play Sutradhara, like Greek Chorus, introduces the content and characters of the play in a very lucid and pointed language and lets the audience know the backdrop of the play. King Yayati,

Prince Pooru and his wife Chitralekha, the Princess of Anga, Queen Devayani, Sharmishtha, the slave to Queen, and Swarnalata speak a language that suits their temperament and character. For instance, Swarnalata reacts against Sharmishtha who has bewitched King Yayati, and talks to Devayani: "That spiteful whore—I would have torn her hair out if you hadn't stopped me. Taught that fiend a proper lesson. A proper lesson. The rakshasi. You heard us, madam…She didn't even spare His Majesty. I…I can't bear it" (7). Even Devayani's condemnation is very sharp and penetrating, "Bitch, I'll kill you. I'll feed you to the…" (13). It's ironical that due to moral transgression Yayati is cursed with old age. He is planning to exchange it with his own son Pooru so as to indulge in filthy sexual gratification knowing the way of immunity: "—the curse will not have its effect on you if a young man agrees to take it upon himself and offers his youth to you in exchange" (44). The protest of Chitralekha is well founded and it imbibes its force and meaning from a very stunning and aggressive language:

> CHITRALEKHA (*Flaring up*): I did not push him to the edge of the pyre, Sir. You did. You hold forth of my wifely duties. What about your duty to your son? Did you think twice before foisting your troubles on a pliant son?
>
> YAYATI (*shouts*): Chitra! Take care…
>
> CHITRALEKHA: Sir! This is my chamber. Only my husband has the right to come in here without my permission. Or to shout out my name when he pleases. I am not aware I have allowed anyone else that freedom.
>
> YAYATI: I apologize…
>
> CHITRLEKHA: Yes, I was keen to become your daughter-in-law. But so were you to accept me as one. Even apart from my family, because of my accomplishments, because of what I am. And now you want me to meekly yield to your demand? (62)

Yayati, Pooru, Chitralekha, Devayani and Sharmishtha all are symbolical representation of lust, obedience, woman's protest, and jealousy. The metaphors used to denote certain peculiar traits of Sharmishtha are: "treacherous hyena" (27), "Satanic" (8), "spiteful whore" (1), "Bitch" (13), "reptile" (30), and "fiend"

(7). Gentleness of Pooru "like a waft of cool breeze"; Rakshasi, guru, Arya, Aryavarta, arti, namaskara, Devi etc. They lend indigenous pulse to the story.

Tughlaq draws its story from Indian history—the reign of Mohammad-Bin-Tughlaq which was remarkable for two reasons: numbers of experiments Tughlaq carried out and his character. Karnad remains close to the original and gives philosophical dimension to the play and psychological depth to the character of Tughlaq—a tortured soul. Apart from structural design, art of characterization, mental and emotional reactions, Natak Company conventions, which the playwright has employed skilfully in the play, language with its various properties has been used to suit the historical context, controversial figure, dialogues, conspiracy, anger, frustration and polarities among characters. Use of Arabic, Persian, Urdu, dialectic words, idioms and phrases, symbols, irony, metaphors, criyptic, sketchy as well as long sonorous poetic sentences have been used to create congenial atmosphere and proper meaning to make the presentation highly awarding. The Announcer has been used as a Greek Chorus that goes on providing basic information hence his language is clear, straightforwad, highly informative and arresting:

> ANNOUNCER: Attention! Attention! The
> Merciful Sultan Muhammad has declared—
> that within the next month every citizen
> of Delhi must leave for Daultabad.
> No one should remain behind in Delhi.
> Anyone who attempts to stay behind or
> To go elsewhere will be severely punished.
> All arrangements have been made to
> Ensure the comfort of citizens on the
> way to Daultbad. All the needs of
> the citizens, regarding food, clothing or
> medicine, will be catered to by the State.
> It is hoped that every citizen will use these

Amenities to the full and be in Daultabad
As soon as possible. Attention! Attention! (46)

The very first line of the play: "God, what's this country coming to!" (1) conveys the anguish of an Old Man of Delhi Sultnate who is generic. Tughlaq has been introduced in a traditional fashion, the language full of adjectives, conceits and pomp: "Attention! Attention! The warrior in the path of God, the Defender of the Word of the Prophet, the friend of the Khalif, the Just, His Merciful Majesty, Sultan Muhammad Tughlaq" (3). At the onset, Tughlaq unlocks his plan of shifting his capital from Delhi to Daultabad. His speech is full of humility, the sentence structure is periodic, the lines are run-on and continuity is maintained artistically:

MUHAMMAD: My empire is large now and embraces the South and
I need a capital which is at its heart. Delhi is too near
the border and as you well know its peace is never
free from the fear of invaders. But for me the most
important factor is that Daultabad is a city of the
Hindus and as the capital it will symbolize the bond
between Muslims and Hindus which I wish to develop
and strengthen in my kingdom. I invite you all to
accompany me to Daultabad. This is only an
invitation and not an order. Only those who have
faith in me may come with me. With their help I
shall build an empire which will be the envy of the
world. (3-4)

In the later scenes when Tughlaq is disillusioned and frustrated his language expresses his tortured soul:

MUHAMMAD: God, God in Heaven, please help me.
Please don't let go of my hand. My skin drips with blood
and I don't know how much of it is mine and how
much of others. I started in Your path, Lord,

> why am I wandering nakd in this desert now?
> I started in search of you. Why am I become a
> pig rolling in this gory mud? Raise me, clean me.
> Cover me with Your Infinite Mercy. I can only
> Clutch at the hem of your cloak with my bloody
> Fingures and plead. I can only beg—have pity on me.
> I have no one but You now. Only You. Only
> You...You...You...You...(67)

Karnad has succeeded in creating a proper Indian atmosphere in the play, i.e., fourteenth century India when Tughlaq reigned by the use of words and idioms and phrases from different sources. Sultan, Jiziya, Kaji-i-Mumalik, dhobi, dar-ul-Islam, Darbar-i-Khas, Allah, Sukrat, Koran, Mussulman, hakim, Kafir, Khalif, Maulvis, Islam and the Muezzin's call for prayer have been wisely given in Arabic: "Alla-Ho-Akbar! Alla-Ho-Akbar...La Elaha Illilah" (41 & 86). Idioms and phrases used in *Tughlaq*: light up our path, went wild, hold your tongue, the end of my tether, to breathe life into, play the game, torn into pieces, backbone of rebels, an incompetent fool, get rid of, an honest scoundrel, crush into dust, get to ooze out spittle, mug's game, etc. "roads lined with skeletons" (70) are an imagery that create an unpleasant and dismal experience. OLD MAN's speech: "I survived. But my family was more fortunate. They all died on the way" (52) and FIRST MAN's reaction: "We starve and they want us to pray. They want to save ours souls" (70) are finest instances of irony and satire.

Symbols in the play enlarge the expressive range of the language due to emotional and associative significance attached to it. The whole play is a symbol of the political situation of India of the sixties that, "...reflects as no other play perhaps does the political mood of disillusionment which followed the Nehru era of idealism in the country:" (Murthy "Introduction" vii-viii). This mood is revealed even in the very first line of the play: "God, what's this country coming to!" (1). Aziz and Aazam symbolize opportunistic and unprincipled people who exploit the liberal ideals and welfare schemes of the government meant for the poor. Chess symbol has a unique significance as it runs through the play. The chess suggests the intrigue in Tughlaq's nature. A skilled chess player, he uses his political opponents as pawn on the chessboard of politics. The Python in Scene Eight symbolizes Tughlaq's barbarity and inhumanity. It is a symbolic of the complete degeneration of his personality from a human being to a wild beast, a huge snake. Daulatabad is a symbol of Hindu-Muslim unity which Tughlaq wants to foster. The vulture and other birds of prey that thrust their beaks into the flesh of Muhammad, so that he knows no peace either by day or night, are also symbolic. They symbolize the frustration of an idealist and visionary, and his spiritual agony. The prayer symbol which has been used as a leitmotif (theme associated with a person or a thought) is highly significant. The Muslim chieftains along with Sheikh Sham-ud-din, a pacifist priest, conspire to murder Tughlaq at prayer time. The use of prayer for murder is reminiscent of what Tughlaq adopted to kill his father. The prayer is symbolic of the fact that his life is corrupted at its very source. Rattan Singh also tries to exploit prayer to murder Tughlaq. Tughlaq is a fanatic about prayer, and when disillusioned about the futility of prayer he prohibits it in his kingdom. The word 'prayer' has been used in an ironical way in the play. It is introduced after an interval of five years. Tughlaq falls into a sound sleep and gets up when the Muezzin's call to prayer fades away; so he fails to offer prayer. The prayer symbol is the very basis of the play.

Hayavadana is based on Thomas Mann's mock-heroic novel *The Transposed Heads*. It rooted in Somedeva's *Katha Saritasagara*, an ancient collection of stories in Sanskrit. It is full of myths, allusions, references, archetypal beliefs, identifiable characters, narrative design and plot rooted in Indian soil. Karnad, in the play, deals with the identity crisis—the mad dance of incompleteness—illustrated through Devadatta, Kapila and Padmini triangle, and a sub-plot in which Hayavadana figures. Bhagavata, Kapila, Padimini, Hayavadana, Ganesha, Kali, Rudra, Indra, Ridhi, Sidhi, Yakshagana, Gandharva, King Vikram, demon Vetal, Vatsyayan, Shakuntala, Uravashi, Yakshini, Indumati, Mt. Chitrakoot, Ujjain, Kashi, Pavan Veethi, Kathakali, pooja, pativrata, punyasthala, arti, dhoti, "*Jhanda Ooncha Rahe Hamara*" (64), "*Sare Jahan se Acchha Hindostan Hamara*" (64), "two pieces of heart" (28), "dog's eye" (31), "apple of every eye" (92), Kapila and Devadatta "Like cocks in a pit" (61) etc. contribute to the richness of language, and develop a distinct sort of the world, different from us—world of incomplete individuals, indifferent gods, dolls that speak and children who cannot, a world indifferent to the desires and frustrations, joys and sorrows of human beings. The image of Ganesha, Kali, Rudra, river and scarecrow, horse rider, Hayavadana extend something deeper associated with theme and characters of the play. Doll I, II, III symbolize the mental dilemma and reactions of Padmini. Like the Sutradhara of *Yayati* and the Announcer of *Tughlaq*, the Story of *Naga-Mandala*, Bhagavata in *Hayavadana* goes on supplying background information and comments on the development of the story. The use of verse and use of prose that is balanced, uniform, precise and pointed, suits the context. The invocation to Ganesha in the opening of Act One is worth quoting:

> O Elephant-headed Herambha
> whose flag is victory,
> and who shines like a thousand suns,
> O husband of Ridhi and Sidhi,
> Seated on a mouse and decorated with a snake.
> O single-tusked destroyer of incompleteness,
> We pay homage to you and start our play. (1)

Therafter Bhagavata introduces the scene and characters of the play in a very lucid and straightforward manner:

> This is the city of Dharampura, ruled by King Dharamsheela...Two youths who dwell in this city are our heroes. One is Devadatta. Comely in appearance, fair in colour, unrivalled in intelligence...Having felled the mightiest pundits of the kingdom in debates on logic and love, having blinded the greatest poes of the world with his poetry and wit, Devadatta is as it were the apple of every eye in Dharampura.

> The other youth is Kapila. He is the only son of iron-smith Lohita...He is dark and plain to look at, yet in deeds which requires drive and daring, in dancing, in strength and in physical skills he has no equal.
>
> [*sings*] Two friends there were
>
> —one mind, one heart—(1-2).

Two friends ironically develop into deadly enemies due to an entangled relationship after transposition, and kill each other. Whenever Karnad has to emphasize anything, he creates space with dashes between the words: "KAPILA: I mean—who—is—it—this—time?" (12). The fear of the Actor has been expressed in a very natural way by the use of broken, criptic and incomplete structure of sentences: "ACTOR: Sir...oh my God!—God!—/ I—I—I—Oh God!" (2). After transposition Devadatta, Kapila and Padmini make a circle and sing a song. Though simple in diction and clear in expression it carries a deeper psychological dilemma they all are facing:

> ALL THREE [*together*].
>
> What a good mix!
>
> No more tricks!
>
> Is this one that
>
> or that one this?
>
> Ho! Ho! (35)

In nature and landscape description Karnad is purely Wordsworthian; he goes beyond physical charm and fascination, and suggests the inner conflict that runs parallel. His language is simple and highly poetic with a touch of emotion:

> the street, and rows of flames of the forest salute it with torches. Then the night comes, a...Long before the sun rises, the shadows of twigs draw *alpanas* on the floor. The stars raise *arti* and go. Then the day dawns and the fun begins. The circus in the tree-tops and the cock-fights in the shower of feathers. And the dances! The tiger-dance, and the peacock-dance, and the dance of the sun's little feet with silver anklets on the river. In the heart of the forest stands the stately chariot of the shield-bearer. It is made of pure

> gold—rows of birds pull it down and our poor baby is tired—so we blow gently and out goes the moon. (52-53)

The image of Ganesha symbolizes perfection and victory, Kali—power; and river and scarecrows in the chorus song, the mental crisis of Padmini, Hayavadana stand for incompleteness, Devadatta's Apollonian tendency and Kaplia's Dionysian tendency, Padmini symbolizing erotic urge, horse energy, and Doll I, II, III symbolizing Padmini's psychic reactions and reverie.

Naga-Mandala which is a richly textured dramatic transmutation of two folk-tales of Karnataka deals with gender-bias, subalternization of women and prospect for their emergence in orthodox Indian society in which patriarchy dominates all the domains of life, i.e., religion, culture, social conventions, beliefs, man-woman relationship. Plot, character and thought have been developed due to dignified composition—consummate excellence in language. Kusbi oil, Ayyo, but'ting, ogress, demon, Naga, Cobra, Yaksha woman, Flames, Indianized similes and metaphors, i.e., "juicy as a tender cucumber" (24), "wife locked up like a caged bird" (30), "Ears like hibiscus. Skin like young mango leaves. Lips like rolls of silk" (32), "change like a chameleon" (51), "spreads hood like an umbrella" (58), and tensferred epithet—"tender bud like you"; and the image of Cobra (58), haunted well (48), Flames floating in the air (23), ruined temple (Prologue) and symbols extend innovativeness and novelty in expression: Ruined temple (dilapidated temple also figures in *Bali: The Sacrifice*) symbolizes seclusion and desperation, Flames represent the socio-psycholgical condition of woman, Naga as a romantic lover or poetic imagination, Rani stands for woman's status, role and emergence, Appanna male-chauvinism, Kappanna filial obligation, Kurudavva's motherly love and worldly wisdom, Village Elders' patriarchy, Dog, Mongoose tools of subjection of women and Rani's tresses—wedded bliss. The introduction of Rani, the protagonist, is very graphic, informative and complete:

> A youg girl...an only daughter, so her parents called her Rani. Queen. Queen of the whole wide world. Queen of the

> long tresses. For when her hair was tied up in a knot, it was as though a black King Cobra lay curled on the nape of her neck, coil upon glistening coil. When it hung loose, the tresses flowed, a torrent of black, along her young limbs, and got entangled in her silver anklets. Her fond father found her a suitable husband. The young man was rich and his parents were both dead. Rani continued to live with her parents until she reached womanhood. Soon, her husband came and took her with him to his village. (27)

Rani is surrounded by the hostile social milieu, and her husband is the cruelest among all the tools of her subjection. She is imprisioned like a caged bird; locked from the outside restricting her meeting with anybody. She is haunted by alienation, develops insomnia, restlessness and hallucination. Karnad has expressed it pointedly:

> RANI: I am so frightened at night. I can't sleep a wink. At home, I sleep between Father and Mother. But here, alone—Kurudavva, can you help me, please? Will you please send word to my parents that I am, like this, here? Will you ask them to free me and take me home? I would jump into a well—if only I could. (32)

The evolution in Rani is noticeable, and Karnad dexterously corelates language with the character. The protest and latent frustration is let loose emphatically to convey it to the audience: "I was astupid, ignorant girl when you brought me here. But now I am a woman, a wife, and I am going to be a mother. I am not a parrot. Not a cat or a sparrow. Why don't you take it on trust that I have a mind and explain this charade to me? Why do you play these games? Why do you change like a chameleon from day to night?" (51). Appanna's anger over Rani's infidelity is expressed by sharp and piercing abuses: "harlot" (52), "slut" (52), and "whore" (53). The imagery of the Cobra is highly thrilling and awesome during the ordeal: "the Cobra slides up her shoulder and spreads its hood like an umbrella over her head. The crowd gasps. The Cobra sways its hood gently for a while, then becomes docile and moves over her shoulder like a garland" (58). Naga's jealousy and sense of loss haunts it with reminiscences that morbidity is poetically drafted by the playwright, "Rani! My queen! The fragrance of my nights! The blossom of my dreams! In another man's arms? In another man's bed? Does she curl around him as passionately every night now? And dig her nails into his back? Bite his lips? ...if I bury my teeth into her breast now, she will be mine—mine forever" (61). It is irony of the whole society that Rani, who indulges in cuckoldry unknowingly, is ready to test her chastity. No one except blind Kurudavva is there to see the libertine, licentious and profiligate nature of Appanna. M.K. Naik has rightly commented: "The play moves at a brisk pace, and the dialogue, which is in clear, simple every day English without any conscious straining after 'Indian-ness', suits the rustic folk-tale it presents as a surface structure, without causing harm to the deep structure of the symbolism beneath" (46).

Tale-Danda is a history play that deals with the problem of caste which has poisoned the Indian life and its institutions. The medieval history of Karnataka, its socio-political milieu, characters rooted in the medieval past of South India, conflict between traditional sanatana dharma and *Lingayat* faith, ideals of new faith—static versus progressive, royal priests, deserve a kind of language that can be a natural vechicle of conveying the vision and thoughts of the playwright and suit the characters and their personalities. Religious fanaticism and its consequences occupy the central position in the play; the character of Basavanna posed a threat to religious fanaticism and the result is awesome. The words and expression of various stocks enrich the text and correspond to the issues, deeds, actions and reactions of the characters: King Bijjala, Sambashiva Shastri, Savitri, Jagadeva, Mallibomma, Sovideva, Damodara Bhatta, Manchanna, Kallaya, Kakkaya, Gangambika, Haralayya, Sheelavanta, Madhuvarasa, Kalavati, Kalyan, "jungle of Uluvi" (90), Ayyo, "*Thoo! Thoo! Thoo!*" (81), "laughing stock" (83), "heap of shit" (83), "ocean of saffron" (74), *Sharanas,* Shiva, Jain, "Om namah Shivaya" (31), untouchables, Nandi, Bhakti, Varna, guru, bhakatas, Darshan, tribals, low-caste, Vedic dharma, *linga,* aryavarta, *Lingayat,* Lord of meeting rivers, Kappadi, "Yuvaraja Kalanjara-Puradhishwara Suvarna-Vrishabha-dhwaja

Someshawara Rajendra Bho parak! Bho parak" (57-58). Even the full-length expression in Sanskrit takes us to the twelfth century Karnataka dominated by Hindu rituals, and marks an instance of Indian imagination:

> Maharaja Kalanjara-puradhishwara Go-Bramana-Pratipalaka Varnasharma-dharma-Rakshaka Dusta-shasana Suvarna-Vrshabhadhwaja Damaru-turyanigro shana Kalchuryavamsha-Kamala-Bhaskara Triambaka-pada-padamamadhupa Parama-maheswara Pratapa-lankeshawara Giridurga-malla Ripu-kari-sandoha-simha Nisshanka-malla Bhujabalachakravarti Someshvara-Rajendra Bho parak—Bho parak. (91)

"Human Body" (29) has been presented as a symbol of holy temple which facilitates our spiritual advancement and well-being of the whole society. "Fire" (91) stands for anger—the anger of Sovideva and the entire Satanatana Dharmi against Basavanna and the forces of change. Killing of Bijjala in the sanctum symbolizes the degeneration of human values similar to the prayer in *Tughlaq*. Mariappa sitting on the shoulders of King Bijjala symbolizes a harmony between low and high castes. Basavanna represents revolution for change, progressive ideas and establishment of egalitarian society. Damodara Bhatt, Manchanna and Sambashiva Shastri stand for traditional values of Hindu religion. Jagadeva and Sovideva symbolize players in power politics. *Linga* (power and generation) and Kappadi (a meeting place of rivers) symbolize peace and spiritual introspection. The similes and metaphors used in the play heighten Indianness: "a woman is just a ripe mango on a roadside tree" (42), "Brahmin like a jackal" (56), "snake" (62)—a metaphor of Sovideva who traps his own father King Bijjala, "city is dead—like a cemetery" (82); the inter-caste marriage of Sheelavanta and Kalavati—"cursed wedding" (48), "absurd wedding" (49), "unnatural alliance" (55) etc. The fear after a violent reaction from brahmins led by Sivideva is exquisitely presented: "GUNDANNA: *Ayyo...Ayyao*...Kala! Malli! I can't bear it. I can't...Mother!" (81). The disgusting and frightening scene has been given melodramatic presentation that makes performance live and very natural:

> GUNDANNA: It's harrowing! A while ago—the King's soldiers arrested Haralaya and took him to the city square. They also brought Madhuvarsa there—And then—as the city watched—they plucked their eyes out—
>
> A reaction of horror from those present
>
> Plucked out their eyes with iron rods—bound them hand and foot and had them dragged through the streets—tied to elephants' legs—*Ayyo*! How can I tell you? Torn limbs along the lanes, torn entrails, flesh, bones—they died screaming! (81)

Uses of capitals, space, italics and dash between the words have been the technique Karnad has used to emphasize the meaning or make the expression forceful throught his plays, here too.

The Fire and the Rain with its solid thematic richness has proved a great success. It draws the story from the myth of Yavakri who figures in the *Mahabharata.* Karnad gives modern meaning to the myth which stresses on the dangers of knowledge without wisdom and power without integrity. Fire sacrifice, origin of drama, and the history of theatre in India, penance, oblation, kriya, Brahma, Lord of All Creations, Vedas, Fifth Veda, Bharata, Hymns, Indra, God of Rain and Sky, demon Vritra, Vishwarupa, Paravasu, Aravasu, Yavakri, Vishakha, Nitillai, Raibhya, Andhak, Braham Rakshasa, adhvaryu, brahmin soul, famine, drought, sudra, outcaste, gurus, mantras, kamandalu, nether world, champak tree, "jack fruit grove" (121), "wheel of Time" (173), "Hell-hole" (176), dhoti, "dogs sniffing around my daughter-in-law's bottom" (138), council of Elders (tribal), "tamarind hill" (143), tribal customs, Vedic practices, Yavakri's rigorous penance for ten years etc. fill life in dry-bones of the age-old myth and vindicate Karnad's interest to revitalize Indian imagination.

The language used in the play has various levels. "Sick of silence" refers to Vishakha's sen se of alienation similar to Rani of *Naga-Mandala*; Yavakri's penance is described in such a way a complete picture is drawn and we are transported to a world of romance, magic and supra-mundane: "Ten years of rigorous penance. And still Lord Indra would not oblige. Finally, Yavakri stood in the middle of a circle of fire and started offering his limbs to the fire—first his fingers, then his eyes, then his entrails, his tongue, and at last, his heart—that's when the god appeared to him. Restored his limbs, and granted him the boon" (115). Simple and stately diction is noticeable in the play. Use of similes and metaphors make the expression more lively and meaningful: "dry like tinder" (103), "dying like a sacrificial animal" (172), "like a bandicoot" (131), "drying up like a dead tree" (142), "a soul locked in nothingness like a foetus stitched up inside its mother's sac" (146), "let's be together like brother and sister" (153), "bodies drenched in blood like rats that pur out during the plague" (154), "like an eunuch" (155), "dance like a celestial being" (161-62), "wave of blood breaking out of the sacrificial enclosure like a flock of fear-crazed jungle fowl" (170); "bitch of yours " (138) refers to Vishakha and "trees loaded with fruits" (121) and "savage" (126) metaphorically represent Vishakha and Nittilai tribal society condemned by brahmins. The words 'bitch' and 'whore' symbolize condemnation of the fair sex by malechauvinists. The 'fire' symbolizes lust, anger, vengeance, envy, treachery, violence and death. The 'rain' symbolizes self-sacrifice, compassion, Divine Grace, forgiveness, revival and life. The image of Brahma Rakshasa (128), Raibhya in meditation (128), big banayan tree (110) and Nittilai's killing (172) are marvellously employed to create a cathartic effect.

Bali: The Sacrifice deals with the instinct of violence and morality of substitution. Inspired by Sanskrit and Kannada epics Karnad delves deep into the problem and treats it in a dramatic manner to expose the ways of violence and hypocrisy involved in it. At the centre it's Bali, i.e., the sacrifice of animals for material gains. The Queen and Mother represent two opposite standpoints whereas the King is in between these two. The Mahout symbolizes the subalternity of the lower class. The instinct of violence, character development and dialogue has been given artistic expression by the use of verse as well as prose that suit the above.

Brilliant use of select words, phrases, similes and metaphors add beauty and power to the play: Bali, Savior, Jain, pallu, dhoti, Mahout, "black and blue" (76), "bazzar woman" (78), namaskara, "World is divided into two orbs...so also the human soul" (74), "ugly as a bandicoot" (75), "ruby lips" (77), "shunned and starved like outcastes" (98), "naked like Saviors" (120), "rainy nights" (125), "Death yields to life like monsoons piled on monsoons so the life follows" (125). The abusing terms like 'harlot' and 'whore' have been used to denote the subalternity of the fair sex.

The imagery supports the meaning and creates a proper background to the context: "inner sanctum of a ruined temple" (73) which also figures in *Naga-Mandala* and *Hayavadana* stands for a haunted place, seclusion and lifelessness, "four armed deity" (74), "replica of cock" (118) etc. The Mahout symbolizes "low-born" (80) and its subalternity, protest and masculinity. Mother Queen has been used as a symbol of traditional practices prevalent in orthodox Hindu society, especially concerned with animal sacrifice. The Queen is quite antithetical to her and symbolizes Jain beliefs. The cock symbolizes hypocrisy involved in rituals.

Certain expressions deserve close scrutiny to endorse Karnad's skill of craftsmanship in language: Night has got a poetic expression, "Nice. The mist's cleared. Nice breeze. It's a beautiful night. Full moon. You can see very leaf in the tree. It's such a bright night; you won't know when it dawns. It'll flow from one into the other, seamlessly" (76). The erotic experience nowhere got such power of words: "Good. Oh God, you are good! uh...uh...uh....You're like no one I know....Oh! you are good—good..." (85). The old belief is treated in the following words: "My maid says that if a boy pees on a bush and then if a girl smells the flowers from that bush, that's how babies are made" (91). The Mahout is ugly because he was born on "full moon. There was an eclipse. As you know, the worst thing you can do to yourself is to be born during an eclipse. The sun or the moon—the god whose eclipse it is—is already in the grips of the demons" (80). The protest of the Queen is remarkable. The language used is quite potent to convey the cinder latent in her mind: "I'll not agree to the sacrifice. I'll never" (114). The acknowledgement of the Mahout's love, the Queen's frankness and courage is expressed in a sponateneous manner: "I do not regret anything that has happened. I will not disown him or anything he gave me....Because it just happened. Without my willing it. It just happened. That's all....And what happened was beautiful" (118-119). The use of verse is highly contextual and throws light on the action of the play. The language used is simple and stately:

> SINGER: Memories slide,
> meld and fuse.
> Discrete moments
> get flung together
> strung in a single moment.
> Then the moment
> Distends, spreads
> Into years.
>
> (The King and the Queen are older) (93)

The Dreams of Tipu Sultan provided an opportunity to Karnad to deal with Tipu Sultan, "one of the most politically perceptive and tragic figures in modern Indian history" ("Preface") and explore his inner world which was recorded by him in his diary. Tipu's valour, political acumenship, struggle against British colonialism, antagonistic forces within the country, innovation in trade and agriculture, famialial love and affection, conspiracy, failures etc. widen the canvas of the play. It is a world of various cultures and practices. People with numerous traits of their personality, political ambitions, wars, psychic reactions, dreams, and the fall of the protagonist—all have been treated by the playwright in a language which unhesitatingly embraces the words, phrases, idioms, similes, metaphors, irony, symbols, imagery from Arabic, Persian, Urdu, Hindi, Sanskrit, Kannada, Marathi etc. They help to develop the proper context and to communicate the ideas implanted in his mind: Nizam, *Arthshastra,* Diwan-i-Aam, Diwan-i-Khas, kebab, Imam, Caliph, caravanserai, Rajah, Quilledar, Sarkar, Goddess Sharda, "*Arre suno—Tum nahin—Han! Tum!*" (10), "*Jee Huzoor*" (10), "*aao dekho. Inko pehchante ho*" (12), "*Han! Han! Yahee hai hamare padshah! Yehi hai—Allah ab kya hoga?*" (12), "*Yeh murdah kya yeh tumhare Sultan ka hai?* " (10), "*Yahan aao…dikhai nahi de rahoa….Andhera*" (10), "*jaldi jaldi*" (13), "*Thehro! Yeh hain*" (13), "*Jee han*" (14), haram, exclamations of horror in Urdu and

Kannada: "*Arre—Roko—Ayyo! Ayyo!Yeh kya kiya?* " (15), "Sarkar-e- Khudadad" (36), "I'm never not serious" (59), Inshallah, Sufi Zikr, zenana, Kaharajas, etc. and the host of dramatis personae soiled in Indian multicultural milieu. They take us back to our history and culture. Use of similes and metaphors is also very apt and they heighten the dramatic effect: "apple's texture...so delicate like a woman's cheeks" (21), "Persian sword" (49), "The English generals squabbling like women in the market" (63), "White Plague" (64). The image of "temple—dilapidated" (18), "White elephant" (20), "English withdrawing" (63), and the dream image artistically fused with the plot:

> HAIDAR: I'm maimed, Tipu. I have no limbs.
>
> TIPU: But you never lost any limb.
>
> HAIDAR: You have maimed me, Tipu. You have cut off my limbs and handed them over to the enemy.
>
> TIPU (*low*): Yes, father. I've done that. Have you come to punish me? (50)

The above dream image also throws light on the psychic disturbances and frustration of Tipu Sultan. "Roar of tigers" (23) symbolizes the ferocity of Tipu Sultan; "fair-skinned and light-eyed-young man" (28) represents the nature of the Marathas in disguise; "white elephant" (20) symbolizes peace and power. The Postscript is full of irony, i.e., how we treat our legendry heroes: "When India became independent in 1947, the families of maharajas who had bowed and scraped before the British masters were granted sumptuous privy purses by the Government of India while the descendents of Tipu Sultan were left to rot in the slums of Calcutta" (65).

The *two monologues, Flowers* and *Broken Images,* mark a significant chnge in subject and form. *Flowers* is a narrative that treats religious devotion and erotic love, finally by the miracle of the *Shivalinga*, the power of the priest's worship is recognized and he is the chosen priest. *Broken Images* discusses the politics of language in Indian literary culture, particularly in relation to literatures of several regions of India, i.e., Indian writings in English versus Bhasha Literatures. The genre in literary writings is another issue that has been highlighted. *Linga, pooja, aarti, dhoti*, flowers common in India—*malligai, sevanti, chandu, hooru, sampigai, kanakambara etc;* and *prasad, pallu,* neem, *Prajata, tritiya, namaskara, gurus,* have been incorporated in the play to accentuate the folklore atmosphere and the obsession with *linga* and *Prasad*. The photographic transcription of the erotic excitement reads like a pornographic video clip, skilfully handled:

> I watched the mole, poised on the inward plunge of her right breast, peering precariously into the darkness of her cleft. I was longing to kiss it, but didn't dare move for fear of disturbing her. Finally when she had fallen into drugged sleep, I laid her back gently on the carpet, still moaning in defiance and resisting sleep like a child. I bent down and kissed the mole. (255)

The priest is a symbol of religious devotion, Chandravati sensuality and *linga* stands for power and divine blessings. "Squabbling like a married couple" (277) is an apt simile. Karnad, in the *Broken Images* has adopted terms used in modern technology; expressions, creative image; self-exploratory reactions used in modern psychology are quite supportive to advance the conflict and focus on the theme of the play. Lapel mike, plasma screen, elephantine lights, headphones, cameras, sound studio, broadcasting studio, *Arthapoorna, artha, Prayaschitta, namaskara*, guru, Literary Agent, hypocrisy of the speaker on the screen, use of paradox, "And this time I had one advantage. She was dead and I was not" (283) and self–isclosure are blended together to justify technological innovation and the dilemma of the protagonist, Manjula Nayak. One instance of self-exploration deserves mention:

> *Namaskara.* I am Manjula Nayak. I must mention that officially I am Mrs. Manjula Murty, but my creative self continues to be Manjula Nayak....The first question—you have probably guessed it already. After having written in Kannada all your life, why did you choose—suddenly—to write in English? Do you see yourself as a Kannada writer or an English writer? What audiences do you write for...Intellectuals whom I respected, writers who were

> gurus to me, friends who I thought would pat me on back and share my delight—they are all suddenly breathing fire. How dare I write in English and betray Kannada. (263)

On the contrary, she betrays Kannada and justifies it. The choice of the words and the beauty of the expression are noticeable: "But my response to the charge that I write in English for money would be: Why not? Isn't that a good enough reason? Would you like to see what royalties I earned when I wrote in Kannada?" (264). The self-image symbolizes the inner self of the protagonist, i.e., Manjula Nayak who broadly represents the crisis the writers of Bhasha literatures are confronting; *Broken Images*, the title itself stands for split-personality, Malini—young talents exploited by kiths and kins for market profitability.

Wedding Album is a dramatic version of marriage in urban middle class family in India which depicts the culture and practices involved in it. The use of self-exploratory, argumentative and reflective style; use of words, phrases, similes, metaphors, symbols, irony and specific expressions augument the atmosphere requisite for the play. The words and phrases from different stocks of Indian languages are dexterously linked with the plot, characters and their mental and emotional make-up: *dupatta, hafta, namaskar, kameez, salwar, pandal, gunas,Amma, bendi, muhurta, Appa, Kanjeevaram Sari, Ma, dhoti, arzee, triphala, vagar, tamasha, Ayyo, avatara,* Sati, Savitri, Shastri; "Oh, god! No. Shiva-Shiva" (48), "God broke this forehead" (21), "cool your top" (22), " make a mountain out of a molehill" (82), "fire altar and seven steps round it" (15), the blend of homour, satire is characteristic of Indian culture and creates the strong feel of our society: "This is India, you know. Not Australia. We have a solution for everything" (49), "they reserve their harassment for Saturday mornings" (28), "hasn't your weekly dispatch arrived" (33), "That's all that remains to me to do now. Sit down. Place a betel leaf on my head, and do penance under the jackfruit tree" (22). The following expression, very obviously expresses the psychic disturbance: "Radhabai, tea, please. Three cups. (*To*

Vidula) It's disaster. Call mother. No. actually don't call her. Not yet. Where is she?" (46).

The play deals with the marriage—both traditional as well as modern, twenty first century marriage. Hence vocabulary and expressions used in modern society are also given due space: "fuck off" (90), "fucking right to harass me" (90), Cooking Quotient, video tapes, SMSes, mobile, phones, video games, dating, tele -serial, ad, laptop, video chatting, camera. Similes and metaphors used are appropriate: "a smile like a toothpaste ad" (11), "Indian women...obedient Sati Savitri" (17), "marriage is a gamble" (27.

Mother symbolizes traditional housewife with progressive ideas, Ashwin—modern young man who believes in "simple registration" (16) for marriage, and "spiritual crisis" (78), Vivan stands for teenage phantasies and sexual urge, Internet Café symbolizes twenty first century culture to find out life partners, the family of Nadkarni—urban middle class family with multicultural and cosmopolitan ideology, Vidula symbolizes modern youth, Hema opposite to Vidula, Gopal touching the feet of Rohit represents culture of marriage and compulsions of a bride's family in marriage.

Works Cited

Aristotle. *Poetics*. Translated by Butcher, S.C. New Delhi/Ludhiana: Kalyani Publishers, 1998.

Karnad, Girish. *Yayati*.New Delhi: Oxford University Press, 2008.

________. *Tughlaq*. (Twenty Second Impression) Delhi: Oxford University Press, 1998.

________. *Hayavadana*. (Fourteenth Impression) Chennai: Oxford University Press, 1998. This impression has been used and reffered.

________. *Three Plays: Naga-Mandala, Hayavadana, Tughlaq*. (Eighth Impression) New Delhi: Oxford University Press, 2002. For *Naga-Mandala* present edition has been extensively used and reffered.

________. *Tale-Danda*. New Delhi: Ravi Dayal, 1993. Subsequent references are from this edition.

________, "Preface" *Bali: The Sacrifice* in *Two Plays by Girish Karnad: The Dreams of Tipu Sultan, Bali: The Sacrifice*. (Fourth Impression) New Delhi: Oxford University Press, 2005. Both the playtexts of this editon have been consuled and reffered.

________. "Preface" *The Dreams of Tipu Sultan* in *Two Plays by Girish Karnad: The Dreams of Tipu Sultan, Bali: The Sacrifice*. (Fourth

Impression) New Delhi: Oxford University Press, 2005. Both the playtexts of this editon have been consuled and referred.

________, *The Fire and the Rain* in *Collected Plays.*Volume Two. (Ed.) Dharwadker, Aparna Bhargava. New Delhi: Oxford University Press, 2005. References are from this edition.

________. *Flowers* and *Broken Images* in *Collected Plays.* Volume Two. (Ed.) Dharwadker, Aparna Bhargava. New Delhi: Oxford University Press, 2005. References of both the monologues are from this edition.

________. *Wedding Album.* New Delhi: Oxford Uiversity Press, 2009.

Murthy. A.R. Ananth. "Introduction" *Tughlaq.* (Twenty Second Impression) Delhi: Oxford University Press, 1998.

Naik, M.K. "Cinderella Still: Recent Indian English Drama" *Littcrit.* Volume 27, Number 1&2, June-Dec, 2001.

11

Conclusion

De-colonization of Indian English drama by Girish Karnad has various connotatations: while the project has analysed his socio-cultural and literary achievements, it will be highly relevant to present day problems Indian society is facing largely: (i) Analysis of Karnad as a postcolonial writer of Indian English Drama will facilitate to see, observe and understand the glory of India's past and its continuity in the present. (ii) It will also give impetus to overcome "colonial neurosis" and recognize indigenous culture, history and literature. (iii) Thematic concerns in his plays will display their urgency in the present context in our country.

The themes of responsibility, human relationship, irresponsible exercise of power and utter forgetfulness of the imperishable values of life (*Yayati*); disintegration of personality, polity in crisis due to internal dissensions and the presence of a powerful alien adversary (*Tughlaq*); mad dance of incompleteness and search for completeness (*Hayavadana*); sexual discrimination (*Naga Mandala*); caste politics and subaltern discourse (*Tale Danda*); lust, anger, treachery, violence, death, sacrifice, Divine grace, forgiveness, revival and life (*The fire and the Rain*); secret inner world of Tipu Sultan and his continual fight against British Colonialism (*The Dreams of Tipu sultan*); non-violence (*Bali:The Sacrifice*); politics of language in literary culture (*Broken Images*); antithesis between spiritual and erotic experiences (*Flowers*), culture of marriage in Indian urban middle class society and its new phases comically treated are highly debatable problems of our country and the work will prove to be a sure guide to tackle these problems. (iv) The project also aims to explain the archetypal patterns embedded in Karnad's plays. Obviously it will be an opportunity to understand Indian myths, legends, folktales, history and culture, narrative design and character-types and feel proud of them. (v) Technique—theatre conventions: folk, classical and modern. Exposition of theatre techniques in Karnad will facilitate enjoying and assessing their validity in the modern context. It will cater to the socio-political, cultural and literary needs of the society. Issues and problems discussed and analysed will enlighten the society and help to meditate on those problems.

Karnad is internationally recognized as a playwright. His plays have been performed in various regional languages, English and German. Even the German, Chinese, French, American and English actors have performed in his plays worldwide. The British Council and the American Center are giving helping hands by arranging the visits of foreign troupses from time to time in big towns. Karnad has represented our country in foreign lands as an emissary of Indian art and culture. He was honoured with Ambassadorship of UNESCO's International Theatre Institute. In 2002, he was offered an opportunity to write The World Theatre Day Message (27 March). Journalistic media has reported his activities on theatre, film and television globally. Haymarket Theatre, Leicester, Warehouse, Croydon London, Deutsches Nationaltheatre, Weimer, Germany, Guthrie Theatre in Minneapolis, USA, Berlin Festival of India, Consulate Auditorium, Dubai, British Theatres and Barbican BITE, Vayu Naidu Company, UK and others have produced all the plays of Karnad several times.

Girish Karnad, a versatile genius, acclaimed as a noted actor, producer, director, TV artist and cultural administrator, occupies a prominent place in Indian English Drama. His plays are the medium where through he discusses socio-political and cultural problems of India conforming to tradition of Henrik Ibsen and G.B. Shaw. He is appreciated as a playwright of myths and legends, history, subalternity, castesim, rituals, feminism, cultural issues and humanism.

Despite these cultural roles Karnad definitely brought revolution in Indian English Drama—discarding Eurocentric models and techniques altogether; boldly advocating and using Indian myths, legends, folk tales, history, socio-political and contemporary issues with Indianized English and folk theatre conventions with the motif to de-colonize Indian English Drama. He gave it a new shape—Postcolonial Indian English Drama. All his plays from *Yayati* to *Wedding Album* illustrate this hypothesis.

Collected Plays of Karnad, in 2 Vols ed. by Aparna Bhargava Dharwadker, *Girish Karnad's Plays: Performance and Critical Perspectives* ed by Tutun Mukherji, *Three Plays of Girish Karnad: A Study in Poetics and Culture* by Vanashree Tripathi, *The Indian Imagination of Girish Karnad* by P. Dhanavel, *Contemporary Indian Drama* ed by Sudhaker Pandey & Freya Taraporewala, *New Directions in Indian drama* ed by Sudhaker Pandey & Freya Barua, *Flowering of Indian Drama: Growth and Development* ed by K. Venkata Reddy & R.K. Dhawan, *Themes and Techniques in the Plays of Girish Karnad & A Survey of Indian English Drama* by Satish Kumar, *Indian English Drama: A Critical Study & A History of Indian English Literature* by M.K.Nayak, *A History of Indian English Drama & Dimensions of Indian English Literature* by S. Krishna Bhatt, *Myth and Symbol in the Plays of Girish Karnad: a Psychoanalytic Approach* by R.S.Bhuvaneshwari, *The Plays of Girish Karnad: Critical Perspectives* ed by Jaideep Sinh Dodia, *Post Colonial Discourse: A Study of Contemporary Literature* ed by R.K.Dhawan, *Indian English Drama: Critical Perspectives* ed by Jaydipsinh K. Dodiya & K. V. Sunderan, *Fifty Years of Indian Writing* ed by R.K.Dhawan, *Indian Drama Today* by Sarat M Babu, *Studies in Indian Drama in English* ed by A.N.Prasad & Saryug Yadav, *Indian Writing in the New Millennium* ed by R.K.Dhawan, *A Thunder on Stage: A Study of Girish Karnad's Plays* ed by C.L.Khatri & Sudhir K. Arora and *Girish Karnad's Plays: Archetypal and Aesthetical Presentations* by Bhagwat Nayak are the seminal texts, editions, reviews and anthologies on Karnad's writings. Literary journals, reviews, introduction to the plays of Karnad, prefaces and online links have advanced the study on Karnad.

A host of scholars on Karnad who have also contributed to literary journals, anthologies, reviews and magazines include

Kirtinath Kurtkoti, G.S. Amur, Jasbir Jain, Seema Suneel, Veena Noble Das, Rajinder Paul, Y. Somalatha, R.G.Joshi, N.S.Jagannathan, Makarand Paranjape, U.R.Ananthamurthy, M. Sarat Babu, Pramod Mutalik, A Jaganmohana Chari, C.P.Rajesh, Jyoti Rane, Indira Nityanand, Pranav Joshipura, Sonal P. Chandervaker, Hitesh Parmer, Saryug Yadav, Hari Padam Rane, Nibir K. Ghosh, P.P. Sharma, S.R. Jalota, Rupalee Burke, Manoj Kumar Sinha, G.D. Barche, Krishna Singh, Bhagwat Nayak, Jaydeep Sarangi, J.D. Soni etc. The scholarly works and articles on Karnad is a success story of Karnad as a de-clonizer of Indian English drama, and his success has motivated the modern generation and paved the way for posterity.

Over the past five decades, Karnad has been recognized nationally and internationally as one of the pre-eminent playwrights in contemporary India. He belongs to the generation of writers who came to maturity shortly after Independence and collectively reshaped Indian theatre as a national institution in the later twentieth century. He secured a high place in multilingual performance culture, the relation of his playwriting to his work in popular media, and his larger-than- life presence as an engaged intellectual in the Indian public sphere.

Karnad's cultural and literary contribution to advance postcolonial discourse, obviously will help to understand his genius as a playwright, purpose of writing plays, his subjects, art of characterization, language, theatre techniques etc. and establish their academic validity. An analysis of—experiments his plot, character, thought, diction and theatre techniques—will help to enlarge the scope of Indian English Drama. The potentiality of Karnad's plays will dwindle the 'sick man' image of Indian English Drama

Karnad contributed to revitalize Indian English Drama and defied the notion of European superiority. His strong advocacy of the purposeful return to its roots in the rich traditions of ancient Indian drama highlights the multidisciplinary relevance of his plays. Vanashree Tripathi has rightly acknowledged the signicance of Karnad's plays:

> Karnad's plays testfy to a larger cultural matrix of mythic modes, oral folk forms and narrative conventions than any other plays written and performed in the recent times. His re-writing of myths and folktales instills unique emotional and intellectual angle to the given prototypes and thus attains a larger frame of reference—psychological complex. The stories of the past from X century B.C. to the present intersect and in displacement and reverberation we sense their presence in our personal and public life in the contemporary world. (19)

Karnad goes back to the myths and legends with a view to make them a vehicle of a new vision. By exploiting the various myths and legends, he shows the absurdity of modern life with all its elemental passions and conflicts, and man's eternal struggle to achieve perfection. In his plays *Yayati, Tughlaq, Hayavadana, Tale-Danda, Naga-Mandala, The Fire and the Rain, Flowers,* he tries to "evolve a symbolic form out of a tension between the archetypal and mythic experience and a living response to life and its values. Contemporaneity in Karnad's plays manifests itself through his operative sensibility in his attempt to give new meaning to the past from the vantage point of the present" (Veena Noble Das 71). He doesn't take the myths in their entirety. He takes only parts of them that are useful to him and the rest he supplements with his imagination to make his plots clear. He has admirably secceeded in his attempt to show the Indian playwright as well as to the world theatre community at large how "our past and present can coalesce to give present day existence meaning and to theatre activity a direction... synthesis of classical, folk and Western—which led to the discovery of a new form as well as a new style of production" (Reddy & Dhawan 23). Obula Reddy has analysed the presentness of the past in Karnad's plays which reveal:

> a healthy tension between tradition and contemporaneity. He borrows from both *Yakshagana* and European *avant-garde.* He goes back to local and folk practices which were part of his childhood environment. Karnad makes it clear that his return to his roots is in reaction to the banality and social irrevelance of modern Indian drama. (36)

Karnad's plays offer together a "re-engagement between the apparently separated worlds and makes the autonomy and accessibility to drama and theatre complementary raher than constrasting domain" (Mukherjee 17). It is remarkable that his plays, irrespective of the source, are deeply grounded in the experiential world of the readers/spectators but transcend cultural specificities to reach out towards a universality of human knowledge. His plays are performed worldwide successfully before audiences of multicultural stock; it proves the validity of his plays. Tutun Mukherjee has made a very pertinent remark: "Girish Karnad's drama reflects both continuity and innovation...Karnad moves on with his creative explorations into new aspects of life and philosophy, art and technology" (55). Karnad has synthesized classical, folk and modern Western theatre traditions, and used them discriminatingly and judiciously which led to a discovery of "a new form and as a result a new style of production—leading to the evolution of Indian drama" (Veena Noble Das 72). Only a few playwrights have exploited the rich cultural heritage of India for the plots and traditional Indian theatre conventions in presentation, and succeesfully attempted new interpretations of Indian myths and legends. Karnad is moulded by Indian tradition and he reciprocally gave it new form and meaning. L.S. Gill has observed the close interaction between Karnad and the Indian tradition:

> Tradition for him is only a corpus of myths, legends and sometimes historically true events from the past. Instead of depending only on the West for his themes and techniques, he experimented with the traditional tales and techniques. As a result, he remains close to tradition as regards his style and contents. He fuses the traditional techniques of Indian theatre with modern Western ideas only to open up new avenues of dramatic possiblities in Indian English drama. (14)
>
> Past and present coalesce to give to our present-day experience a new meaning. For Karnad, they go together and only thus they hold complete meaning. Indeed, he doesn't think of new stories but harvests episodes from the bottomless treasure-chest of mythology and history.

> Tradition itself becomes the stage for him upon which modernity enacts itself in terms of dramaturgy. (46)

Karnad has made an effort, comments N.M. Nigam, "to fight the legacy of colonialism by upholding Indian values and its cultural ethos. The themes do have contemporary significance but the main focus is on the presentation of complex cultural fabric of India" (35). Resistance to colonialism and its colonial discourse is sufficely manifested through his choice of the subjects for his plays, i.e., myths, legends, folklore and history of India, character delineation—rooted in cultural soil of India, puffed with Indian sensibility, technique—conventions of dramatic performance: folk, classical and modern. His emphasis is on the indigeneous conventions though he has fused the classical and modern conventions as was required by the context; use of English—erstwhile master's language nativised it and made it convenient to express the thought embedded in the play. Use of Indianised vocabulary, metaphors, similies, irony, imagery and humour etc. create a distinct identity to his play, "Indian" through and through. He was quite successful in de-colonizing Indian English Drama and gave it recognition in the international arena. He is justly eulogized as a cultural administrator and "Renaissance Man" (Kalidas & Merchant).

Works Cited

Das, Veena Noble. "Experiment and Innovation in Modern Indian Drama in Translation: The Plays of Mohan Rakesh, Badal Sircar, Vijay Tendulker and Girish Karnad" *Contemporary Indian Drama.* (Eds.) Pandey, Sudhaker & Taraporewala, Freya. New Delhi: Prestige, 1990.

Gill, L.S. *Girish Karnad's Hayavadana: A Critical Study*. New Delhi: Asia Book Club, 2005.

Kalidas, S. & Merchant, Rehmat. "Renaissance Man" <India-today.com/itoday/.../arts.html> 20.10.2010.

Nigam, N.M. "Myth and Folklore in Girish Karnad's *The Fire and the Rain*" *Perspectives and Challenges in Indian-English Drama.* (Ed) Tondon, Neeru. New Delhi: Atlantic Publishers and Distributors, 2006.

Reddy, Venkata K & Dhawan, R.K. *Flowering of Indian Drama: Growth and Development.* New Delhi: Prestige, 2004.

Tripathi, Vanashree. *Three Plays of Girish Karnad: Hayavadana, Tale-Danda, The Fire and the Rain.* New Delhi: Prestige, 2004.

Reddy, Obula P. "Cultural Heterogeneity in Indian Drama" *Flowering of Indian Drama: Growth and Development.* (Eds) Reddy, Venkata K. & Dhawan, R.K., New Delhi: Prestige, 2004.

Mukherjee, Tutun. (Ed) *Girish Karnad's Plays: Performance and Critical Perspectives.* Delhi: Pencraft International, 2006.

Select Bibliography

Primary Sources: Plays by Girish Karnad

Yayati. Kannada version published by Manohara Granth Mala, Dharwad, 1961 and English Version published by OUP, 2008.

Ma Nishad written in 1964. Published in *Ekaanka Sangraha,* ed. Sinduvalli Anantha Murthy, New Delhi: Sahitya Akademi, 1986.

Tughlaq. New Delhi: OUP, 1964.

Hayavadana. Chennai: OUP, 1971.

Anjumallige. Kannada version published by Manohara Grantha Mala, Dharwad, 1977. The English translation by the playwright as "Driven Snow" is as yet unpublished.

Hittina Hunja. 1980, published as *Bali: The Sacrifice* [along with *The Dreams of Tipu Sultan*] New Delhi: OUP, 2003.

Naga-Mandala: A Play with a Cobra. OUP, 1990.

Tale-Danda. New Delhi: Ravi Dayal, 1993.

The Fire and the Rain. New Delhi: OUP,1998.

"The Dreams of Tipu Sultan," *Theatre India*. No.1 May 2000: 47-85.

The Dreams of Tipu Sultan and Bali: The Sacrifice. New Delhi: OUP, 2004.

Two Monologues: Flowers and Broken Images. OUP, 2005.

Wedding Album. OUP, Nov. 2008.

Articles and Lectures

"Caste and Conflict in Kannada Cinema," First Ritwik Ghatak Memorial Lecture, *Kino:* Journal of the Cine Club of Calcutta: 8-21, 1980.

"Bhavabhuti's *Uttara Rama Charita:* A Play about a Playwright," Conference on Indian Literatures for the festivals of India, 1986.

"Culture," *India Briefing*. (Ed.) Marshall M. Boulton. Boulder & London: Westview Press, 1987.

"In Search of New Theatre," *Contemporary Indian Traditions*. (Ed.) Carla Bourdan. Washington: Smithsonian Press, 1988: 93-105.

"Theatre in India," *Daelous*. Fall 1989: 331-56.

"Masks of Reality," *Little India*: August 31, 1991.

"Entertaining India," Satyajit Ray Memorial Lecture, Nehru Centre, London, 1993.

"Citizen/ Soldier," *Economic and Political Weekly,* 15 March, 1997.

"The Arts and Social Change in India: India's Culture in Motion," Royal Tropical Institute (KIT) Amsterdam, 1998.

"World Theatre Day—27 March 2002," *Theatre India,* No 5 May 2002: 6-7.

"A Playwright—A Discussion with U.R. Anantha Murthy, Prasanna, Girish Karnad," *Indian Literature,* No. 169, Sept-Oct. 1995.

"Culture and Colonialism," British Asia/ Asian British symposia, Southampton University, 2003.

Editions, Selections and Anthologies of Plays by Karnad

Collected Plays, Volume One, with an Introduction by Aparna Bhargava Dharwadker, New Delhi: OUP, (Fourth Impression) 2008. The Volume contains *Tughlaq, Bali: The Sacrifice* and *Naga- Mandala: Play with a Cobra.*

Collected Plays, Volume Two, with an Introduction by Aparna Bhargava Dharwadker, New Delhi: OUP, 2005. The Volume contains *Tale-Danda, The Fire and the Rain, The Dreams of Tipu Sultan, Two Monologues: Flowers* and *Broken Images.*

Secondary Sources

Abidi, S.Z.H. Plenary Lecture in International Conference on "Postcolonial Literatures and Transnational" at C.C.S. University, Meerut, April 9-10, 2010.

Abrams, M.H. *A Glossary of Literary Terms.* (Seventh Edition), Singapore: Thomason Asia Pvt. Ltd., 2003.

Akshara, K.V. "The Dreams of Kannada Theatre: A Turn of the Century Narrative", *Theatre India* No 2 Nov. 1999:120-151.

Ali, Syed Mashkoor. (Ed.) *Indian Writing in English: A Critical Response.* NewDelhi: Creative Books [Creative New Literatures Series-47], 2001.

Anantha Murthy, U.R. "A Note on Karnad's *Hayavadana*", *Literary Criterion* 12: 2-3:37-43.

_________. Introduction. *Tughlaq.*by Girish Karnad. Delhi: OUP,1994.

Aristotle. *Poetics.* Translated by Butcher, S.C. New Delhi/Ludhiana: Kalyani Publishers, 1998.

Arora, Sudhir K. "Spiritualising the Aesthetics (of Flowers) versus Breaking the Ethics (of Image): A Critical Study of Karnad's Two Monologues *Flowers and Broken Images, " Thunder on Stage: A Study of Girish Karnad's Plays.* (Eds.) Khatri, C.L. & Arora, Sudhir K. Jaipur: Book Enclave, 2008.

Ashcroft, Bill, Gareth Griffiths and Helen Tiffin. *Key Concepts in Post-colonial Studies.* London and New York: Routledge, 1998.

_________. *The Empire Writes Back: Theory and Practice in Post-colonial Literatures.* (2nd edition) London/New York: Routledge, 2010.

_________. *The Post-colonial Studies Reader.* (2nd edition) London/New York: Routledge, 2006.

Awasthi, Suresh. "Theatre of Roots", Encounter with Tradition, TDR (1988) Vol. 33, No. 4 (Winter, 1989).

Babu, M. Sarat. *Indian Drama Today: A Study in the Theme of Cultural Deformity*. New Delhi: Prestige Books, 1997.

Balme, Christopher. "Indian Drama in English: Transcreation and the Indigenous Performance Tradition," *(Post) Colonial Stages: Critical & Creative Views on Drama, Theatre & Performance.* (Ed) Helen Gilbert, West Yorkshire: Dangaroo, 1999:146-160.

_________. *Decolonizing the Stage: Theatrical Syncreticism and Post-Colonial Drama.* London: & New York: OUP, 1999.

Barry, Peter. *Beginning Theory: An Introduction to Literary and Cultural Theory.* (Second Edition). Chennai: T.R. Publications Pvt. Ltd., 2004.

_________. (Ed.) *Issues in Contemporary Critical Theory*. Macmillan Casebook, 1987.

Bhabha, Homi K. (Ed.) *Nation and Narration.* London: Routledge, 1990.

Bharatmuni, *Natyasastra.* Trans. Manomohan Ghosh. Calcutta: Asiatic Society, 1961.

Bhatt, S.K. "Indo-Anglian Drama: A Critical Study" <yabaluri.org/TRIVENI/CDWEB> 12.02.2011.

Budholia, O.P. "Dramatic Art of Girish Karnad", and "Myth as Symbol: An Interpretation of Girish Karnad's 'The Fire and the Rain'." *Critical Essays on Indian English Literature.* Jaipur: Book Enclave, 2003: Chapter 11 and 12.

Burke, Rupalee. "India Then and Now: The Contemporary Relevance of Girish Karnad's *Tale-Danda*" *Studies in Indian Drama in English.* (Eds.) Prasad, Amar Nath and Yadav, Saryug. Bareilly: Prakash Book Depot, 2003.

Chandrashekhar, K. "Before the Curtain Call, " *The Hindu.* New Delhi, March 21, 1999.

Changule, R.B. "Girish Karnad's *The Dreams of Tipu Sultan*: A Critical Introduction" <englishcyberliterature.net> 18.01.2011.

Chari, A. Jaganmohana. "Girish Karnad's *Hayavadana* and *Nagamandala*: A study of Postcolonial Dialectics, " *Postcolonial Discourse: a Study of Contemporary Literature.* (Ed.) R.K. Dhawan. New Delhi: Prestige Books, 1997.

Chaturvedi, Vinayak. *Subaltern Studies and Postcolonialism.* Verso, 2000.

Crow, Brian and Chris Banfield. "Girish Karnad and an Indian Theatre of Roots", *An Introduction to Postcolonial Theatre.* (Eds) Brain Crow and Chris Banfield, New York: CUP, 1996.

Das, Bijay Kumar. *Postmodern Indian English Literature*. New Delhi: Atlantic Publishers & Distributors Pvt. Ltd., 2006.

_________. *Twentieth Century Literary Criticism*. (Fifth Revised and Enlarged Edition) New Delhi: Atlantic Publishers & Distributors Pvt. Ltd., 2007.

Das, Veena Noble. "A Re-Reading of Girish Karnad's Plays with Reference to Myth and Folktale" *Flowering of Indian English Drama: Growth and Development*. (Eds.) Reddey, Venkata K & Dhawan, R.K. New Delhi: Prestige, 2004.

Deopti "Wedding Album" <banglore.metblogs.com> 18.01.2011

Despande, G.P. (Ed) *Modern Indian Drama: An Anthology*. New Delhi: Sahitya Akademi,1990.

"Development of Theatre in India" *<www.Indianetzone.com>* 12.02.2011.

Devy, G.N. (Ed.) *Indian Literary Criticism: Theory and Interpretation*. Hyderabad: Orient Longman, 2007.

Dhanavel, P. *An Indian Imagination of Girish Karnad: Essays on 'Hayavadana'*. New Delhi: Prestige, 1998.

Dharwadker, Aparna Bhargava. (Ed.) With an Introduction *Collected Plays.* Volume One: *Tughlaq, Hayavadana, Bali: The Sacrifice, Naga-Mandala*. New Delhi: O.U.P., Fourth Impression, 2008.

_________. (Ed.) With an Introduction Collected Plays. Volume Two: *Tale-Danda, The Fire and the Rain, The Dreams of Tipu Sultan, Two Monologues, Flowers, Broken Images*. New Delhi: O.U.P., 2005.

_________. "Performance, Meaning and Materials of Modern Indian Theatre: An Interview with Girish Karnad," *New Theatre Quaterly,* Vol.XI. No.44 November,1995:355-370.

_________."Historical Fictions and Postcolonial Representation: Reading Girish Karnad's *Tughlaq*". *PMLA* 110-1, 1995: 43-58.

_________. "Diaspora, Nation and the Failure of Home: Two Contemporary Indian Plays", *Theatre Journal* 50.1, 1998: 71-94.

_________. "Playwriting and Criticism: Another Look at Girish Karnad." *Theatre India*. No.1 May 1999: 83-90.

Dhawan, R.K. (Ed.) *Postcolonial Discourse: A Study of Contemporary Literature*. New Delhi: Prestige Books, 1997.

_________. (Ed.) *Indian Writing in the New Millennium*. New Delhi: Indian Association for English Studies, 2000.

_________. "Girish Karnad: The Man and the Writer, " *The Plays of Girish* (Ed.) Dodiya, J. Prestige: New Delhi, 2009.

Dodiya, Jayadipsinh. (Ed.) *The Plays of Girish Karnad: Critical Perspectives*. New Delhi: Prestige Books, 1999.

_________. and K.V. Surendran. (Eds.) *Indian English Drama: Critical Perspectives*. New Delhi: Sarup & Sons, 2000.

Dwivedi, A.N. (Ed.) *Studies in Contemporary Indian English Drama*. New Delhi: Kalyani Publishers, 1999.

Edison, Thomas. "Back on Stage: *A Heap of Broken Images* and Odakalu Bimba," *Times News*. Network, March 21, 2005.

Ellis-Fermor, Una. *The Frontiers of Drama.* (Second Edition) New Fetter Lane: Meuthen & Co. Ltd. 1964.

"Express News Service" <*www.Indianewsexpress.com*> 18.01.2011.

Fanon, Frantz. *The Wretched of the Earth.* Trans. Constance Farrington. New York: Grove Press, 1990.

Gandhi, Leela. *Postcolonial Theory: A Critical Introduction.* (Sixth Impression). New Delhi: OUP, 2005.

Gargi, Balwant. *Folk Theatre of India.* Calcutta: Rupa & Co., 1991.

George, K.M. (Ed.) *Modern Indian Literature: An Anthology.* Vol.III Plays and Prose. New Delhi: Sahitya Akademi, 1995.

Ghosh, Nibir Kanti. "Girish Karnad's *Tughlaq*: History in the Future Tense," *Fifty Years of Indian Writing.* (Ed.) R. K. Dhawan. New Delhi: Indian Association for English Studies, 1998.

Gill, L.S. *Girish Karnad's Hayavadana: A Critical Study.* New Delhi: Asia Book Club, 2005.

"Girish Karnad" <karnatakavision.com/girish-karnad.php> 20.10.2010.

Goel, Savita. "Folk Theatre Strategies in *Hayavadana*" *The Plays of Girish Karnad: Critical Perspectives.* (Ed) Dodiya, Jaydipsinh. New Delhi: Prestige, 2009.

Gowda, H.H.Annaiah. "Karnad's *Tughlaq* and Ramanujan's Relation," *The Literary Half-Yearly.*Vol. XIV No.1 Jan 1973.

_________. *Indian Drama.* Mysore: 1974.

_________. "Indian Drama in English: Some Highlights", *Indian Writing in the New Millennium.* (Ed.) R.K. Dhawan. New Delhi: Indian Association for English Studies, 2000.

Granville-Barker, H. *Study of Drama.* London: Sidgwick & Jackson Ltd., 1931.

Griffin, Gabriale. *Research Methods for English Studies.* Jaipur: Rawat Publication, 2007.

Guha, Ranjit. "On Some Aspects of Historiography of Colonial India," *Writing on South Asian History and Society.* (Ed.) Guha. Delhi: OUP, 1982. 108, Vol. 1 of *Subaltern Studies.*

Guha, Ranjit & Spivak, G.C. *Selected Subaltern Studies* (Paperback). Forwad Edward Said. New York: OUP, 1988.Guha, Ranjit et al. (Eds.) *Subaltern Studies.* (Vol. 1-10: Paperback). Delhi: OUP, 1999.

Gupta, Bharat. *Dramatic Concepts: Greek and Indian.* New Delhi: Printworld, 1994.

Gupta, Chandra Bhan. *The Indian Theatre.* New Delhi: Munshiram Manoharlal Publishers, 1991.

Iyenger, K.R. Srinivasa. (Ed.) *Indian Literature since Independence.* New Delhi: Sahitya Akedemi, 1973.

________. "Drama in Modern India and the Responsibility in a Changed World". (Symposia at the Fourth P.E.N. All-India Conference), Bombay: The All-India Centre, 1961.

________. *Indian Writing in English.* (Revised and Updated Edition). New Delhi: Sterling, 1995.

Jagamonarchari, A. "Karnad's *Hayavadana* and *Naga-Mandala*: A Study in Post Colonial Dialectics", *New Directions in Indian Drama.* (Eds.) Pandey, Sudhaker & Barua, Freya. New Delhi: Prestige, 1994.

Jain, Nemichandra. *Indian Theatre: Traditions, Continuity and Change.* New Delhi: Vikas Publishing House, 1992.

Joshipura, Pranav. "*Tale-Danda:* A Problem Play", *Indian English Drama: Critical Perspectives.* (Eds.) Dondiya & Sunderan. New Delhi: Sarup & Sons, 2000.

Kale, M.R. "Introduction: The Sanskrit Drama", *The Abhjnasakuntalam of Kalidas.* Delhi: Motilal Banarsidas Publishers, 2005.

Kalida & Rahmat "Renaissance Man" <India-today.com/itoday/.../arts.html> 20.10.2010.

Karnad, Girish. "Preface", *Yayati.* New Delhi: Oxford University Press, 2008.

________."Inroduction" to *Three Plays: Naga-Mandala, Hayavadana, Tughlaq.* New Delhi: O.U.P., 2002. *Naga-Mandala* has been extensively used and referred from this edition.

________. "Preface" *Dream of Tipu Sultan* in *Two Plays: Dream of Tipu Sultan, Bali: The Sacrifice.* New Delhi: O.U.P., Fourth Impression, 2005.

________. "Preface", *Tale-Danada.* Delhi: Ravi Dayal, 1993. This edition has been extensively used and referred in.

Keith, A.B. Sanskrit Drama: *Its Origin, Development, Theory and Practice.* Delhi: Motilal Banarasidas Publishers Pvt. Ltd., 1998.

Khanna, Anshuman. "Dialogic Ramifications in Karnad's Bali: The Sacrifice" Thunder on Stage: A Study of Girish Karnad's Plays. (Eds.) Khatri, C.L. & Arora, Sudhir K. Jaipur: Book Enclave, 2008.

Khatri, C.L. and K. Arora. (Eds.) *A Thunder on Stage: A Study of Girish Karnad's Plays.* Jaipur: Book Enclave, 2008.

Krishanamayi. "Redefinig the Insurgent Female Psyche in an Androcentric milieu" *The Indian Journal of English Studies.* Vol. XLI, 2003-04.

Kumar, S. Nanda speaks with Girish Karnad <*www.deccan* herald.com/ mar27 2005/ac1.asp) 20.11.2009.

Kumar, Satish. *A Survey of Indian English Drama.* Bareilly: Prakash Book Depot, 1993.

________. "Girish Karnad's Dramatic Technique", *Creative Forum*, Vol. 1, No. 2, June, 1988.

________. *Themes and Techniques in the Plays of Girish Karnad.* Bareilly: Student Store, 1987.

Kurtkoti, Kirtinath. "Introduction," *Hayavadana*. New Delhi: OUP, 1985.

________. "Nataka Shilpa: A Study of the Structure of Girish Karnad's *Tughlaq*". *Manvantara* Combined issue 5 & 6.

Kushwaha, M.S. (Ed.) *Dramatic Theory and Practice: Indian and Western* (Creative New Literature's Series-37) Delhi: Creative Books, 2000.

________. (Ed.) *Indian Poetics and Western Thought*. Lucknow: Agro Publishing House, 1988.

Lal, Ananda. (Ed.) *Rasa: The Indian Performing Arts in the Last 25 Years*. Vol.II. Calcutta: Anamika Kala Sangam, 1995.

————, (Ed.) *The Oxford Companion to Indian Theatre*. New Delhi: OUP, 2004.

Lodge, David. (Ed.) *Modern Criticism and Theory: A Reader*. (Second Edition) Revised and Expanded by Nigel Wood. Delhi: Dorling Kindersley (India) Pvt. Ltd., 2007.

Loomba, Ania. *Colonialism / Postcolonialism*. London: Routledge, 1998.

Mee, Erin B. "Contemporary Indian Theatre: Three Voices", *PAJ: A Journal of Performance and Art*. PAJ 55 (Volume 19, Number 1, The MIT Press), January 1997: 1-5.

________. "Girid Karnad : Decolonizing Ways of Seeing in *Hayavadana*". *Performance Studies* International, Arizona, 2000.

________. (Ed.) *Drama Contemporary: India*. (Reprint) New Delhi: OUP, 2002.

Mishra, Shubha. "Reading and (Mis) reading Girish Karnad'a *Bali: The Sacrifice* in the Light of Foucault's Panopticism", *Thunder on Stage: A Study of Girish Karnad's Plays*. (Eds) Khatri, C.L. & Arora, Sudhir K. Jaipur: Book Enclave, 2008.

Mishra, Vinod. "Girish Karnad's *Bali: The Sacrifice*: A Voice of Reason against a Saga of Myth", *Thunder on Stage: A Study of Girish Karnad's Plays*. (Eds.) Khatri, C.L. & Arora, Sudhir K.Jaipur: Book Enclave, 2008.

Mohan, Deepa "Wedding Album at Chowdiah" <banglore.citizenmatters.in> 17.01.2011.

Mukherjee, Tutun. (Ed.) *Girish Karnad's Plays: Performance and Critical Perspectives*. Delhi: Pencraft International, 2006.

________. "Persistence of Classical Categories in Modern Indian Drama: Girish Karnad's *Hayavadana*", *Literature and Popular Culture: A Festschrift for Isaac Sequeira*. (Eds.) R.S. Sharma et al. Hyderabad: Cauvery Printers, 1987: 131-139.

________. (Ed.) "Language as Gesture: A Conversation with Girish Karnad," *Periphery to Centre stage*. New Delhi: Prestige Books, 1998: 218-220.

Murthy, U.R. Anantha. "Introduction", *Tughlaq*. Chennai: Oxford University Press, 1998.

Nayak, Bhagwat. "Indian English Drama: Tradition and Individual Talents", *The Critical Endeavour,* Volume XIV May, 2008.

________.*Girish Karnad's Plays: Archetypal and Aesthetical Presentations.* Delhi: Authors Press, 2011.

Naik, M.K. *A History of Indian English Literature*. New Delhi: Sahitya Akademi, (Reprint) 2009.

________. *Studies in Indian English Literature*. New Delhi: Sterling, 1977.

________. "Cinderella Still: Recent Indian English Drama", *Littcrit*, 51&52 Vol. 27, No. 1&2, June- Dec. 2001. 44-60.

________. and S.Mokashi-Punekar. (Eds.) *Perspectives on Indian Drama in English*. Madras: OUP, 1977.

________. and Shyamala A. Narayan. *Indian English Literature 1980-2000: A Critical Survey*. New Delhi: Pencraft International, 2001.

Nayar, K. Pramod. *Literary Theory Today*. New Delhi: Prestige/Asia Book Club, 2002.

Nicoll, Allardyce. *Theatre and Dramatic Theory*. London: George G. Harrap & Co. Ltd., 1962.

Nigam, N.M. "Myth and Folklore in Girish Karnad's *The Fire and the Rain*", *Perspectives and Challenges in Indian-English Drama*. (Ed.) Tondon, Neeru. New Delhi: Atlantic Publishers and Distributors, 2006.

Padma Rani, P. Hari. "The Form of Indian drama in English: A Few Problems" *Indian English Drama: Critical Perspectives.* (Eds.) Dodiya, K. Jaydipsingh and Surendran, K.V. New Delhi: Sarup and Sons, 2002.

Pandey, Sudhaker and Freya Taraporewala. (Eds.) *mporary Indian Drama*. New Delhi: Prestige Books, 1990.

________. and Freya Barua. (Eds.) *New Directions in Indian Drama*. New Delhi: Prestige Books, 1994.

Pathak, Malvika. "A Profile of Girish Karnad" www. Soas.ac.uk/Religions/ comeandmeet/2000 Karnad.htm., 2004.

Pickering, Kenneth. *Studying Modern Drama.* (Second Edition) New York: Palgrave/ Macmillan, 2003.

Prasad, Amar Nath & Yadav, Saryug. (Eds.) *Studies in Indian Drama in English*. Bareilly: Prakash Book Depot, 2003.

Quatson, Ato. *Postcolonialism: Theory, Practice or Process?* Cambridge: CUP, 2000.

Rao, P. Mallikarjuna et al. (Eds.) *Postcolonial Theory and Literature.* New Delhi: Atlantic Publishers & Distributors, 2003.

Ramaswamy, S. "Indian Drama in English: A Tentative Reflection", *Makers of Indian English Literature.* (Ed.) Narasimhaiah, C.D. Delhi: Pencraf International, 2000.

________. "The New and the Old: Indian Writing at the Turn of the Century", *Indian Writing in the New Millennium.* (Ed.) Dhawan, R.K. New Delhi: Indian Association for English Studies, 2000.

Raykar, Shubhangi S. "The Development of Girish Karnad as a Dramatist: *Hayavadana*", *Contemporary Indian Drama.* (Eds.) Pandey, Sudhaker & Taraporewala, Freya. New Delhi: Prestige, 1990.

Reddy, Obula P. "Cultural Heterogeneity in Indian Drama", *Flowering of Indian Drama: Growth and Development.* (Eds.) Reddy, Venkata K. & Dhawan, R.K., New Delhi: Prestige, 2004.

Reddy, Venkat K. and R.K. Dhawan. (Eds.) *Flowering of Indian Drama: Growth and Development.* New Delhi: Prestige Books, 2004.

Richmond, Farley et al. (Eds.) *Indian Theatre: Traditions of Performance.* Honolulu: University of Hawai Press, 1990.

Sagar, Prem. (Ed.) *Girish Karnad: Naga-Mandala.* Agra: Lakshmi Narain Agarwal, n.d.

Said, W. Edward. *Orientalism: Western Conceptions of the Orient* (1978). New Delhi: Penguin Books India Pvt. Ltd., 2001.

Satchidanandan, K. *Indian Literature: Positions and Propositions.* Delhi: Pencraft International, 1999.

Singh, Avadhesh K. *Interventions: Literary and Critical Discourses.* New Delhi: Creative Books, 2007.

_________. Presidential Address: "Writing Postmodernism and Postcolonialism in India" in National Seminar (February 6-7, 2009) at Nabira Mahavidyayalaya Katol, Nagpur.

Singh, Krishna."Sexual Politics in Girish Karnad's *Naga Mandala*". *The Critical Endeavour,* Vol x, December, 2004 & *The Atlantic Critical Review*, Vol 3, Number 3, July-September, 2004.

_________."Girish Karnad's *Tale-Danda*: A Subaltern Discourse". *The Critical Endeavour*, Vol xii, December, 2006 & *The Atlantic Critical Review*, Vol 6, Number 1, January-March,2007.

_________. "Archetypal Criticism of Karnad's *Hayavadana*". *The Atlantic Literary Review,* Vol 7, Number 3, July-September, 2006.

Singh, Saurabh Kumar. "Theatre of Roots: A Resistance to Colonial Discourse", *The Atlantic Literary Review,* Volume 8, Number 1, January-March 2009.

Sinha, A.K. "Thematic Concerns and Technical Features in Girish Karnad's Plays", *The Plays of Girish Karnad.* (Ed.) Dodiya, J. New Delhi: Prestige, 2009.

Sinha, M.P. *Research Methods in English.* New Delhi: Atlantic Publishers & Distributors Pvt. Ltd., 2004.

Soloman, Rakesh. "Culture, Imperialism, and Nationalist Resistance: Performance in Colonial India", *Theatre Journal* 46 (1994): 323-347.

Somalata, Y. "Girish Karnad's *Tale-Danda:* Painful Rite of Passage", *Flowering of Indian English Drama: Growth and Development.* (Eds.) Reddey, Venkata K & Dhawan, R.K. New Delhi: Prestige, 2004.

Soni, J.D. "Girish Karnad's *Naga-Mandala*: An Experiment in Technique", *Indian Writing in the New Millenium.* (Ed.) Dhawan, R.K. New Delhi: Indian Association for English Studies, 2000.

Srinivasan, Amrit. "Foreward", *Wedding Album*. New Delhi: Oxford University Press, 2009.

Sundararaman, M.N. "Tradition and Modernity in Indian English Drama". *The Indian Journal of Indian Writing in English*, 21: 1. January 1993.

Suneel, Seema. "Karnad's *Yayati* Reconsidered" *Contemporary Indian Drama*. (Eds.) Pandey, Sudhaker & Taraporewala, Freya. New Delhi: Prestige, 1990.

Tandon, Neeru. (Ed.) *Perspectives and Challenges in Indian-English Drama*. New Delhi: Atlantic Publishers & Distributors (P) Ltd., 2006.

Tiffin, Helen. "Post-colonialism, Post-Modernism—Rehabilitation of Post Colonial History" *Journal of Commonwealth Literature*. 23.1, 1988.

Tilak, Raghukul. *Tughlaq: A Critical Study*. New Delhi: Rama Brothers, 1998.

Tripathi, Vanashree. *Three Plays of Girish Karnad: A Study in Poetics and Culture: Hayavadana- Tale-Danda-The Fire and the Rain*. New Delhi: Prestige Books, 2003.

Trivedi, Harish. *Colonial Transactions: English Literature and India*. Calcutta: Papyrus, 1993.

Turner, Victor. *Dramas, Fields and Metaphors*. Ithaca: Cornell University Press, 1974.

Una, Ellis-Fermor. *The Frontiers of Drama*. Fetter Lane: Methuen & Co. Ltd, 1964.

Van Erven, Eugene. *The Playful Revolution: Theatre and Liberation in Asia*. Bloomington: Indiana University Press, 1992.

Varadpande, M.L. *History of Indian Theatre: Lok Ranga*. New Delhi: Abhinay Publishers,1992.

wa Thiong'o, Ngugi. *Decolonizing the Mind: The Politics of Language in African Literature*. Portsmouth N.H.: Heinemann, 1994.

Wadikar, Shailaja B. "Background of Indian Theatre", *Flowering of Indian Drama: Growth and Development*. (Eds.) Reddy, Venakata K. & Dhawan, R.K. New Delhi: Prestige, 2004.

Walder, Dennis. *Post-Colonial Literatures in English: History, Language, Theory*. (Second Indian Reprint) New Delhi: Atlantic Publishers & Distributors Pvt. Ltd., 2005.

Whitfield, George. *An Introduction to Drama*. Oxford: Oxford University Press, n.d.

Wikipedia "Girish Karnad"<en.wikipedia.org/wiki/Girish_Karnad> 21.08.2010.

Wikipedia: <The Free Encyclopedia/Girish Raghunath Karnad.htm> 16.09.2009

Yadav, Saryug. "Indian English Drama: Tradition and Achievement", *Indian English Drama: Critical Perspectives*. (Eds.) Dodiya, K. Jaydipsingh and Surendran, K.V. New Delhi: Sarup and Sons, 2002.

Index